JUDICIAL RETIREMENT LAWS
OF THE FIFTY STATES
AND THE DISTRICT OF COLUMBIA

Judicial Retirement Laws
of the Fifty States
and the District of Columbia

BERNARD S. MEYER

FORDHAM UNIVERSITY PRESS
New York
1999

LC 99-28273
ISBN 0-8232-1925-9 (hardcover)
ISBN 0-8232-1926-7 (paperback)

Library of Congress Cataloging-in-Publication Data

Meyer, Bernard S.
    Judicial retirement laws of the fifty states and the District of Columbia
/ Bernard S. Meyer.
        p.   cm.
    ISBN 0-8232-1925-9 (hc.).—ISBN 0-8232-1926-7 (pbk.)
    1. Judges—United States—Retirement.   2. Judges—
United States—States—Retirement.   I. Title.
    KF8776.M49   1999   99-28279
    347.73'14—dc21   CIP

99   00   01   02   03   5   4   3   2   1

First Edition

CONTENTS

Foreword   ix

Acknowledgments   x

How to Use This Report   xi

Part I: Why Judicial Retirement Laws Should Be Changed: A
Comparison of the Laws of the Fifty States and the District of
Columbia   1
   Inconsistencies Abound   3
   The Many Exceptions to Mandatory Age Retirement   4
   Involuntary Disability Retirement Provisions Are Equally
     Diverse   7
   Involuntary Retirement for Accidental Disability   8
   Burden of Proof of Disability   9
   Periodic Examination of, and Income Reporting by, Disability
     Retirees   9
   Most Retirement Laws Apply Uniformly to All State Court   9
   Optional Retirement for Age and/or Service   10
   Voluntary Retirement for Disability   12
   Termination or Reduction of Disability Benefits   14
   Voluntary Retirement for Accidental Disability   14
   Cost of Living Adjustment of Benefit   15
   Exemption of Benefits from Taxation or Legal Process and
     Unassignability of Benefits   17
   Service After Retirement   18
   Practice of Law by Retired Judges   19
   Assignment to Judicial Duty of Retired Judges   19
   Title of Retirees Performing Judicial Duties   20
   Appeal of Retiree's Decision   20
   Assignment of Retiree as Master or Referee   21
   Alternate Dispute Resolution Service by Retiree   21
   Courts on Which a Retiree May Serve   22

How Long a Retiree May Continue in Service   23
Continuing Education Requirement   23
Pay for Retiree's Service   24
Cost of Living Adjustment   25
Pay for Retirees Serving Part Time   26
Service Credit for Retiree's Service   26
Facilities Provided for Retiree Serving After Retirement   27
Emoluments Available to Retiree Serving After
    Retirement   27

Part II: How Judicial Retirement Laws Should Be Changed   29
Abolish Mandatory Retirement for Age   31
Require Biennial Physical and Mental Examinations   32
Define Mental and Physical Disability More Clearly   32
Burden of Proof of Disability   33
Service Credit for Disability Retirement   34
Voluntary Retirement for Disability   34
Accidental Disability Retirement   35
Voluntary Retirement for Age and/or Service   35
Cost of Living Adjustment of Retirement Benefit   36
Exemption of Benefits from Taxation or Legal Process and
    Unassignability of Benefits   37
Service After Retirement   37
Practice of Law by Retired Judges   38
Assignment to Judicial Duty of Retired Judges   38
Alternate Dispute Resolution Service by Retiree   39
Title of Retirees Performing Judicial Duties   39
Pay for Retiree's Services   39
Facilities Provided for Retiree Serving After Retirement   40
Emoluments Available to Retiree Serving After
    Retirement   41

Part III: Constitutional, Statutory, and Regulatory Provisions of
the Fifty-One Jurisdictions   43
Alabama   45
Alaska   50
Arizona   53
Arkansas   56
California   59

Colorado   64
Connecticut   67
Delaware   70
District of Columbia   74
Florida   77
Georgia   83
Hawaii   87
Idaho   90
Illinois   94
Indiana   97
Iowa   102
Kansas   106
Kentucky   110
Louisiana   114
Maine   120
Maryland   123
Massachusetts   126
Michigan   130
Minnesota   133
Mississippi   138
Missouri   144
Montana   149
Nebraska   153
Nevada   156
New Hampshire   161
New Jersey   166
New Mexico   170
New York   175
North Carolina   180
North Dakota   187
Ohio   192
Oklahoma   196
Oregon   200
Pennsylvania   205
Rhode Island   209
South Carolina   215
South Dakota   218
Tennessee   222
Texas   230

Utah   236
Vermont   241
Virginia   245
Washington   249
West Virginia   257
Wisconsin   264
Wyoming   270

FOREWORD

The author of this valuable report, Bernard S. Meyer, is a highly respected judge of the Court of Appeals of the State of New York, now retired. In the main body of this report Judge Meyer surveys, with appropriate constitutional and statutory citations, the judicial retirement provisions in each of the fifty states and the District of Columbia. In each jurisdiction he identifies, for example, existing provisions for mandatory retirement on account of age, for retirement for disability (voluntary and involuntary), and for further judicial service after retirement.

In an initial section entitled "Why Judicial Retirement Laws Should be Changed," Judge Meyer takes an overall look at the great variety and assortment that exist in the judicial retirement provisions of the fifty-one jurisdictions. Then he follows, in a section entitled "How Judicial Retirement Laws Should Be Changed," with an explication of the principles that in his judgment should guide a model state judicial retirement law.

Judge Meyer's report brings together, for the first time, a comprehensive survey of existing state retirement laws, with the carefully considered judgment of a prominent member of the judiciary on how those laws should be changed for the improvement of the administration of justice.

One of Judge Meyer's proposals would, for example, enable states to make fuller use of retired and senior judges in continued judicial service. This reservoir of available judicial man power is going unused or underused in many states. The judicial leaders in each of the fifty-one jurisdictions can with profit reexamine its judicial retirement laws in light of what other jurisdictions are already doing and with the further benefit of Judge Meyer's thoughtful proposals.

Judge Meyer has conducted his survey and prepared his report as vice-chair of the Judiciary Committee of the ABA Senior Lawyers Division. That committee and the ABA Joint Judicial Division/Senior Lawyers Division Committee on Senior and Retired Judges have combined to serve as an ad hoc peer review group for the report.

Vincent McKusick
Chief Justice (ret.), Maine Supreme Judicial Court

ACKNOWLEDGMENTS

Assistance in the preparation of this volume has been provided by a number of individuals from legal organizations and law schools. From the American Bar Association's National Conference of State Trial Judges, Hon. James E. Barlow, and from its Judicial Division, Luke Bierman, Jeremy Persin, Cindy Reich, and Hon. Mattie Belle Davis; from the National Center for State Courts, Larry L. Sipes; from the New York County Lawyers Association, Hon. Walter M. Schackman and Hon. Alfred H. Kleinman; from the New York University School of Law, Gary Alperson.

The initial research of the constitutions, statutes, and rules of the fifty states and the District of Columbia was provided by Troy Cady of Hofstra University School of Law, by Steven J. Duskie, Stanley Petrusiak, and West Winter of St. Mary's University School of Law; by Jane Baumann, Lisa Bianculli, Thomas Crino, Laura Corvo; Elizabeth Engert, Michael Fiure, Thomas Martin, William Matarkoudis, William McLane, Lavinia Mears, Rudolf Riley, Dana Scancerella, Jessica Stein, and Douglas A. Wheeler of Seton Hall University School of Law's Legislative Bureau; and Alessandro L. Antonacci of Touro College Law Center.

Work on this project began in 1995 and has been concluded some two-and-a-half years later in 1998. Without the assistance of those listed above, it would not have been possible for a retired judge now practicing law to have brought the work to conclusion in twice that amount of time.

I am deeply grateful.

HOW TO USE THIS REPORT

Each of the reports on the constitutions, statutes, and rules of the fifty states and the District of Columbia hereafter set forth contains five sections.

The first—Mandatory Retirement Provisions Applicable Generally—deals with involuntary retirement for age, involuntary retirement for disability;[1] the procedural provisions applicable to the latter, and notation of decisions of the jurisdiction's courts relating to the constitutionality of such provisions or procedures under it. To be noted, however, is that Gregory v. Ashcroft, 501 U.S. 452, upholding the constitutionality of Missouri's mandatory retirement for age, is not referenced except in the Missouri report, but that its reasoning supports the constitutionality of mandatory retirement for age in other jurisdictions imposing such a requirement at least until such time as medical evidence with respect to mental ability of the elderly makes a legislative determination with respect to a particular age unreasonable.

The second section—Retirement Provisions re Particular Courts—as its title indicates, reports on the rules governing retirement from those particular courts that differ from the generally applicable rules. Only a few states differentiate between courts as to retirement.

The third section—Optional Provisions for Retirement—reports on voluntary retirement for age and/or service and voluntary retirement for disability and the procedures related thereto. It does not discuss the amount of either form of retirement benefits, except to note those provisions that equate retirement for disability with voluntary retirement for age and/or service. It also does not as a general matter discuss insurance benefits, survivor benefits, death benefits, or deferred compensation plans, although some reports contain reference to one or more of such provisions.

The section does, however, report provisions authorizing cost of living increase in such benefits, and those that protect such benefits from various

---

[1] In some states involuntary retirement for disability is dealt with in the same statute concerned with impeachment. However, impeachment is not discussed in the reports.

forms of legal process and prohibit assignment, except for amounts due from the retiree to the retirement system or for child or spousal support pursuant to court judgment or decree.

The fourth section—Service After Retirement—deals with the extent to which the state permits retired judges to function in a judicial capacity: whether as senior judge, special judge, surrogate judge, temporary judge, judicial hearing officer, or other titles, how long after retirement the retiree may continue in that capacity, and the extent to which continuation is dependent upon periodic mental and/or physical examination, and whether a retiree so serving is required to attend continuing education courses. It also reports on provisions that permit a retiree to serve as an arbitrator or mediator in a court-related or privately sponsored alternative dispute resolution proceeding, or as a member of a commission or other body related to the judiciary.

The fifth section—Pay and Emoluments—concerns how a retiree is compensated for service after retirement, whether he or she is entitled to credit for such service toward receiving maximum retirement benefits if he or she retired at an earlier age or with fewer years of service than required for that purpose, whether only time spent in hearing is compensated or whether time in research and preparation of a decision is also paid for, whether travel and expenses are compensated, and whether such a retiree continues to be included in health or other insurance programs.

With respect to the five paragraphs preceding this one, it should be noted that if a particular state report does not discuss an item referred to in those paragraphs, such as cost of living increase in retirement benefits, exemption of such benefits from tax or legal process, continuing education for retirees serving after retirement, no such provision has been found in the state's constitution, statute, or rules.

Production of this volume was begun in 1995 and completed in mid-1998, but in view of the large number of constitutional and statutory provisions and court rules covered, it has not been possible to bring each such provision up to date of publication of this volume by searching for possible change after the report was put in final form. Therefore, users of this volume interested in a particular provision or rule should review the state's post-1996 legislative materials for possible repeal, revision, or amendment.

A word should be said concerning the research supporting the fifty-one reports contained herein. When the research by students and others was done, the format of the reports had not been developed. When it was decided to use the format as a basis for preparing proposed uniform provisions, follow-up research was done for each of the fifty-one jurisdictions to be sure that all relevant provisions were included. That research began with the General Index and covered all relevant index headings, the constitution or statute provisions thus uncovered and the annotations thereto, and legislative materials enacted or adopted thereafter up to the time of preparation of the report for the particular state.

The sections of this volume that follow set forth:

1. a review of the retirement provisions in the fifty-one jurisdictions, titled "Why Judicial Retirement Laws Should Be Changed";
2. a section titled "How Judicial Retirement Laws Should Be Changed," proposing simplification and, to the extent possible, uniformity in those provisions;
3. the fifty-one reports that form the basis for the study and the simplification proposals.

I

Why Judicial Retirement Laws Should be Changed: A Comparison of the Laws of the Fifty States and the District of Columbia

When should a judge be forced to retire? To what extent should he or she be permitted to serve after retiring? When should he or she be permitted voluntarily to retire? A review of state and federal judicial retirement law reveals a host of inconsistencies in the way these questions are answered.

The anomaly of requiring retirement at a particular age is illustrated by the U.S. Supreme Court's decision of Gregory v. Ashcroft, 501 U.S. 452[1] upholding Missouri's mandatory requirement that judges retire at age seventy. That decision held (p.473) that "the people of Missouri rationally could conclude that the threat of deterioration at age 70 is sufficiently great and the alternative of removal sufficiently inadequate that they will require all judges to step aside at age 70." Yet because the U.S. Constitution allows all federal judges to serve on all trial and appellate levels without limitation to age, of the seven justices who concurred in that decision, two (White and Brennan) were over seventy and two of the dissenters (Blackmun and Marshall) were eighty-two. Of interest also is the decision of the New Hampshire Supreme Court which in Grinnell v. State, 121 N.H. 823, 435 A.2d 523 reached the same conclusion notwithstanding that the court recognized that mandatory retirement deprived the bench of many able jurists who are forced to retire at the height of their intellectual creativity.

An equally glaring example involves James Kent, known as New York's "great chancellor." When he was appointed to that office in 1814, New York's 1777 Constitution compelled retirement of all judges at age sixty, which age Kent attained in 1823, after but nine years of service. Yet Kent lived until 1847 and during those twenty-four years wrote *Kent's Commentaries*, which to this day is referred to in opinions, articles, and texts and taught in law schools as much as many modern texts.

Moreover, the anomaly exists not only with respect to federal judges, but also in relation to the thirteen states whose constitution and statutes include no compulsory retirement provisions (California, Delaware, Idaho [which earlier had such provision but repealed it], Kentucky, Maine, Mis-

---

[1] Citations are given for case law referred to in this section, but are not given for provisions of constitutions, statutes, or rules, since they can be found in the reports concerning the particular state set forth in the later section of this volume.

sissippi, Nebraska, Nevada, New Mexico, Oklahoma, Rhode Island, Tennessee and West Virginia).

THE MANY EXCEPTIONS TO MANDATORY AGE RETIREMENT

Further, the provisions of jurisdictions that mandate retirement for age are far from consistent, although it is highly doubtful that geographic location has any direct effect upon mental or physical ability. Nor are they clearly inconsistent with provisions, considered below in relation to Service After Retirement, which permit retirees to serve after retirement without age limitation. Thus, twenty-four states (Alabama, Alaska, Arizona, Arkansas, Connecticut, Florida, Hawaii, Kansas, Louisiana, Maryland, Massachusetts, Michigan, Minnesota, Missouri, New Hampshire, New Jersey, New York, Ohio, Pennsylvania, South Dakota, Vermont, Virginia, Wisconsin and Wyoming) require retirement on attaining seventy, or at the end of the year in which age seventy is attained, but a number of those provisions are not absolute. And, in the instance of a judge who fails to retire on attaining age seventy, at least three are so phrased as to provide for loss of retirement benefits but return of the judge's contributions (Alabama), or simply to mandate loss of retirement benefits (Arkansas), or require forfeiture of salary and retirement compensation (Missouri). An exception to the latter rule, however, is made for a retiree under seventy-six years of age who serves as appointed defense counsel for indigent persons facing a criminal charge! By implication, therefore, a judge who is well enough off financially not to need salary or retirement benefits can continue to serve in those states, unless for some reason other than age he or she is impeached, although no case so holding has been found.

Sixteen of the states prescribing retirement at age seventy make exceptions to that requirement. Thus, Arkansas permits a judge who is not eligible to retire at seventy to continue to serve until completion of the term of office in which he or she receives sufficient service credit to retire without losing such benefits. Connecticut permits the chief justice, or a judge of the supreme court, a judge of the superior court, or a judge of the court of common pleas who after seventy has become a state referee to exercise the powers of the superior court or court of common pleas on matters referred to him or her as a state referee, apparently without limitation as to age. Florida permits a judge who has turned seventy to complete the term of office one-half of which he or she has served when he or she became seventy, or to serve upon temporary assignment.

Kansas law permits an incumbent judge who becomes seventy, if he or she so desires, to finish the term during which he or she became seventy. Louisiana law provides that the judicial service rights of a judge in office or retired when the 1974 Constitution was adopted shall not be diminished, and that a judge who was over the age of seventy on December 1, 1974 could remain in service until he or she has served twenty years or until the age of eighty, whichever first occurs. And Michigan's case law has held that a judge in office when its 1974 Constitution was adopted could serve until the end of his or her term (Ball v. Thomas, 1 Mich. App.1, 133 N.W.2d 218).

Minnesota law permits any judge who becomes eligible for retirement within three years after expiration of the term to which elected, and who applies to the governor for extension of the term, stating his or her intention to retire when eligible, to have his or her time extended by the governor for three years or such part thereof as is necessary for eligibility to retire. As above noted, Missouri excepts a retiree under seventy-six who serves as appointed defense counsel for indigent persons facing criminal charges; and New Hampshire's age seventy retirement provision has been held not applicable to justices of the peace (Keniston v. State, 63 N.H. 37).

New York law requires retirement at the end of the year in which the judge becomes seventy, but permits a judge of its appellate division or supreme court (New York's highest trial court) to serve for six years thereafter if he or she is found at the end of the year in which the judge became seventy, and at the end of the second and fourth years thereafter, to be mentally and physically fit, and a judge of the Court of Appeals who retires at seventy as required, to return to the supreme court for six years, subject to the same biennial examinations. New York law permits no such extension for its numerous judges of other trial courts, yet inconsistently imposes no retirement age on retirees serving as Judicial Hearing Officers or on justices of the peace. Ohio law proscribes election or appointment as a judge of a person who reaches seventy on the day before he or she would assume office; but since it has no mandatory retirement provision, a person who would not reach seventy until the day of assumption of office or thereafter apparently may serve the full term of the judgeship to which appointed or elected. And South Dakota law permits a judge who reaches age seventy to conclude matters then pending before him or her, unless the supreme court makes provision for other disposition of the matters.

Vermont's Constitution requires retirement of all judges at the end of the calendar year in which age seventy is reached, or at the end of the term during which the judge reaches seventy, and establishes a six-year term of office which may be extended for another six years unless a majority of the General Assembly vote against extension. Apparently, therefore, a justice or judge elected or continued in office at age sixty-nine may retain office until age seventy-six, although no court decision so holding has been found. Virginia law requires all judges who attain seventy to retire twenty days after the convening of the next regular session of the General Assembly. Wisconsin's Constitution requires retirement on the July 31 following the date on which the person attains the age of not less than seventy years, which the legislature shall prescribe. The legislature has not prescribed a higher age beyond which regular justices or judges cannot serve; but as to reserve judges (defined in the Wisconsin report below) it was held in State ex rel Godfrey v. Gollman, 76 Wis.2d 417, 251 N.W.2d 438, that reserve judges, as distinguished from regular justices and judges, could serve after the age of seventy; and Wyoming's Constitution provides that the office of every justice or judge becomes vacant when the incumbent reaches the age of seventy, as the legislature may prescribe. However, Wyoming statute mandates retirement of supreme court and district court judges at age seventy, but has enacted no mandatory provisions as to county judges, municipal judges, and justices of the peace.

Finally, to be noted with respect to mandatory retirement for age are the states of Colorado, Iowa, North Carolina, and South Carolina, where the mandatory age is seventy-two; North Dakota where it is seventy-three; the District of Columbia where it is seventy-four; and the states of Georgia, Illinois, Indiana, Louisiana, Oregon, Texas, Utah, and Washington where judges are not required to retire until attaining seventy-five years of age. A number of those states' statutes contain exceptions even to that age. Thus, Iowa, which prior to July 1, 1965, did not require retirement until seventy-five, in that year reduced the age to seventy-two, but provided that the reduced age applied only to judges appointed after July 1, 1965. North Carolina's law mandates retirement on the first day of the month next succeeding age seventy-two. North Dakota's statute provides that a judge who fails to apply for retirement prior to attaining seventy-three waives all retirement benefits unless he or she has not served ten years at seventy-three, in which case he or she does not waive benefits, provided he or she retires at the expiration of the term. Georgia's statute requires a judge of the court of appeals or a justice of the supreme court to file a notice of election to retire on or before the day on which he or she reaches seventy-five, or on the last day of the term that he or she is serving when he or she attains age seventy, whichever is later, but a trial judge is required to retire on the first day of the calendar month following that in which he or she reached age seventy. Illinois requires judges to retire only at the end of the term during which they reached seventy-five, but in Anagnost v. Laglie, 230 Ill. App.2d 109, 595 N.E.2d 109 it was held that a seventy-eight year old former judge was a proper candidate for reelection, since the retirement statute imposed no bar concerning who could run for election to judicial office. Utah's statute mandates retirement at seventy-five but permits a judge or justice who is sixty-five or older on July 1, 1996, to serve until December 31 of the year in which he or she would have been subject to retention election. However, it bars a county judge who reached seventy-five before that date or before the first Monday in February, 1999, as well as a municipal justice court judge who reached seventy-five before that date or before the first Monday in February 2000, from reelection or reappointment.

Involuntary Disability Retirement Provisions Are Equally Diverse

Similar diversity infests the provisions that deal with involuntary retirement for disability. The statutes of Arizona, Georgia, and New York make no provision for involuntary retirement for disability, although New York judges or justices permitted to serve beyond age seventy can serve only for three two-year terms and must pass physical and mental examination before the beginning of each two-year term.

A number of state provisions speak of disability which seriously interferes with the performance of the judge's duties and is, or is likely to be, permanent (Alaska, California, District of Columbia, Hawaii, Idaho, Indiana, Kansas [so incapacitated as to be unable to perform duties adequately], Kentucky [which authorizes its commission to order temporary or permanent retirement], Louisiana [as to judges who are members of the State Employee Retirement System], Maryland, Minnesota, Mississippi, Nebraska, New Mexico, Rhode Island {seriously interferes and will continue to interfere with performance of duties], South Dakota {which, however, contains no language with respect to permanence], Texas [which, however, only requires that the disability is likely to become permanent], Utah, Virginia, and Wyoming). Iowa's provision is identical except that it substitutes "substantially interferes" for "seriously interferes," but the District of Columbia, Maryland, Mississippi, and Rhode Island laws each include an alternate definition listed below.

Other states' definitions are more absolute, referring to a judge who is physically or mentally unable to perform the duties of the office (Alabama, Illinois, and Louisiana [as to Judicial Retirement System members]), to a physical or mental disability which so incapacitates the judge that it is impossible for him or her to perform the duties of office (Maine), which prevents the performance of judicial duties (Michigan), prevents proper performance of duties and is, or is likely to be, permanent (Nevada), to total and permanent disability which prevents rendering useful and efficient service (Florida), or is so disabled as to prevent the carrying out of duties for ninety days or more (Tennessee).

Some state definitions speak of permanent sickness (Missouri), habitual intemperance (District of Columbia, Michigan, Mississippi, South Dakota), advanced age (Massachusetts, Nevada, West Virginia [but the West Virginia Supreme Court Rules limit such retirement to a judge who is eligible to receive retirement benefits]), or to incompetence or any other cause rendering a judge incapable of performing judicial duties (Oregon). At least one state (Ohio) distinguishes between permanent mental disability, which prohibits discharging the duties of the office, and physical disability, which so impairs the judge's facilities as to prevent the proper discharge of judicial duties for six months.

INVOLUNTARY RETIREMENT FOR ACCIDENTAL DISABILITY

New Hampshire authorizes retirement for accidental disability, defined as total and permanent mental or physical incapacity for duty as the natural and proximate result of an accident occurring while in the actual performance of duty, without willful negligence on the judge's part. Vermont's provision differs only in that it speaks of "accidental and occupationally related disability," defined as an accident occurring at a definite time and place during the course of performance of duty and was not the result of his or her negligence or willful misconduct. Many states' provisions protect the judge's interests by expressly stating that though involuntarily retired, the judge's retirement is to be considered voluntary (Alaska, Arkansas, California, Hawaii, Iowa, Kentucky, Minnesota, Mississippi, Nebraska, Nevada, New Mexico, North Dakota, Pennsylvania, Utah, Virginia, Washington, and Wyoming) and two also require the state to pay the judge's counsel fee if the complaint concerning disability is dismissed (Rhode Island and Wisconsin).

Burden of Proof of Disability

Clear and convincing evidence of disability is required by the laws of New Mexico, Ohio, and Pennsylvania, but in Ohio and Pennsylvania the unjustified refusal to submit to medical examination is evidence of disability. Under the Wisconsin statute the disability must be proved to a reasonable certainty by clear, satisfactory, and convincing evidence.

Periodic Examination of, and Income Reporting by, Disability Retirees

Several state statutes protect the state's interest by requiring the disabled judge to submit to periodic medical examination (Vermont) or to report income earned during disability retirement (Pennsylvania and South Dakota) and New Hampshire's law makes clear that the pension of a judge on disability retirement who is engaged in or able to engage in a gainful occupation may be reduced and that if he or she is restored to service, the pension ceases.

Most Retirement Laws Apply Uniformly to All State Courts

Only eighteen of the fifty-one jurisdictions distinguish between courts with respect to retirement. Some involve courts generally thought to require knowledge of a particular area of law: District of Columbia (tax court); Rhode Island (workers compensation judges). Most, however, relate to judges sitting in a court that serves a limited geographic area: Alabama (permits municipalities to enact their own retirement provisions); California (case law holds that a former justice court judge is not eligible for assignment after retirement); Indiana (a person may not run for judge of the county court or for judge of the superior court in four named counties if he or she will be seventy or older before the term of office begins); Kansas (permits district magistrate judges to elect to become members of the retirement system); Minnesota (service of municipal court judges after retirement is limited to judges of the municipal court of Hennepin County); New Jersey (a judge of the county court, county district court, and the juvenile and domestic relations court of any county who was not eligible to retire when these offices were abolished, permitted to apply for retirement at age sixty); New Mexico (has a separate Magistrate Retirement Act, largely though not entirely identical in language to the Judicial Retirement Act); New York (town justices of the peace and village police justices are not subject to retirement laws); South Carolina (probate judges may elect between retirement systems); Tennessee (city judges may become members of the state's consolidated retirement system if the municipality so provides by resolution; judges of a general sessions court, a trial justice court, a county judge, a probate judge, or a judge of the juvenile and/or domestic relations court whose compensation is paid wholly by the county may become members of the state's consolidated system); Utah (bars a county or municipal justice court judge who reached seventy-five before July 1, 1996 or specified later dates from reelection or reappointment). One state, Nevada, by providing that during twelve months after retirement a district court judge who retired in good standing may sign any records left unsigned at the time he left office, protects the interests of the state and of the litigants.

OPTIONAL RETIREMENT FOR AGE AND/OR SERVICE

Optional retirement for age and/or service is dealt with in equally diverse fashion. In part this results from the fact that a judge may qualify for retirement under more than one system of retirement (Florida, Louisiana, Montana, Washington, and West Virginia).

The earliest age provided for is forty-five (New Hampshire), and the latest is seventy (Alabama, California, Rhode Island, South Carolina, Utah, and Wyoming). With respect to years of service, one (New Jersey) permits any judge who attains age sixty while serving as a judge to make written application for retirement, but specifies no years of service requirement, while Idaho provides that judges of the supreme court and district court may retire at age sixty-five with but four years of service, Mississippi permits judges of any court to retire at sixty with four years service credit, and Wyoming allows judges of the county and municipal courts and justices of the peace to seek early retirement at or after sixty-five years of age with at least four years of service.

Service alone without regard to age may be the basis for retirement after thirty years of service in Connecticut (ten years of which must be as a judge), Florida (but only twenty years for circuit judges), Louisiana, Montana, Vermont, and Washington; after twenty-five years in Hawaii, Iowa, and Mississippi; after twenty-four years of service in Delaware, New Mexico, and North Carolina; and after twenty years of service in Arkansas, Connecticut (all as a judge), and Idaho. The specified years of service must be consecutive under the laws of Iowa and Wyoming. Under the Texas statute only the most recent ten years must be continuous, but in the District of Columbia, Hawaii, New Jersey, and Virginia such service need not be continuous, and the New Jersey provision expressly states that years of employment by the state in other occupations than as a judge are to be credited.

With respect to the age a judge must have attained in order to seek retirement, a number of states specify but one age: Connecticut (sixty-five), Colorado (sixty), Delaware (sixty-two), Idaho (sixty-five), Illinois (sixty-two), Indiana (sixty-two, but he or she may not be receiving a salary from the state other than for service as a judge pro tempore or senior judge), Kentucky (sixty-five), Maryland (sixty), Virginia (fifty-five). Others specify various complex combinations of service and age as to which no useful purpose would be served by analyzing them here, other than to note that three statutes permit retirement at or after age and service together total eighty (Oklahoma), eighty-five (Kansas), or eighty-eight (North Dakota). One state (Washington) defers payment of retirement benefits until age sixty for anyone who leaves office before that age, and another (West Virginia) states that the judge need not be in office when the pension begins. Seventeen states permit retirement on a reduced pension at an age below that required for full retirement benefits (Florida, Illinois, Kansas, Maine, Mississippi, Montana, Nebraska, Nevada, New Hampshire, New Mexico, Rhode Island, South Dakota, Texas, Vermont, Washington, and Wisconsin). Oklahoma's statute provides that in computing the periods of time served a major fraction of a year is counted as a whole year, but Pennsylvania allows fractional points for fractional parts of a year of service. One state (Oregon), which provides for retirement at sixty-five, permits retirement on reduced benefits at age sixty but requires that a judge who retires at sixty must serve without compensation as a judge pro tempore for thirty-five days per year for a period of five years from date of retirement.

VOLUNTARY RETIREMENT FOR DISABILITY

Voluntary retirement for disability is not dealt with by Rhode Island's statutes. Of those jurisdictions that provide for such retirement, Colorado's statute expressly states that there is no service requirement and Kentucky statute states that the eight-year service requirement on which normal retirement depends does not apply to disability retirement. Of those jurisdictions that impose a service requirement, the requirements for disability retirement vary from 180 days to fifteen years. Thus, North Dakota requires for judges retiring under the Public Employee Retirement System at least 180 days of eligible employment, that the disability have occurred during eligible employment, and that application be made within twelve months after termination of employment. Alaska, California (for judges who become such prior to January 1, 1989), and Illinois (for temporary total disability) require two years; Arkansas, Maryland, three years; California (for judges who became such after January 1, 1989), Idaho, and Mississippi, four years, but an Idaho judge who has less than four years who seeks disability retirement can get a refund of contributions to the system, plus interest. Disability retirement is conditioned upon five years service in California (for members of Judicial Retirement System II), the District of Columbia, Florida (for members of the Retirement System who become such prior to July 1, 1980), Nevada, New Mexico (but its service requirement may be waived if the disability arises solely out of judicial duty), North Carolina (as to judges who entered into office on or after January 1, 1974), Pennsylvania, South Carolina, Vermont, and Wisconsin (but Wisconsin statute provides that its five year-service requirement is inapplicable to an application for disability retirement made prior to the judge's normal retirement date). Six years service is required in Iowa; seven years in Texas and eight years in Michigan, in North Carolina (as to judges who entered into office prior to January 1, 1974), and Tennessee. Florida's service requirement is ten years for members of the Retirement System who became such after July 1, 1980; Georgia's is ten years for trial judges but Hawaii's is ten years for all judges, as is Louisiana's, New Hampshire's, and West Virginia's. However, Massachusetts and Minnesota impose what appears to be the longest service requirement (fifteen years in Massachusetts; one full term and seventy years of age, or two full terms, in Minnesota).

The definitions of disability with respect to voluntary retirement are as many and various as those for involuntary disability retirement, and in some states definition of the term for voluntary retirement differs from its definition for involuntary retirement. Thus, South Dakota leaves it to the board to set criteria for defining disability but requires that the method of doing so be applied uniformly and consistently and that no such application be determined until after the employer has certified that it is unable to provide comparable level employment; and Wyoming requires permanent disability for involuntary retirement but permits voluntary retirement for partial disability, defined as a condition that renders a member unable to perform the occupation for which he or she is reasonably suited by training or experience but still allows him or her to function in other employment, and which is reasonably expected to last at least twelve months.

A number of states condition retirement on permanent incapacitation or disability (Arizona, Arkansas, Colorado, Delaware, Idaho, Iowa, Kansas, Nevada, New Hampshire), but some require only that the disability "is or is likely to be permanent" (Alaska, Kentucky, Louisiana, Maryland, Mississippi, Utah, Vermont, Virginia), or reasonably likely to become permanent (Indiana, Nebraska), or is of permanent or extended duration (Montana). In many states the incapacity must be total (Florida, Georgia, Indiana, Louisiana, Massachusetts, New Mexico, North Carolina, South Carolina, Wyoming), or prevent further performance of judicial duties (Hawaii, Texas), proper performance of such duties (Oklahoma), or make it *impossible* for the judge to perform his or her duties as such (Maine). Many states have less stringent criteria, however: that the judge is unable for an extended duration to perform any work for which qualified (Oregon); that the disability prevents proper performance of his or her duties (Oklahoma); that the judge is incapacitated "to the extent that public service suffers therefrom" (Minnesota); that he or she is permanently unable to carry out his or her duties on a full-time basis (Alabama); or unable to fulfill adequately the duties of office (Connecticut); or unable reasonably to perform the duties of office (Illinois); or incapacitated from full and efficient performance of such duties (New Jersey, Washington) or the discharge of such duties efficiently (California, North Carolina); or that the disability seriously interferes with such performance (District of Columbia, Tennessee).

California requires that the disability arise out of and in the course of judicial service. New Jersey and Washington provisions refer to a judge "physically or otherwise incapacitated," and New York requires that the judge file a petition stating that he or she "is, for reasons specified, incapacitated to perform the duties of the Office." Almost all other states' governing provisions define disability to mean physical or mental incapacity, but the South Carolina statute speaks of a member "totally and permanently disabled, physically or mentally, or both." The Tennessee statute provides that when medical factors alone are not determinative, vocational factors, including age, education, training, and work experience must be considered, and Wyoming authorizes its board to require functional capacity evaluations and vocational examinations.

TERMINATION OR REDUCTION OF DISABILITY BENEFITS

In Colorado, if the board determines that the judge has recovered, the disability benefit continues until he or she has been reinstated in his or her former position or has accepted public or private employment, the compensation for which, together with the disability benefit, equals or exceeds the compensation last earned as a member. Several states require reevaluation after one year (New Mexico), or periodic examination of a judge after disability retirement and discontinue the retirement benefit until such examination occurs or revoke the benefit if the refusal to be examined continues for a year (New Hampshire, Vermont), or discontinue (New Mexico, Washington) or reduce (New Hampshire) the benefit if the member is found able to engage in a gainful occupation,[2] or revoke the benefit if found able to perform his or her former duties and is restored to service (Montana, Ohio, cf Missouri). New Mexico, Pennsylvania, and South Dakota also require the judge to report periodically all employment income earned and suspend the benefit until such report is filed (South Dakota) or revoke it if the refusal to file continues for six months.

VOLUNTARY RETIREMENT FOR ACCIDENTAL DISABILITY

Separate provisions with respect to accidentally incurred disability are contained in the statutes of Massachusetts, New Mexico, New York, Oregon,

---

[2] In Washington the benefit of a member found to be gainfully employed ceases unless the compensation from such employment is less than the member earned at date of disability, in which event it is reduced to an amount which, together with the compensation earned, equals the judge's compensation at the date of disability retirement.

South Carolina, South Dakota, Utah, Washington, and West Virginia. Each of those states requires that the disability be incurred during active service. Each requires bodily injury, except Massachusetts (which refers to "personal injury sustained or hazard undergone at some definite time or place"), New York (which requires only incapacity resulting from "an incident"), and Oregon and West Virginia (whose statutes include "injury or disease").

New Mexico, South Dakota, and West Virginia, each of which has a service requirement for disability retirement, waive that requirement if the disability is the direct and proximate result (New Mexico) or natural and proximate result (West Virginia), or the member was disabled by accident while performing his or her usual duties (South Dakota). New Mexico requires further that the disability arise solely and exclusively out of and in the course of such service. Under Utah's statute the injury must be the sole cause of disability and must result from external force or violence. And the West Virginia statute adds that the judge must have received workers compensation on account of the physical or mental disability. In three states the incapacity must have been incurred "without serious or wilful misconduct on the judge's part" (Massachusetts), "not by his [or her] own wilful negligence" (New York), and "not self-inflicted" (Oregon).

COST OF LIVING ADJUSTMENT OF BENEFIT

Cost of living adjustment of the retirement benefit is provided for by twenty-eight jurisdictions. Generally, only adjustment by way of increase is authorized, but the statutes of five states (New Mexico, Oregon, Tennessee, Vermont, Wyoming [as to judges of the supreme court and district court]) provide not only for increase but also for decrease of such benefits. The most common provision is for an annual increase based upon the increase in a specified index of the United States Department of Labor's Consumer Price Index (District of Columbia, Kentucky, Minnesota, Oregon, Virginia, Washington) or on the Consumer Price Index and other specific statutory provisions for increase (Mississippi, Nevada, North Carolina, Ohio) or on eighty percent of the Consumer Price Index, but not to exceed in total sixty-five percent of the initial benefit (Missouri), but Wyoming's increase is determined by its State Division of Economic Analysis, and New Hampshire's statute directs that the increase be actuarially computed.

Several states relate the increase of a retiree's allowance to the salary of a judge holding the same position the retiree held when he or she retired (Maryland), or to the increase for judges of a specified court during the prior twelve months (Wyoming), or with respect to a disability retiree that there be only such increase as the legislature grants (Montana).

Some states make an increase of a retiree's allowance available only after a number of months or years after retirement: twelve months (Tennessee); two years or one full calendar year (New Mexico); three years (Montana, Rhode Island); or six years (Nebraska); or make availability of an increase contingent upon whether the investment gain in reserves for retired members or beneficiaries exceeds accrued liabilities for the preceding fiscal year (Mississippi), or turn on the effect it will have on the retirement fund (Oklahoma).

Annual or total limitations on the adjustment are imposed by Montana (1.5 percent annually), Wyoming (1.5 percent annually, but excess may be accumulated and used in a subsequent year to bring the increase for that year to 1.5 percent), Illinois (three percent cumulative of all prior increases), Nebraska (three percent annually, total not to exceed $250 per month), New Mexico (three percent cumulatively, but the retiree may decline the increase), Ohio (three percent annually, provided that the excess may be accumulated and used in any subsequent year to bring the increase for that year to three percent, and provided further that the benefit does not exceed the limit established by 26 U.S.C.A. §415 [relating to state pension plans]), Rhode Island (three percent annually but *not* compounded), Virginia (three percent, plus half of the increase over three percent up to seven percent), Utah (four percent of the monthly allowance, but the excess may be accumulated and used in any subsequent year to bring the increase to four percent), and Missouri (total increase in benefit may not exceed sixty-five percent of the initial benefit).

Statutes enacting particularized methods of computing benefit increase exist in Iowa (based on date of retirement, years of service and stated percentages), North Dakota (for members employed prior to January 1, 1996, an increase of two percent beginning August 1, 1993 and of one percent beginning January 1, 1994), Oregon (as to judge who retired in 1984 or thereafter in varying percentages based on when the judge retired), and South Dakota (monthly increase on or after July 1, 1979, for members who were receiving or were eligible to receive a retirement allowance as of June 30, 1974).

Exemption of Benefits from Taxation or Legal Process
and Unassignability of Benefits

Tax exemption of retirement benefits, exemption from legal process, and unassignability of such benefits are provided for in thirty-six states.

The taxability of retirement benefits is dealt with by the laws of twenty-six states, two of which (New Mexico and North Dakota) repealed preexisting exemptions, and the statute of one of which (Vermont) expressly provides that such benefits are *not* exempt from taxes, including income taxes. One state (Wisconsin) exempts such benefits from "any tax, other than a tax on income levied by the state or any subdivision of the state." However, most of the provisions exempt from state and local taxes, state and municipal taxes, state, county, or municipal taxes, or state, county, municipal, or local taxes (Kansas, Kentucky, Louisiana, Montana, Nevada, New Hampshire, New Jersey, New York, Pennsylvania, Rhode Island, South Carolina, South Dakota, Tennessee, Texas, Utah, Virginia, Washington, West Virginia, Wyoming), but Mississippi's law goes beyond that to specify "any state, county or municipal ad valorem taxes, income taxes, premium taxes, privilege taxes, property taxes, sales and use taxes or other taxes not so named." Particular taxes are excepted from the exemption by the laws of some of those states: estate or inheritance tax (New York, Oregon, South Carolina, *cf* Utah [which includes within its exemption payments to a beneficiary]; personal income tax (Oregon, Rhode Island, South Carolina); school tax (Ohio). Montana grants only a partial exemption: neither an annuity in excess of $3,600 nor the refund of a member's contributions to the retirement system made after June 30, 1985 are exempt. Utah's statute also contains a somewhat esoteric exception from its exemption of any benefits subject to federal income tax which have not been taxed.

With respect to exemption of retirement benefits from legal process and the unassignability of such benefits, no provision has been found in the statutes of Alabama, Alaska, Arizona, Arkansas, California, Connecticut, Florida, Georgia, Hawaii, Indiana, Maine, Massachusetts; and although the statutes of Delaware, Idaho, Iowa, Nevada, and Rhode Island contain such provisions with respect to retirement benefits of state employees other than judges, no such provision with respect to judges has been found. In the statutes of the states that exempt judges' retirement benefits, the usual provision exempts from execution, levy, garnishment, attachment, bankruptcy or insolvency proceedings, or other legal process (Colorado, District of Columbia, Illinois, Kansas, Kentucky, Louisiana, Maryland, Minnesota, Mississippi, Missouri, Montana, New Jersey, New York, Ohio, Pennsylvania, South Carolina, South Dakota, Texas, Vermont, West Virginia, Wisconsin, Wyoming), although the statutes of some of those states do not include some of those processes (e.g., bankruptcy or insolvency). In a number of these states the statute excepts from the exemption a qualified domestic relations order, a child support order, a marital property settlement, or money due to the retirement system or to the state (Colorado, Louisiana, Maryland, Minnesota, Mississippi, Missouri, Montana, Nebraska, Nevada, New Mexico, Tennessee). To be noted, however, is that the wording of the exception from the exemption varies in some of the statutes of those states and that the New Hampshire statute grants an exception only to the extent that benefits under a private retirement system are exempted.

The statutes of Colorado, District of Columbia, Illinois, Iowa, Kansas, and Minnesota also proscribe any assignment of such benefits, while those of other states, although containing such a proscription, exempt from it specified items. Thus, Montana exempts a rollover allowed by the Internal Revenue Code, payment to an employer of an employment-related claim, or a group insurance premium which the retiree elected to have withheld; New York exempts insurance and medicare premiums and the employees' membership organization dues; Pennsylvania exempts an assignment to a credit union as security for a loan or to the retirement board which has satisfied such a loan and money due the state on account of employment; and those of North Carolina, Oklahoma, Oregon, Pennsylvania, South Carolina, South Dakota, Tennessee, Utah, West Virginia, Wisconsin, and Wyoming exempt assignment pursuant to qualified domestic relations orders, for support of a spouse, former spouse, child or other dependent, or pursuant to a settlement agreement incident to a matrimonial action, or with respect to claims of the retirement system for overpayment of benefits, or of the state arising out of employment, although not all of the above-listed states' statutes exclude all of the foregoing assignments.

SERVICE AFTER RETIREMENT

Service after retirement is authorized by all fifty-one jurisdictions, all but two of which require the consent of, or an application by, the retired justice or judge. Idaho requires any retired justice or judge to sit as a district court judge or magistrate when so directed by the chief justice of the supreme court, and Virginia's statute provides that a retired district court judge under seventy years of age when called upon by the chief justice *must* perform such judicial duties as the chief justice deems necessary for a period not to exceed ninety days at any one time.

PRACTICE OF LAW BY RETIRED JUDGES

The practice of law by a justice or judge serving after retirement is expressly dealt with by the laws of nineteen states. Twelve states preclude such practice altogether while so authorized (Alabama, Connecticut, Delaware, Florida, Iowa, Maryland, Massachusetts, Nevada, New Jersey, South Carolina, Virginia, Wyoming), two only while so serving (Hawaii, Tennessee), Georgia permits practice if the retired judge resigns his or her senior judgeship, Pennsylvania requires the retired judge to agree not to engage in law practice now or in the future, Texas conditions assignment on the retired judge's agreement not to appear in any Texas court for two years, Utah requires that the retiree not have practiced law since retirement and not practice while a senior judge, but the Kentucky Supreme Court has held that a special judge pro tempore is *not* barred from practicing law while serving as such a judge, and Hawaii's statute concerning appointment of a per diem district court judge, while it does not mention retired judges, is broad enough to include them and permits such a judge to engage in private practice during his or her term of service as such.

ASSIGNMENT TO JUDICIAL DUTY OF RETIRED JUDGES

The statutory provisions for assignment of retired justices or judges to judicial duty are too many and varied to warrant complete classification. To be eligible for assignment, a retired justice or judge must have served as a justice or judge for various periods: two years, except three years for judges serving in Baltimore or named counties (Maryland); at least four years (Wisconsin), for service as a private judge (Indiana), for service as a district court judge of the Philadelphia Municipal Court (Pennsylvania), or for service as a district judge outside the First Judicial Region (Texas); at least five years, but less than ten (Florida); five years, but not more than ten years since retirement (North Carolina); six years for a judge required to retire at age seventy; eight years (Mississippi, Montana) or for a judge of the supreme court or circuit court (Wisconsin); ten years (Georgia, New Hampshire, Pennsylvania); or twelve years (Missouri, Texas [for judges in the First Judicial Region]).

Physical or mental capacity to perform the duties of office is an express condition of assignment in a number of states (Alaska, Arizona, Arkansas, District of Columbia, Idaho, Maryland, New York, Utah), but Tennessee's statute requires only that the retired judge seeking to serve as a senior judge present evidence only that he or she is not disabled so as to substantially interfere with the performance of his or her duties as such. Also ineligible for assignment is a judge defeated in a retention election or who fails of reelection to office under the statutes of Florida, Maryland, Mississippi, Nevada, Wisconsin, but the Oklahoma Supreme Court has ruled that defeat for reelection does *not* bar assignment of a retired district judge as a temporary judge or a judge pro tempore.

TITLE OF RETIREES PERFORMING JUDICIAL DUTIES

The title of the office held by a retired judge assigned to duty after retirement may be senior judge, special judge, private judge, judge pro tempore, surrogate judge, temporary judge, judicial hearing officer, special magistrate, judicial referee, master, or commissioner. The common element of the private judge, the judge pro tempore, the temporary judge, and the special magistrate is that they became such by agreement of the parties: private judge (Indiana), judge pro tempore (Arizona, Arkansas, Colorado, Florida, Idaho, Michigan, Ohio, Rhode Island, Tennessee, Texas, Washington); temporary judge (California); special magistrate (Minnesota). Although the statutes of Arizona, Arkansas, California, Colorado, Florida, Idaho, Nevada, and New Mexico make no express references to retired judges, the text of each concerning eligibility is broad enough to include them, and a California case has so held with respect to its statute. A unique provision is that of West Virginia, which authorizes a circuit court judge who finds that the public interest requires a special term to so direct, but provides that the judge to hold such term shall be elected by the attorneys practicing in the circuit court. The statute does not mention retired judges, but its language is broad enough to include them.

APPEAL OF RETIREE'S DECISION

Under the statutes of Indiana, Ohio, Rhode Island, Tennessee, and Texas the award or judgment of the retired judge so designated by the parties or attorneys is appealable, but the Michigan statute expressly states that *no* appeal will lie from such an award or judgment. The compensation and expenses of a retired judge designated by the parties or attorneys are paid by the parties under the express provisions of the Colorado, Idaho, Minnesota, Ohio, and Rhode Island statutes.

ASSIGNMENT OF RETIREE AS MASTER OR REFEREE

Master or referee status is provided for by the statutes of California, Connecticut, and New Hampshire. The California statute authorizes the supreme court or any court of appeals to appoint a retired judge master or referee in any proceeding pending before the court or before the Commission on Judicial Performance. Connecticut makes a judge who is retired at age seventy, unless for disability, a state referee for the balance of his or her term of office and eligible for appointment as such referee thereafter for life. It also permits a retired judge of the court of common pleas or superior court to act as a state referee in small claims matters. Under New Hampshire's statute, a justice of the supreme court or superior court, and each full-time justice of the district courts, upon retirement becomes a judicial referee who may be assigned to hear and determine nonjury cases in any court, and permits a probate judge to appoint as a *master* in any contested case any former judge retired from that court for age, but in another section provides that a probate judge retired for age becomes a *referee* empowered to act as such in the probate court.

New York's judicial hearing officer (JHO) statute and rules permit a judge of any court other than a town or village court who no longer holds judicial office to apply for designation as a judicial hearing officer. The designation is for a two-year term and is renewable for additional two-year terms without limit as to age. Nonjury matters are assigned to a JHO to hear and report or, with the consent of the parties, to hear and determine. A JHO may also be assigned to pre-argument screening of pending appeals. Nevada by supreme court rule permits a senior judge to be assigned as a settlement judge in any state court designated by the chief justice.

ALTERNATE DISPUTE RESOLUTION SERVICE BY RETIREE

Service as a court-appointed arbitrator or in private alternate dispute resolution matters is permitted by the laws of Alaska (although the statute does not specifically mention retired judges), Connecticut (provided the senior judge has performed duties as such for at least seventy-five days during each preceding year except the first), Iowa (but not when assigned to judicial service or when to do so would interfere with an assignment to judicial service and shall not use the title senior judge while so acting), South Carolina (if parties to an appeal agree to arbitration of the appeal, retired justice or judge may act as arbitrator), and Texas (in civil or family law matters, if parties agree, retired judge who has developed substantial experience in such areas of specialty may be appointed special judge under Alternate Methods of Dispute Resolution Act).

COURTS ON WHICH A RETIREE MAY SERVE

Assignment of a retired judge may be to any court in many states (Arizona, California, Colorado, Florida, Georgia, Illinois, Kansas, Kentucky, Louisiana, Maine, Missouri, Oregon, South Dakota, Tennessee, Utah), any court at or below that on which the retired judge served (Nevada), any court on which the retired judge sat or could have sat (Delaware), any court as to retirees from specified courts (Minnesota as to supreme court retirees, Nebraska as to retirees from the supreme court or district court), any court except as specified (Alaska—district court judge in district court only; Maryland—any court except orphan's court; Minnesota—judge retired from a court other than Supreme to any court except Supreme and retired district court judge to serve only in that court; New Jersey—judge retired from a court other than Supreme to any court except Supreme; Wisconsin—retiree from any court of record may serve on any court except the supreme court). A number of other states' statutes contain multiple provisions concerning the courts to which a retired judge may be assigned, which appear to relate to the retiree's experience while an active judge (Hawaii, Idaho, Indiana, Iowa, Mississippi, Montana, Nebraska, North Carolina, Rhode Island, South Carolina, Vermont, Washington, West Virginia). One state (New Mexico) limits assignment of a judge retired from any court to a particular court (district court), one permits assignment of a retired judge of a court as an administrative judge (Iowa), and two authorize assignment outside the judicial system (Missouri—as a member of the retirement system board or investigator for the Ethics Commission and North Dakota—as legal counsel to an executive or legislative body).

How Long a Retiree May Continue in Service

The period of time during which a retired judge may serve by assignment is unlimited in many states. Georgia's statute expressly provides that a retired judge may serve as a senior judge for life, and Michigan case law holds that there is no age restrictions on assignment of a retired judge. A number of states fix a limited term but provide that the term may be renewed, without limitation as to the number of renewals: Alaska (two years), Arizona (six months), District of Columbia (four years up to age seventy-four, then two years), Maine (seven years); Massachusetts (two years), Missouri (one year), New York (JHO, two years), North Dakota (one year), Utah (three years); two states (Indiana, Texas) make the period of service turn on the time specified in the retired judge's application.

Service by a retired judge is, however, limited by many other states: California (five years), Colorado (three-year term renewable, but not for more than twelve years), Iowa (twelve months until the twelve-month period during which the retiree becomes seventy-eight years of age), Kansas (two years renewable, but not for more than twelve years), New York (supreme court, appellate division, and court of appeals retiree sitting as trial judge, two years renewable, but not for more than six years). Service during each year of the period fixed is full time in California, as designated in the assignment order in Oregon, and for a minimum of thirteen weeks in Iowa, but in the following states is limited to stated periods: Indiana (sixty days with exceptions), Kansas (not more than 180 days), Massachusetts (no single assignment of more than ninety days), North Carolina (not exceeding six months), Wisconsin (six months).

Continuing Education Requirement

Attendance at continuing education courses is required of judges serving after retirement in the following states: California (once in every two years), Colorado (forty-five units within three years until age sixty-five); Florida (thirty hours in three years); Minnesota (forty-five units within three years, but may be waived); Mississippi (while serving as a senior judge); North Carolina (thirty hours every two years, but may be waived); North Dakota (forty-five hours every three years); Ohio (twenty-four hours every two years, but temporary exemption may be granted); Texas (completion each year of the educational requirements for active judges); West Virginia (thirty hours every two years); Wisconsin (five credits to be eligible for appointment or reappointment, unless waived for good cause, but does not apply during six months after appointment). Continuing education requirements of the following states do not specifically mention retired judges but based on the wording of the provision would appear to include them: Delaware (thirty hours every two years, but can be waived); Iowa (fifteen hours per year required of every person licensed to practice law); New York (twenty-four hours every two years); Nevada (twelve hours each calendar year, except for those seventy years of age or for undue hardship); Wyoming (fifteen hours required). Query whether the following continuing education requirements apply to retirees: Rhode Island (as to a retired judge sitting by assignment for less than full time, the continuing education requirement being unapplicable to judges whose duties are full time); Utah (whose continuing education rule does not mention retired judges, in light of the statute which provides for payment to retired judges for attendance at education functions); or under Louisiana's court rule which applies to "all attorneys."

PAY FOR RETIREE'S SERVICE

In several states no pay is received for after-retirement services by any retired justice or judge or by a justice or judge retired from a particular court: Alabama (probate judges); Indiana (special judges assigned to criminal trials in the county of his or her residence, temporary judge when serving as a judge pro tem or special judge); Iowa (district associate judge over seventy years of age); Missouri (retired judge serving as a member of the Citizens Commission on Compensation); Oregon (judge who retires at sixty years of age must serve without compensation for thirty-five days a year for five years after retiring, but is reimbursed for expenses); South Carolina (retiree serving as active associate justice or judge receives no pay for first three months of service, but receives expenses); South Dakota (no provision relating to compensation other than retirement benefits has been found); Wyoming (no provision re judge of county court, district court, or justice of the peace has been found).

In the states that do provide compensation for judges serving after retirement, the provisions are many and various. Some relate the pay to the current salary of a judge of the court from which the retiree retired (Delaware, Idaho, Maine, Maryland, Massachusetts, Missouri, Nevada, New

Hampshire, New Jersey, Pennsylvania, South Carolina, Washington),[3] others relate it to the current salary of a judge of the court to which the retiree is assigned (Alaska, Arizona, Colorado, District of Columbia, Hawaii, Iowa, Illinois, Louisiana, Michigan, Minnesota, Montana, Nebraska, North Carolina, North Dakota, Ohio, Tennessee, Texas, Wyoming); one state (Rhode Island) to what a judge or justice with comparable service time is receiving as a justice or judge of the court to which the retiree is assigned or a justice or judge of the court from which the retiree retired, whichever is greater; one (California) to the pay of a judge of the court to which assigned, or from which retired, as the retiree elects; one (Connecticut) salary plus retirement benefit not to exceed during the fiscal year the highest salary on which his or her retirement salary is based; one (Oregon) to the pay of a regularly elected judge of the court to which assigned but not to exceed for the calendar year, when added to the retirement benefit, the salary of a judge of the court from which the retiree retired; one (Vermont) to the pay of a judge of the court to which assigned but when added to retirement benefits not to exceed in total the annual salary of a judge of its superior court; and one (Wisconsin) to the pay of a judge of the court to which assigned but the monthly amount of which, when added to retirement benefits, does not exceed one-twelfth of the yearly compensation of a circuit court judge.

Cost of Living Adjustment

The statutes in many states modify the reference to the compensation of a judge of the court from which retired or to which assigned with the adjective "current," but the statutes of states that do not should, in any event, be construed as implicitly referring to the compensation then being paid to a judge of the court referred to, notwithstanding the absence of that adjective. However, a cost of living increase in the compensation of a retired judge assigned to active duty is provided for by the statutes of Pennsylvania and Wisconsin based upon the U.S. Department of Labor Consumer Price Index for the most recent twelve-month period for which the index has been reported (Pennsylvania) or upon the total percentage increase in circuit court judges' salaries during the preceding twelve-month period ending on August 1 (Wisconsin).

---

[3] At least one, but not necessarily all, of the judgeships in the state referred to in this paragraph is governed by the respective rule stated.

PAY FOR RETIREES SERVING PART TIME

The basis for arriving at daily salary as stated in the Colorado, Montana, Nebraska, North Dakota, and Oregon statutes is one-twentieth of the monthly salary, and in Nevada's statute as five percent of gross monthly salary based presumably upon court sessions on twenty days a month, but Hawaii's statute states that a month equals twenty-one days. Other states arrive at daily rate of pay of the retired judge on the basis of the following proportions of annual salary: 1/235th (Missouri); 1/250th (Kentucky, Michigan, Washington); 1/260th (Mississippi); or 1/320th (Massachusetts). Or they fix a per diem by statute: Delaware ($150 per day); Florida (not less than $200 per day or part of a day); Georgia ($165 per day); Maine ($150 per day or $90 per half day); Michigan ($200 per day or part of a day); North Carolina ($200 per day); Oklahoma (not more than $200 per day); Virginia ($250 per day). New York pays its judicial hearing officers $250 a day, but for judges permitted to continue serving after age seventy on the appellate division or trial bench pays them the full salary of the office until age seventy-six, if permitted after biennial physical and mental examination to continue to sit until then, after which they may serve as a judicial hearing officer.

SERVICE CREDIT FOR RETIREE'S SERVICE

A few states deal explicitly with whether an assigned retired judge is entitled to credit for such service. Arkansas and the District of Columbia give no credit for such service, Nebraska gives no such credit but provides that contributions to the retirement fund are excused during such service, and the Texas statute states that a senior district judge receives no credit for assigned time served. Alaska gives credit for each day served by a retiree who has not received maximum service credit but only until the maximum is reached, Florida gives credit to a judge who became seventy before the maximum service credit accrued and whose assignment followed immediately after his or her last full term preceding retirement and only as necessary to vest retirement benefits, Hawaii gives credit for such service in the determination of the judge's retirement allowance but the judge receives no retirement pay during service as an assigned retiree, and Michigan gives credit to a retiree performing judicial duties for each thirty days during which he or she performed such services on twenty days.

FACILITIES PROVIDED FOR RETIREE SERVING AFTER RETIREMENT

In addition to pay, expenses of an assigned retiree are reimbursed by most states, some more openhandedly than others. Thus Tennessee's statute includes office space and equipment, secretarial and research assistance, a law library, and, if assigned to a court outside the county of residence, travel expenses as provided to an active justice or judge; Iowa's statute includes a court reporter and, if assignment is to an appellate court, a law clerk; Minnesota's, a court reporter, deputy clerk, bailiff, and a courtroom; New Hampshire's, office rent; Virginia's, office, telephone, and supplies; Oklahoma's, office, equipment, and support staff; the District of Columbia's and Kansas', secretarial services. The statutes of other states are more general and more limited. Some provide for reimbursement of necessary expenses (Kentucky, Vermont, West Virginia), necessary expenses including travel, meals, and lodging (Michigan), expenses that are necessary and reasonable (Alabama, Louisiana, Maine), that are necessary and proper (Arkansas), that are necessary travel expenses (Florida, Mississippi, North Dakota), or simply that are reasonable (New Jersey). Others provide for reimbursement of actual expenses (Montana, New Hampshire, North Carolina, South Carolina), actual and reasonable expenses (Maryland), actual and necessary expenses (Ohio, New York re JHO's), actual and necessary expenses, plus mileage (Colorado), actual expenses for travel and living when sitting outside the retiree's county of residence (Texas, Wisconsin). Others reimburse for expenses while sitting outside the county of the retiree's residence (Massachusetts, Oklahoma), for travel and subsistence while sitting outside the county of residence (Arizona, Idaho, Missouri, *cf* Washington), or simply for travel expenses or mileage while so sitting (Nevada, *cf* Connecticut). One is phrased in terms of mileage and reasonable expenses, including meals and lodging (Indiana). And a few states provide reimbursement for a retiree as with other state employees (Nebraska), or for travel as received by an active judge or justice (Wyoming), or as determined by its supreme court (Oklahoma, South Dakota).

EMOLUMENTS AVAILABLE TO RETIREE SERVING AFTER RETIREMENT

Finally, a retiree sitting by assignment is also entitled to medical, accident, or life insurance, or a death benefit in the following states: medical insurance but only during the period of assigned service (Alaska); hospital insurance (Michigan); hospital, medical, and surgical insurance (Alabama); group health insurance (Connecticut, Illinois, Vermont); group health, part of which is paid for by the retiree (Maine, Michigan); group health and accident insurance, part of which is paid for by the retiree (Arizona); accidental death insurance of $5,000, part of which is paid for by the retiree (Massachusetts); life insurance (New Jersey); life insurance of $5,000 if the retiree has twenty years of service (Vermont); life insurance reduced to $5,000 at age sixty (Connecticut); a death benefit of $4,000 if claimed within three years of death (Oklahoma); a death benefit for the beneficiary of a disability retiree who dies before age sixty (New Jersey).

II

How Judicial Retirement Laws Should Be Changed

Abolish Mandatory Retirement for Age

The major change that should be made is the abolition of mandatory retirement for age, or to phrase the suggestion differently, to authorize imposition of involuntary retirement only when mental or physical disability warrants doing so. Age alone should play no part, even advanced age, whatever that term contained in the Massachusetts, Nevada, and West Virginia statutes means. The facts that federal judges may serve for life[1] and thirteen states have no mandatory age requirement, and that many other states permit retired judges to continue serving full or part time without age limitation, without any suggestion that litigants in those jurisdictions have suffered in any way as a result, strongly suggests that the changes hereafter proposed in the laws of the other jurisdictions is desirable, the more particularly since under the present system in those states overcrowding of court calendars is a continuing problem.

This is not to suggest that retirees should be permitted to serve for life without any check on ability to serve other than that resulting from a complaint by a litigant or by others serving in the judicial system. It is, rather, to suggest a system similar to that in New York which requires mental and physical examination every two years, but without its limitation as to age seventy-six. Doing so should sufficiently protect the interest of litigants, since it is reasonable to expect that any claimed aberrational conduct occurring during any such two-year period would be brought to the attention of the judicial system and, as appropriate, would result in an involuntary disability proceeding. Moreover, except as may be required by federal or state constitutional provisions protecting sitting judges against reduction of the term for which elected or appointed, there should be no provision in the statute that a judge has the right to serve until the end of the term for which elected or appointed. Such a provision protects the interest of the sitting judge with respect to his or her pension, but does nothing to protect the interests of the litigants. In any event, such a provision is unnecessary in a system that permits involuntary retirement only for physical or mental disability, provided the statute contains a provision

---

[1] As Alexander Hamilton expressed it in *The Federalist*: "Next to permanency in office, nothing can contribute more to the independence of judges than a fixed provision for their support." Shrager & Frost, *The Quotable Lawyer*, p. 68.51.

that states that although involuntarily retired, the judge's retirement is to be considered voluntary (see pages 8–9 above), thus protecting the judge's pension interest.

REQUIRE BIENNIAL PHYSICAL AND MENTAL EXAMINATIONS

A more difficult problem is how to define the disability on which involuntary retirement is to be based. In a system that calls for physical and mental examination every two years at the expense of the state by a physician and/or psychiatrist who reports to the board or other body considering involuntary retirement, there is no need to distinguish between temporary and permanent disability provided only that an involuntarily retired judge who believes himself or herself sufficiently recovered to warrant restoration to service can request physical and mental examinations at any time at the expense of the judge, refundable to him or her, however, if the judge is then found by the board restorable to service. Appointment of a physician and/or psychiatrist to make such examinations at the request of the state or of the judge should be by the chief judge of the state's highest court or by the body responsible for administration of the courts, and the decision of the board should in any event be subject to court review. Biennial examinations should continue as long as the retiree continues to sit, terminating only when he or she resigns the position of senior judge.

DEFINE MENTAL AND PHYSICAL DISABILITY MORE CLEARLY

The age at which such periodic examinations should begin could then remain at seventy if the state believed the additional costs to it to be justified, but it may be inferred from the federal experience and that of the states that impose no mandatory retirement age that disqualifying disability does not often occur, if at all, until substantially later in life. A legislative determination to fix the age for beginning the examination process at seventy-six, seventy-eight, or even eighty should be upheld.[2] While the definition of disability should continue to cover both mental and physical

---

[2] That age alone does not determine functional ability and that there is on the average no decline in intelligence until at least eighty, see Stuadinger, Cornelius & Baltes: "The Aging of Intelligence: Potential and Limits, 503 the Annals 43, 44–45," cited in Severson, Age Discrimination Law, 17 Wm. Mitchell L.R. 858, fn 9.

disability, a distinction between the two, similar to that of the Ohio statute, should be made. Mental disability should be defined as one that so
obfuscates or slows down the judge's thought process as to materially affect
the discharge of judicial duties, while physical disability should be defined
as one that prevents efficient performance of judicial duties for ninety calendar days or more (see the Florida and Tennessee definitions at page 8
above. Although the professionals who do the mental and physical examinations should be asked to express an opinion concerning whether a disabling condition is, or is likely to be, permanent, the board or other body
considering involuntary retirement should have discretion to determine
that although the disability has continued, or is expected to continue, for
ninety calendar days or more (e.g., a back operation which has necessitated,
or will necessitate, time in the hospital, in rehabilitation service, and at
home for more than ninety days), the judge remains mentally capable of
rendering service efficiently, and the present condition of the calendar in
the court in which he or she sat prior to disability does not necessitate
termination of his or her judicial services. Moreover, an involuntarily retired judge should have the right to apply at any time for reexamination
and to be restored to his or her judicial position if later found on further
examination to be sufficiently recovered from the disabling condition to
warrant restoration. That the disabling physical or mental condition as
thus defined resulted from accident should have no bearing with respect to
involuntary disability, although it may play a part with respect to a judge
who could be restored to service after involuntary retirement but opts
instead to remain retired as hereafter described, and has an important effect
as to voluntary disability retirement as hereinafter noted.

BURDEN OF PROOF OF DISABILITY

The government's burden of proof as to involuntary disability retirement
should be preponderance of proof, rather than clear and convincing evidence as some states now apparently require, for while the heavier burden
protects the judge's interest in continuing in office, the preponderance
standard is more protective of the interests of litigants whose rights are
involved in matters that come before the judge. However, a judge's unjustified refusal to submit to examination by medical or psychiatric professionals should be deemed evidence of disability, and repeated failure to appear

for such examination or examinations should be presumed to constitute unjustified refusal. If a judge who has been involuntarily retired for disability is restored to judicial service as a result of later examination(s), the pension he or she received as a result of involuntary retirement should cease.

SERVICE CREDIT FOR DISABILITY RETIREMENT

The judge should receive service credit for the period of involuntary retirement and if he or she has reached the age which together with the thus enhanced period of service permits retirement, and he or she elects to remain retired, should receive a pension computed on the basis of his or her age and enhanced years of service. Service credit for the years during which the judge is involuntarily retired is justified, however, only if the judge is barred during retirement from other gainful employment or the pension payment is reduced in the proportion that the amount earned per year from such employment bears to pension payments received during that year. To that end, in view of the provision that involuntary retirement for disability is to be treated as voluntary (see page 32 above), a judge retired for disability should be required to report income earned from such employment during the fiscal year during which the pension benefit was paid to the judge, measured from the date of inception of the disability pension.

VOLUNTARY RETIREMENT FOR DISABILITY

Voluntary retirement may be for disability, for age, for service, for age and service, or for accident. The definitions of physical and mental disability should be the same as above set forth (pp. 32–33, compare pp. 12–14) for involuntary retirement, but there should be no requirement that the disability have been caused by judicial service, nor should there be any service requirement for voluntary disability retirement, the provision for examination by state employed professionals and for such examination biennially being sufficient to protect the retirement fund against feigned disability. There should, however, be provisions, as above suggested for involuntary disability retirement, for cessation of retirement benefits based on continued refusal of such examination(s), for cessation of benefits and restoration to former employment if the judge is found to be sufficiently recovered, or for reduction of benefit if found capable of gainful employment, and for reporting of income from employment during such retirement. Vocational factors, as provided for in the Tennessee and Wyoming statutes (see p. 14), to the extent that they have been considered in relation to the appointment or election of the judge, should play no part in the determination of voluntary disability retirement of a judge. The burden of proof as to disability will be that of the judge seeking voluntary retirement, but the standard—preponderance of evidence—should be the same as for involuntary disability retirement.

ACCIDENTAL DISABILITY RETIREMENT

Accidental disability retirement should require a mental or physical disability as above defined, resulting from force, not self-inflicted, incurred while performing judicial duties or as a direct and proximate cause thereof, without willful misconduct on the part of the judge. Negligence on the judge's part should not be a disqualifying factor, however, in view of the affirmative requirements that there be force inflicted by someone other than the judge, nor should the statute include, as does the present West Virginia statute, both injury and disease, the probability that disease will be accidentally incurred being highly unlikely. The statute should also make clear that a judge retired for accidental disability should be deemed to have voluntarily retired, and is therefore required to submit to biennial examinations and to make periodic reports of employment income.

VOLUNTARY RETIREMENT FOR AGE AND/OR SERVICE

Voluntary retirement for age and for service refers to the point at which a judge who opts to leave judicial service will receive a pension. Service years in nonjudicial employment that is part of the state's retirement system, or, if a separate system, that is required to transfer the judge's contributions during the nonjudicial employment to the judicial system, should be credited to the judge seeking retirement. Retirement on the basis of service alone should be permitted at any time after completion of twenty years of service, which need not be continuous, fractional parts of differing services being counted in computing years of service. Retirement for age alone should not be permitted, however, and the earliest age at which retirement with a pension should be permitted should be fifty-five with at least ten years service credit. There should, however, be no provision for retirement at an earlier age with a reduced pension, nor should any distinction be made between courts with respect to the age and/or service requirements for optional retirement.

Cost of Living Adjustment of Retirement Benefit

Except with respect to judges who retire voluntarily prior to the age when periodic examinations begin, provision for adjustment of the pension benefit would not be required with respect to the years prior to the beginning of periodic examinations, for until that time the judge will be continuing in office and receiving the full salary of his or her office, including any cost of living adjustments of the salary of the office. Increase of pension benefit from and after the beginning of periodic examinations of the judge, or for a judge who voluntarily retires prior to the beginning of periodic examinations, should be provided for by relating the increase to that of the increase in salary of a judge holding the position the retiree held when he or she retired, without time limit, however, on when after retirement the increase provision be given effect. If such a provision is enacted, there should be no need for a percent limit on the amount of the annual increase of the benefit since the current salary of the judge holding the office that the retiree held will have been fixed after full consideration of the budget consequences. If a percentage increase is enacted, however, it should permit any excess over the permitted percentage of increase to be used in subsequent years in which the increase would be less than the permitted percent.

In many states, however, the statute could not provide for decrease of such benefit because, in the interest of preserving judicial independence, the state has a constitutional provision that proscribes the decrease of judicial salaries (cf, e.g., N.Y. Constitution, Article XIII, §7). In states the constitution of which does not bar a decrease in pension, the statute should provide with respect to a decrease that a subsequent increase in the Consumer Price Index will not result in an increase in the pension until the C.P.I. is above the point it had reached when the decrease was imposed.

EXEMPTION OF BENEFITS FROM TAXATION OR LEGAL
PROCESS AND UNASSIGNABILITY OF BENEFITS

Under a system such as herein proposed, the judge continues in office subject to periodic examination, receiving the salary of his or her office and subject to contribution to the retirement fund unless retired for disability, involuntarily or voluntarily. Only as to a judge retired for disability, or who opts for retirement on the basis of age and/or service, or who fails of reelection or reappointment after having become eligible for age and/or service retirement, are provisions needed with respect to taxability, prohibition of assignment, and protection from legal process of retirement benefits.

The laws of the fifty-one jurisdictions covered by this study with respect to taxation are so varied as to make problematical the adoption of a proposed uniform provision other than one stating that the benefits received by a judge serving after retirement shall be taxable by the state or a county, or municipality thereof only to the extent that such benefits of a state, county, or municipal employee other than a judge would be subject to such tax or taxes. With respect to legal process and assignability, while the exceptions from the exemptions discussed at page 17 ff. above vary somewhat (e.g., a rollover allowed by the Internal Revenue Code, Medicare, or other insurance premiums), the proposed uniform statute should exclude—and thus permit assignment of, and legal process in relation to—all of the items referred to in the statutes of the states there discussed.

SERVICE AFTER RETIREMENT

The uniform act should permit service after retirement by any retiree who has served at least five years as an active judge, upon application by the retired judge or a judge who failed of reelection or reappointment, made within five years after his or her active service ended and upon his or her submission to mental and physical examination with respect to capacity, if at the time the application is made he or she has attained the age at which such examinations of an active judge would be required. The application should also specify whether the retiree seeks assignment as a full-time senior judge or for some lesser period of weeks or months during a calendar year and is aware that if assigned full or part time that he or she may not engage in the practice of law, but if assigned part time only, the assignment may be not only to sit as a member of an appellate or trial court but also to act as a settlement judge with respect to cases yet to be tried or those on appeal, or to preside over accounting or discovery proceedings and the like. Assignments should be made by the chief judge or justice of the state's highest court or by the chief administrative judge and should be for two year periods, renewable without limitations other than passing mental and physical examinations when of an age to require such examinations or when complaint as to the particular judge's capacity is made, and the completion each year of continuing judicial education requirements for active judges of the court to which assigned.

PRACTICE OF LAW BY RETIRED JUDGES

Service as a senior judge, whether full or part time, should be conditioned upon the retiree, whether previously a trial or appellate judge, not engaging in the practice of law, for the Code of Judicial Conduct, Canon 5F, proscribes such extrajudicial activities by a judge. Although Canon 5E proscribes a judge acting as an arbitrator or mediator, the proposed statute should authorize appointment of a senior judge as a mediator or arbitrator in a court-mandated alternative dispute resolution program, provided it is subject to court review or appeal. Because court-mandated mediation or arbitration is reviewable or appealable, it can be likened to appointment to hear and report, or as a referee or special master, and is consistent with the general practice of using retired judges who also practice law as private judges, even though in most jurisdictions a private judge's decision is not reviewable or appealable, for that strongly suggests that most litigants do not view the practice of law by a private judge as disqualifying. Of course, whether serving full time or part time, a retired judge should inform all parties of, and offer to disqualify himself or herself with respect to, assignment of a case that may involve a conflict of interest resulting from his or her present or prior law practice, *cf* Code, Canon 3D.

ASSIGNMENT TO JUDICIAL DUTY OF RETIRED JUDGES

Assignment should be to any court at or below the court or courts on which the retiree sat during active service, except when a judge of an appellate court is temporarily disabled or otherwise disqualified, in which case the statute should provide that the vacancy may be filled by a retired member of either an appellate or a trial court. The statute should also provide that assignment to a matrimonial or family court, a worker's compensation court, or a court whose jurisdiction is limited to estate and trust matters should be limited to a judge who has sat at least three years as an active judge of the court to which assignment is made and that assignment of retirees from such specialty courts should be limited to the court on which he or she served as an active judge, unless his or her prior experience included at least three years on a trial or appellate court. The proposed statute should also provide that a retired judge may also be assigned to a court-mandated alternative dispute resolution program, subject to the same limitation to judges of specialty courts as to such a program maintained by such court.

Alternate Dispute Resolution Service by Retiree

A senior judge who accepts assignment by the chief justice or chief administrative judge, whether serving full or part time, should not be permitted to serve as an arbitrator or mediator, except in a court-mandated alternative dispute resolution program, and in view of Canon 5E of the Code of Judicial Conduct that rule should apply, even though all parties to a justiciable controversy consent to such service.

Title of Retirees Performing Judicial Duties

The title of the office held by a retiree so assigned should be simply senior judge, rather than the many differing titles used in presently existing statutes, but a retired judge serving in an alternate dispute resolution program maintained outside the courts should be referred to as a private judge. However, decisions of a senior judge sitting in trial court should be appealable.

Pay for Retiree's Services

With respect to pay and emoluments, if the proposed system is enacted, a judge who continues to serve full time in the office to which elected or appointed, until retired for disability or until he or she voluntarily retires based upon age and/or service, will continue to receive the compensation of the office and the emoluments (e.g., life insurance, health insurance) provided for the office. A judge who wishes to serve less than full time can do so if he or she is eligible for age and/or service retirement under the proposed statute, provided the statute also requires that the judge's application so state and set forth the portion of each year during which he or she wishes to serve, as well as the judge's understanding that he or she remains subject to biennial mental and physical examination respecting capacity to serve as a part-time senior judge. Application should be made to, and assignments of part-time judges should be made by, the chief justice or chief administrative judge.

There should be no requirement of service without compensation by a retiree, but the retiree should not have the right to refuse an assignment within the period designated by him or her for part-time service, except for disqualifying conflict of interest.

Payment for a retiree's service should be based upon $1/235$th of the annual salary of a judge of the court to which the retiree is assigned, computed on the basis of the number of days on which courts sit (five days a week, fifty-two weeks per year = 260), minus fifteen days for public holidays and two weeks (ten court days) for vacation during the year. The compensation should be based on the compensation of a judge of the court to which assigned because a retiree may be assigned to a court below, or in some instances above, that on which the retiree sat when he or she retired. Retirement pay should be continued notwithstanding such service, but no deduction should be made for contribution to the retirement fund. And since assignment may be to a court below or above that from which the judge retired, his or her total compensation and retirement benefit for the year should not exceed the current salary of a justice or judge of the court to which assigned or a justice or judge of the court from which retired, whichever is greater. However, credit for such service should not be given.

FACILITIES PROVIDED FOR RETIREE SERVING AFTER RETIREMENT

Because judges other than voluntary retirees continue to serve in the office to which elected or appointed, they will continue to occupy courtrooms and chambers and be provided law clerk, secretarial, and other services. A voluntarily retired judge should be provided similar services but on a pool basis with other retired judges and when assigned to a court in a county other than the judge's residence should be entitled to travel and subsistence expenses.

EMOLUMENTS AVAILABLE TO RETIREE SERVING AFTER RETIREMENT

Finally, a retiree sitting by assignment should receive the same emoluments by way of health, accident, and life insurance as are provided for active judges.

Part III

Constitutional, Statutory, and Regulatory Provisions of the Fifty-One Jurisdictions

ALABAMA

Mandatory Retirement Provisions Applicable Generally

Constitution section 6.16, as enacted by Amendment 328, empowers the legislature to provide by law for the retirement of judges, including supernumerary judges,[1] with such conditions as it may prescribe, but the section also provides that a judge over the age of seventy may be appointed a supernumerary judge if he or she is not eligible to receive state judicial retirement benefits. Section 12-18-7(c) of the Alabama Code provides that a justice of the supreme court or judge of a court of appeals or circuit court who becomes seventy years of age during the term for which elected, who is qualified to be retired (as to which see Optional Provisions section, below) and who does not, at or before the expiration of the term, file a written declaration of intention to retire at the end of the term shall be deemed to have forfeited the right to retirement benefits but shall be entitled to refund of his or her contributions to the retirement fund. Const. Amdt 328, §6.15 fixes the term of office of each judge of Alabama's judicial system at six years.

Sections 6.17 and 6.18 of the Constitution as enacted by Amendment 581 authorizes the Judicial Inquiry Commission to investigate complaints concerning any judge and if its members find a reasonable basis to charge that the judge is physically or mentally unable to perform his or her duties to file a complaint with the Court of the Judiciary. That court, after notice and public hearing, may suspend without pay or retire a judge who is physically or mentally unable to perform his or her duties. The judge may then appeal to the supreme court which reviews the record on the law and the facts.

---

[1] Supernumerary judges were not appointed after September 18, 1973, but the laws as to such judges remain in effect until all such judges as of that date are deceased. See Code §§12-2-50, 12-17-40.

RETIREMENT PROVISIONS RE PARTICULAR COURTS

As to municipal judges, §12-14-33(c) states that the municipality may provide for their retirement, with such conditions as it may prescribe. The analysis of codes of all Alabama municipalities has not been undertaken, but from inquiry of municipal judges in Birmingham, Mobile, and Montgomery, it was learned that none of those cities had enacted retirement provisions for such judges.

Optional Provisions for Retirement

Under Code §§12-18-4, 12-18-6(a) and 12-18-7(a) any justice of the supreme court, judge of one of the courts of appeals, or of a circuit court may elect to retire by filing a written declaration of intention with the chief justice of the supreme court. Any such justice or judge may elect to be retired if he or she has served for twelve years on such courts and is sixty-five or older, or has so served for fifteen years and is sixty-two, less one year for each year of service in excess of fifteen, or has so served for ten years and is not less than seventy, or has served for not less than eighteen years or a time equal to three full terms as a justice or judge of such courts, Code §12-18-6, but except for disability no such judge is eligible for retirement pay prior to attaining sixty years of age, Code §12-18-40. Moreover, if he or she has served less than a full term on the court from which he or she seeks to retire, he or she is only entitled to retire from any previous judicial office in which he or she served a full term, *id.*

Former county court judges and full-time municipal judges commissioned as district court judges pursuant to the October 10, 1975 amendment of the constitution who elected to serve under the judicial retirement system, and all district court judges appointed or elected after October 10, 1975, may request retirement, Code §§12-18-50, 12-18-51, 12-18-55, as may probate judges, Code §§12-18-84, 12-18-85.

Judges may also elect to be retired for disability. A justice of the supreme court or judge of a court of appeals or circuit court who has served as much as five years on any two or more of said courts consecutively and has become permanently physically or mentally unable to carry out his or her duties on a full-time basis as certified by three reputable physicians may elect to be retired, Code §12-18-6(a)(1) and (b)(1) as may also a district judge, Code §12-18-55(1), or a probate judge, Code §12-18-84(1).

A judge retired for disability who has served for ten years receives a disability allowance equal to seventy-five percent of the salary payable for the position he or she held at the time of retirement, or if he or she has served less than ten years, equal to twenty-five percent of such salary plus ten percent thereof for each year of service in excess of two years, but in no event less than thirty percent of the annual salary being paid to a full-time justice or judge, Code §12-18-10 (as to justices of the supreme court and judges of the court of appeals and circuit court), §12-18-59 (as to district judges), §12-18-87(c) (as to probate judges).

SERVICE AFTER RETIREMENT

Section 6.10 of the constitution, as enacted by Amdt. 328, authorizes the chief justice of the supreme court to "assign supernumerary justices and judges and retired trial judges and retired appellate judges for temporary service in any court." A judge of the supreme court or judge of a court of appeals or circuit court must take the oath of office as a retired judge and thereafter on request of the chief justice or the presiding judge of one of the courts of appeals or the governor may serve on the supreme court, on either court of appeals or on any circuit court, or in other courts when assigned by the chief justice to special temporary duty in such courts, Code §12-18-7(b), see §12-18-10(e), unless the chief justice transfers him or her to inactive status upon his or her request or as the chief justice finds required in the public interest, Code §12-18-10(f),(g),(h). Retired justices or judges who perform active service for the supreme court or one or both of the courts of appeals are assisted by not more than two confidential secretaries employed by the administrative director of the courts, Code §12-5-21. The chief justice may also call a district court judge to temporary active duty in any court, Code §12-18-61 and a probate judge to active duty status as a probate judge, Code §12-18-88.

Also to be noted is that the supreme court is authorized by Code §12-1-14 to appoint special circuit judges, special district court judges, or special probate judges for temporary service when need therefor arises, provided the person so appointed possesses the qualifications of the judgeship to which he or she is appointed. The section makes no mention of retired judges, but its qualification language is broad enough to permit appointment of a retired judge as a special judge.

Although §6.08(a) of Amdt 328 to the Constitution makes no specific mention of retired justices or judges or special judges, its provision that "[n]o judge of any court of this state shall, during his [or her] continuance in office, engage in the practice of law" is broad enough to cover them.

PAY AND EMOLUMENTS

A supreme court justice or judge of a court of appeals called back to active status receives for each month of active service such amount, when added to his or her retirement benefit, as would amount to $250 per month less than the salary paid to a justice or judge of the appellate court from which he or she retired, Code §12-18-10(e), first paragraph, but note the apparent inconsistency in the second paragraph of that section which states that when a retired justice or judge of an appellate court serves as an active member of the supreme court or one of the courts of appeals, he or she shall receive, during such service, compensation equal to that due a regular justice or judge for the performance of such duties. When serving on a circuit court, however, such justice or judge receives the same compensation as a regular judge of that circuit, *id*, first paragraph.

A retired judge of the circuit court called to active service with the supreme court or a court of appeals is paid the salary paid a circuit judge in the circuit from which he or she retired, but when recalled to serve as a circuit judge is paid the same salary as a circuit judge of the circuit to which he or she is assigned, or in the circuit from which he or she retired, whichever is greater (*id*).

A retired district court judge recalled to temporary active duty in any court is paid the same salary as a district judge in the district from which he or she retired or in the district to which he or she is assigned, whichever is greater, subject, however, to the limitation that the total paid a retired district judge on active duty during any calendar year may not exceed a sum which is $1,000 less than the compensation received by a regular judge in the district from which the judge retired, Code §12-18-61.

Notwithstanding the provisions of the above-cited Code sections concerning circuit and district court judges, the *1996 Survey of State Judicial Fringe Benefits, Second Edition*, published by the ABA National Conference of State Trial Judges, states that the retirement system interprets those provisions as inapplicable to such judges and that "in most instances, the judges serve without additional compensation." No regulation or administrative or court opinion is cited for that statement.

A retired probate judge recalled to active duty receives only reimbursement for all reasonable and necessary expenses, including travel, Code §12-18-88, no provision for salary as such being contained in the Code and Const, Amdt 328, §6.08, providing that no judge shall receive any remuneration for judicial services except the salary and allowance authorized by law.

Finally as to compensation, Code §12-1-14, which provides for appointment of special circuit, district, or probate judges, limits the compensation of such a judge to a sum not exceeding $100 a day as established by rule.

All enrolled justices or judges, as well as special court judges, are entitled, in addition to compensation as above set forth, to necessary and reasonable expenses, Code §12-1-18 (as to circuit, district, and municipal judges), §12-18-88 (as to probate judges), §12-1-14 (as to special judges).

All retired and supernumerary justices and judges are also entitled to group hospital, medical and surgical insurance, Code §12-1-15(a).

ALASKA

Article IV, Section 11, of the Alaska Constitution provides that justices and judges shall be retired at the age of seventy "except as provided in this article," and Alaska Statutes, §22.25.010(a) fixes the time of retirement as "the date that the justice or judge reaches the age of 70." The exception apparently refers to a judge retired by rejection in a retention election (Const. Art. IV, §§6, 7) or retired for disability by the Judicial Conduct Commission (Const. Art. IV, §10).

A justice or judge may be retired for disability which interferes with the conduct of his or her office and that is or may become permanent, either upon the judge's written application or when an allegation as to his or her incapacity is made to the Judicial Conduct Commission, Statutes, §22.25.010(b) and (c), after hearings by the commission and its recommendation to the supreme court that he or she be retired for disability which seriously interferes with the performance of his or her duties and that is or may be permanent, Statutes, §22.30.011 and 22.30.070(c); but §22.30.070(d) expressly provides that "a judge retired by the supreme court shall be considered to have retired voluntarily." The commission may request the judge to submit to physical or mental examination and, if the judge refuses to do so, must determine the disability issue adversely to him or her, Statutes, §22.30.066(b). A judge or justice retired for disability is entitled to retirement pay if he or she has served for two years or more, Statutes, §22.25.010(b).

RETIREMENT PROVISIONS RE PARTICULAR COURTS

No distinction drawn.

OPTIONAL PROVISIONS FOR RETIREMENT

Voluntarily at any time, with retirement pay if judge has served five years or more, the pay to commence at age sixty, or if the justice or judge elects to accept a lesser sum, to commence immediately if he or she has reached age fifty-five or served twenty years as a justice or judge; Statutes, §22.25.010(d). All service in any court, including service as a magistrate or deputy magistrate, is included in computing time served; Statutes, §22.25.010(f).

As to voluntary retirement for disability, see Mandatory Retirement Provisions above.

SERVICE AFTER RETIREMENT

Const. Art. IV states that retired judges shall render no further service on the bench except for special assignment as provided by court rule. By appointment of the chief justice or his designee, a retired justice of the supreme court or retiree of the court of appeals or superior court who consents to such appointment, may sit in any court as a senior justice or judge; but a retired judge of the district court may only be appointed to sit in district court, Rules Governing Administration of the Courts, Rule 23(a), except that where the assignment of a retired district judge is temporary (i.e., for ninety days or less) he or she may be appointed to serve on the superior court (Kouchutin v. State of Alaska, 739 F.2d 170).

Appointment of a retired judge by the chief justice may be for a specified case or a specified time up to two years, or until the matter before him or her is completed and an appointment may be renewed, Rule 23(a), *supra*, unless the chief justice determines, based on a performance evaluation conducted every two years by the judicial council and the presiding judges under whom the retired judge has served, that his or her service should not be continued, Rule 23(b). A judge or justice retired for incapacity is ineligible for appointment unless found eligible by a licensed physician to perform judicial duties efficiently, and a judge or justice rejected in a retention election or removed from office by the Judicial Conduct Commission remains ineligible for appointment unless thereafter nominated and reappointed to the bench, Rule 23(a), *supra*.

Although the section does not mention retired judges, Statutes, §44.102(5) which provides for court-appointed arbitration apparently would permit appointment of a retired judge.

PAY AND EMOLUMENTS

The pay of a retired justice or judge is the same as a judge of the court in which he or she served for the period of such service, less the retirement pay, if any, received by him or her, plus full medical insurance coverage for the period of service as a retiree, Rule 23(c). Furthermore, if he or she has not accrued maximum service credit toward retirement, he or she is entitled to such credit for each day of retired service until the maximum is reached, Rule 23(d).

Compensation of a nonvolunteer arbitrator is governed by Statutes, §44.102(5)(b) and Supreme Court Rule 11.100. The Rule does not fix compensation; rather it directs that the arbitrator must keep the total charges for service and expenses reasonable and consistent with the nature of the case or other statutory payment limits.

ARIZONA

The Arizona Constitution requires that justices and judges of courts of record be retired upon reaching the age of seventy, except those who were serving in 1974 who may serve until the end of the term during which they became seventy years of age, Art. VI, §§20, 35, 39.

Although Arizona statute provides for voluntary retirement for disability (see Optional Provisions for Retirement below) no statutory or constitutional provision for mandatory retirement for disability has been found.

Retirement Provisions re Particular Courts

None.

Optional Provisions for Retirement

Normal retirement means any judge or justice who has attained age sixty-five with five or more years of credited service, age sixty-two with ten or more years of such service, or age sixty with twenty-five or more years of such service, Ariz. Rev. Stat. Annot. §38-805(A). A judge with at least ten years of credited service may take early retirement at age fifty.

The Elected Official Retirement Plan defines "elected official" to include justices of the supreme court, judges of the court of appeals, and judges of the superior court, Ariz. Rev. Stat. Annot., §38-801(5)(C), and provides in §38-806 that a judge who either personally or by a guardian submits an affidavit as to the nature of his or her incapacity, and is found to be permanently mentally or physically incapacitated from performing the duties of his or her office after examination by a board of three doctors, may receive disability retirement benefits, but may be required by the retirement fund manager to be thereafter medically examined if the manager has reason to believe that a member retired for disability but not yet eligible for normal retirement may no longer be incapacitated. If he or she is found by a board of three physicians to be capable of performing his or her duties as a judge, or refuses to submit to such an examination for one year or more, the manager may revoke his or her pension.

SERVICE AFTER RETIREMENT

A retired justice or judge of any court of record who is drawing retirement pay may serve as a justice or judge of any court, Constitution, Art.VI, §20, and if physically and mentally able, may be called by the supreme court or its chief justice to assist the supreme court or superior court as directed by the supreme court, Ariz. Rev. Stat. Annot., Title 38, Chap. 5, Art. 3, §38-813(A), but may not serve as a member of the Commission on Judicial Conduct, Const., Art. VI.1, §1(A).

Constitution, Art. VI, §31 authorizes the legislature to provide for appointment of judges pro tempore of courts inferior to the supreme court. Judges pro tempore have all the powers of a regularly elected judge, Const., Art. VI, §31; Amoole v. Maricopa County, 177 Ariz. 185, 866 P.2d 167. Arizona Rev. Statutes Annotated, Title 12, Chap. 1, Art. 3, §12-141 authorizes the chief justice of the supreme court, on request of the presiding judge of the superior court in any county, to appoint such a judge, provided the appointee has resided in the state and been admitted to practice there for not less than five years, *id*, §12-142, subject to approval of the board of supervisors of the county for a period not to exceed six months for any one term, and the chief justice may reappoint such a judge, *id*, §12-144(B). He may also terminate the term of such a judge at any time, *id*. Like provisions for appointment of judges pro tempore for a division of the court of appeals, by the chief justice of the supreme court on request of the chief judge of such division of the court of appeals, and prescribing a six-month term, and for reappointment of such judge are contained in *id*, §§12-145, 12-146 and 12-147(b). Although the provisions of the constitution and statutes relating to judges pro tempore do not specifically refer to retired judges, they would appear to be eligible for pro tempore appointment if they meet the practice and residence qualifications for such appointment. Judges pro tempore are not, however, subject to any provision of law relating to the retirement of judges, Ariz. Rev. Stat. Annot., §§12-142, 12-146.

Pay and Emoluments

A retired judge temporarily called back to active duty receives the same compensation and expenses as other like active judges, less any amount received for such period in retirement benefits and, when serving outside the county of his residence, receives his or her necessary traveling and subsistence expenses, Const., Art. VI, §20; Ariz. Rev. Stat. Annot., Title 38, Chap. 5, Art. 3, §38-813(B). A retired judge is, however, entitled to continue receiving retirement benefits, Ariz. Rev. Stat. Annot. §38-804(E). He or she is also entitled to group health and accident insurance, *id*, §38-817, but may provide for payment of the premiums therefor by deduction from his or her retirement benefits, *id*, §38-651.01.

Judges pro tempore are paid for the period of appointment based on an annual salary equal to that of a judge of the court to which he or she was appointed, Ariz. Rev. Stat. Annot. §§12-142, 12-146.

ARKANSAS

Mandatory Retirement Provisions Applicable Generally

Statutes, 24-8-215(c)(3) fixes the age for mandatory retirement at seventy on penalty of losing retirement benefits; but if the judge/justice was serving prior to July 1, 1965, he or she may continue to serve until any age and upon retirement will be eligible for retirement benefits (*id*), and, if not eligible to retire at seventy, may continue to serve until completion of the term of office in which he or she receives sufficient service credit to retire without losing such benefits, Statutes 24-8-215(c)(2). Amendment 66 to the constitution establishes a Judicial Discipline and Disability Commission with authority to recommend by majority vote to the supreme court that a justice or judge be removed for physical or mental disability that prevents the proper performance of judicial duties; but also provides that a "judge or justice retired by the supreme court shall be considered to have retired voluntarily as provided by law."

Retirement Provisions re Particular Courts

No distinction drawn; see Statutes, 24-8-214(a).

Optional Provisions for Retirement

Any judge or justice with a minimum of ten years of credited service may voluntarily retire upon or after reaching age sixty-five, Statutes 24-8-215(a). Any judge or justice with a minimum of twenty years of service may retire regardless of age and, if he or she has served at least fourteen years, is eligible for retirement benefits upon reaching sixty-five years of age, Statutes 24-8-215(b). If elected after July 1, 1983, the judge or justice must have a minimum of eight years actual service as a justice of the supreme court or a judge of the circuit or chancery courts or of the court of appeals, Statutes 24-8-215(d).

However, Statutes 24-8-216 permits a judge of the circuit or chancery court who has fourteen years or more of credited service in the Arkansas Judicial Retirement System established by Acts 1953, No. 385, to retire after reaching age sixty-two and before reaching age sixty-five at a retirement benefit reduced 6 percent for each full year and proportionately for any part of a year that the judge retires before reaching age sixty-five.

Any judge or justice may voluntarily request that the Judicial Discipline and Disability Commission recommend that he or she leave because of a mental or physical disability, Amend. 66, subd (b). That subdivision states that grounds for leave or removal from office shall be determined by legislative enactment; and Statutes 24-8-217 provides that any member of the Arkansas Judicial Retirement System who has served a minimum of three consecutive years shall receive retirement benefits if any incapacitating disability shall occur during any term for which the judge has been elected, the three-year service requirement being applicable only to judges elected after July 1, 1983. Subdivision (c) of that section requires that the Judicial Discipline and Disability Commission act only upon proper certification of incapacity by two or more physicians, and that the commission should not grant a judgment of disability until reasonably assured of the judge's permanent physical or mental incapacity to perform the duties of his or her judicial office. Under Rule 11(F) of the Judicial Discipline and Disability Commission it may, upon finding mental or physical disability, recommend to the supreme court that the judge be granted leave with pay, or that he or she be retired and be considered eligible for benefits under §24-8-217.

The retirement benefit payable to a judge or justice retiring voluntarily under either of the above provisions is one-half the annual salary payable to the last judicial office held and is payable for the recipient's life, Statutes 24-8-218.

SERVICE AFTER RETIREMENT

Any retired judge may, with his or her consent, be recalled for temporary service by the chief justice, Statutes 24-8-221(a), except a judge receiving disability benefits, Statutes 24-8-221(b). But note that a retired judge or justice recalled pursuant to subdivision (a) cannot temporarily replace a circuit judge who has recused himself or herself, even if assigned by the chief justice, since the retired judge's term having expired he can only serve in replacement of a recused judge if designated as provided in Arkansas

Constitution, Article 7, §§21 and 22B, that is, either by election as a special judge by the regular practicing attorneys in attendance at that court, or by a judge on the court of a different circuit, Burris v. Britt, 281 Ark. 225, 663 S.W.2d 715, modified as to costs, 287 Art. 215, 667 S.W.2d 367. Constitution Art. 7, §21 provides that if the office of a judge of the circuit court is vacant at the beginning of a term of court, or a judge is sick or unable to continue, the attorneys regularly practicing in that court may meet on the second day of the term and elect a judge to preside, "and the attorney so elected shall have the same power and authority as a regular judge," which, however, terminates at the end of the term.

To be noted also are Const. Art. 7, §§7 and 36 and Statutes 16-10-115. Const. Art. 7, §7 empowers the governor, when one or more supreme court justices are disqualified in any case, to appoint the necessary number of persons to sit in that case; and Const. Art. 7, §36 gives the Governor similar power when a county or probate judge is disqualified in a given case. Neither section excludes retired judges from an appointment under its provisions.

Statutes 16-10-115 permits any court, except in a criminal case, upon stipulation of the parties litigant, to order a cause to be tried before an attorney licensed to practice in Arkansas, who upon being sworn is empowered to act until final determination of the cause. The section does not exclude retired judges or justices from its provisions.

PAY AND EMOLUMENTS

A recalled judge receives such pay, including any retirement pay he or she receives, as equals that of a full-time judge serving at the time in the same or similar capacity, Statutes 24-8-221(c), and the same reimbursement for necessary and proper expenses as a full-time judge serving in the same or similar capacity, Statutes 24-8-221(d). Temporary service does not, however, modify the retirement benefits to which entitled, regardless of age at retirement, Statutes 24-8-221(e).

The stipulation of the parties providing for trial before an attorney pursuant to court order must include the amount to be paid to him or her and the method of payment, Statutes 16-10-115(b).

CALIFORNIA

Constitution, Article VI, Section 20 states that "[t]he Legislature shall provide for retirement, with reasonable allowance, of judges of courts of record for age or disability", but no mandatory provision as to age has been enacted.

With respect to disability, Const., Art VI, §18, subds. (b) and (d) provide that the Commission on Judicial Performance may retire a judge for disability that seriously interferes with the performance of the judge's duties and is, or is likely to, become permanent; but subd. (e) states that "a judge retired by the commission shall be considered to have retired voluntarily." As to voluntary retirement for disability, see Optional Provisions for Retirement, below.

Government Code §§68701 and 68701.5 provide that the commission may investigate the conduct or performance of any retired judge serving on senior judge's status and may order the retired judge's senior judge status terminated for incapacity.

Retirement Provisions re Particular Courts

A former justice court judge who has withdrawn from active service but receives neither a retirement allowance under the Public Employees' Retirement System, nor under the retirement plan of the county in which he was employed, is not a retired justice court judge within the meaning of Constitution, Art. VI, Sec. 6 and Government Code Sec. 68543.5 and, therefore, is not eligible for assignment, Stewart v. Bird, 160 Cal.Rptr.660, 100 Cal.App.3d 215.

Optional Provisions for Retirement

A judge may retire at age sixty-five with twenty years or more of service, or at age seventy with five or more years of service, Government Code,

Sec. 75522(a); but if he or she does not retire prior to commencement of the term of office after the term during which he or she reaches seventy, the retirement allowance shall not exceed fifty percent of the judge's final compensation, Government Code, Sec. 75522(d)(2), unless this provision is held to be in violation of federal law. Judges are, however, encouraged to retire at or before seventy years of age by statutes reducing retirement benefits of those who chose not to retire at or before seventy, Government Code §§75075-75079, and those provisions do not violate the equal protection provisions of the Fourteenth Amendment to the U.S. Constitution, Rittenband v. Cory, 205 Cal.Rptr. 576, 159 Cal.App.3d 410.

A judge who is a member of the Judicial Retirement System and who became a judge between January 1, 1980 and December 31, 1988 and had at least two years of credited judicial service, or who became a judge after January 1, 1989 and was credited with at least four years of judicial service, or in either case whose disability resulted from injury or disease arising out of and in the course of judicial service, may retire voluntarily by presenting to the Commission on Judicial Performance a written application and the written statement of a physician or psychiatrist that he or she has personally examined the judge and is of the opinion that the judge is unable to discharge efficiently the duties of his or her office by reason of mental or physical disability that is or is likely to become permanent, may, with the approval of the chief justice or acting chief justice and of the commission, be retired from office, Government Code §§75060, 75061. The commission may require any judge receiving a disability allowance who is under the age of sixty-five to undergo medical examination, and if the commission determines on the basis of the examination that the judge is not so incapacitated, he or she shall be a judicial officer exercising powers as such only when assigned to a court by the Chairman of the Judicial Council, Government Code §75060.6; Davis v. Commission on Judicial Qualifications (as it was then called), 141 Cal. Rptr. 75.

Essentially similar provisions for voluntary disability retirement of judges who are members of Judicial Retirement System II, except that such judges must have at least five years of credited service to be eligible to retire for disability, are contained in Government Code §§75502, 75560-75560.6.

Disability retirement under the Retirement System is subject to Division IV of the Rules of the Judicial Performance Commission, which provide that within 120 days of the first commission meeting after receiving the judge's application and medical records, the commission may request one or more examinations of the judge by independent medical examiners or consultants, and that it may provide on a case by case basis when the judge should be reexamined, pursuant to §75060.6.

SERVICE AFTER RETIREMENT

A retired judge who consents may be assigned to any court, Constitution, Art. VI, Sec. 6. Upon retirement prior to January 1, 1997, but not thereafter, Government Code §75028.6, a judge may apply to the chairperson of the Judicial Council for senior judge status. When serving in senior judge status, he or she shall serve full time, as assigned, for up to five years, but, by accepting senior status, waives the right to refuse any assignment, as well as to any retirement allowance, except health and welfare benefits. Such status terminates at the end of five years, unless terminated sooner by request of the judge, by his or her failure to perform service as assigned, or by order of the Commission on Judicial Performance. However, on termination he or she may elect to receive the retirement benefits to which he or she was eligible when senior status was elected, Government Code §§75028.1-75028.5.

Effective January 1, 1996, the chief justice adopted "Standards and Guidelines for Judges Serving on Assignment," which provide that: a retired judge must file an application with the Administrative Office of the Courts each year by January 15 for eligibility to serve on temporary assignment; the presiding judge of the court to which assigned must file a confidential evaluation of each assigned retired judge on or before December 31 of the calendar year; a retired judge who serves on assignment must participate in continuing judicial education for retired judges at least once every two years; and a judge who retires or resigns is ineligible for assignment, unless a certificate has been obtained from the Commission on Judicial Performance indicating that there was no formal disciplinary proceeding pending at the time of retirement or resignation, Standards, I(D); Code of Civil Procedure, §2093(c).

A judge retired for disability may engage in the practice of law or other gainful occupation while less than seventy years of age, but his or her retirement allowance ceases permanently. If such a judge becomes entitled to a salary for assignment to a court after retirement, his or her retirement allowance is, during the time he or she is entitled to such salary, reduced by the amount of the salary, Government Code §75080(a). Subdivision (b) of that section provides, however, that a judge retired for disability may engage in the practice of law while less than seventy years of age, without loss or reduction in allowance, as long as the amount earned in any month when combined with the allowance does not exceed seventy-five percent of the salary payable to the judge holding the judicial office to which the retired judge was last elected or appointed, the retirement allowance being reduced by the amount of earnings in excess of that amount.

Under either the Judicial Retirement System or Judicial Retirement System II, a retired judge may be appointed by the supreme court or any court of appeal, or division thereof, to act as master or referee in any proceeding pending before any such court or before the Commission on Judicial Performance, Government Code §§75083, 75583.

Const. Art. VI, §21 provides that on "stipulation of the parties litigant the court may order a cause to be tried by a temporary judge who is a member of the State Bar, sworn and empowered to act until final determination of the cause." Although the section does not expressly refer to retired judges, a stipulation naming a retired judge as a temporary judge would appear to be within its terms, cf In Re Marriage of Assemi, 30 Cal. Rptr.2d 265, 872 P.2d 1190.

To be noted also is Government Code §68543.8(b), which directs the judicial council to contract with up to ten retired judges to be assigned up to 110 court days each year for the purpose of reducing delay in civil trials in counties requesting such assignment.

PAY AND EMOLUMENTS

A retired judge who elects prior to January 1, 1997 to be available for full-time service on senior status after retirement is compensated at a rate equal to the full compensation of a judge of the court from which he or she retired or, at the judge's election, at a rate equal to the full compensation of a judge of the court to which he or she is assigned, Government Code §75028(b). A judge serving in senior judge status is also eligible for travel, board, and lodging expenses, (id).

A retired judge who serves in a trial court on assignment is paid, in addition to the retirement pension, ninety-two percent of the salary of the court to which assigned, for each day of service in court, based on a 250-day year for service in a superior court, Govt. Code, §68543.7 (see also

§68543.5), but is not compensated for time spent in travel or to research or write a decision on matters submitted to him or her.

A retired judge appointed as master or referee pursuant to Government Code §75083 or §75583 is paid while so acting, in addition to his or her retirement allowance, the difference, if any, between the retirement allowance and the compensation of a judge of the court from which he or she retired, and when appointed to act as referee in a county other than that in which he or she resides, also receives necessary expenses for travel, board, and lodging incurred in discharge of the appointment (*id*).

A judge assigned pursuant to §68543.8(b) receives one-half the daily salary of a superior court judge for each day of service, in addition to retirement benefits and travel, board, and lodging expenses, §68543.8(c) and (d).

COLORADO

MANDATORY RETIREMENT PROVISIONS APPLICABLE GENERALLY

The Colorado Constitution provides that a judge or justice of a court of record must retire on attaining the age seventy-two, Art. 6, §23.

A Commission on Judicial Discipline has been created and may recommend to the Colorado Supreme Court that a judge be retired for good cause. *Id.* The Commission on Judicial Discipline may recommend that the supreme court retire a judge for a disability which is, or is likely to become, of a permanent character, Colorado Court Rule 36(b).

RETIREMENT PROVISIONS RE PARTICULAR COURTS

None.

OPTIONAL PROVISIONS FOR RETIREMENT

A judge is eligible to retire if he is sixty years old or older and is not a member of a county or a city and county retirement plan, or if a member of such plan, is not entitled to receive a deferred annuity, Colo. Rev. Stat., §13-3-109.

Members of the judicial division are eligible to apply for disability retirement without regard to the amount of earned service credit, Colo. Rev. Stat., §24-51-701. A medical or psychological examination may be required by the board. A judge may be retired for disability if found by the board to be permanently disabled, *id*, §24-51-702, 703(1) or if so found by the supreme court, *id*, §703(2). However, if the board determines that a disabled member has recovered, the disability benefit continues until the member has been reinstated in his or her former position or has accepted public or private employment in which the compensation for such employment, combined with the disability benefit, equals or exceeds the compensation last earned while a member, *id*, §24-51-707(1).

Retirement benefits are increased annually as of March 1, by the lesser of (a) the total percentage determined by multiplying 3.5 percent compounded annually times the number of years the benefit was effective after March 1, 1993, and (b) the percentage increase in the Consumer Price Index from 1992, or the year in which the benefit became effective, whichever is later, to the year preceding March 1, Colo. Rev. Stat., §§24-51-1001-1003. Retirement benefits are not assignable, nor are they subject to execution, levy, garnishment, bankruptcy proceedings, or other legal process, except for a qualified domestic relations order or for child support purposes, Colo. Rev. Stat., §24-51-212.

SERVICE AFTER RETIREMENT

The chief justice of the supreme court may assign a retired judge, who consents, to temporarily perform judicial duties if he deems it necessary to aid in the prompt disposition of judicial business, Colorado Constitution, Article VI, §5(3); Col. Rev. Stat., §13-3-110.

Whenever the chief justice of the supreme court deems assignment of a judge necessary to the prompt disposition of judicial business, the chief justice may assign any retired judge of the court of appeals, who consents, to temporarily perform judicial duties in any court of record, Colo. Rev. Stat, §13-4-104.5. Any retired county judge licensed to practice law in Colorado for five years may be assigned by the chief justice of the supreme court, pursuant to section 5(3) of article VI of the state constitution to perform judicial duties in any district court, probate court of the city and county of Denver, or the juvenile court of the city and county of Denver, Colo. Rev. Stat., §13-6-218.

In addition to recall by the chief justice, Colorado statutes provide that retirees of the judicial division may return to temporary judicial duties, pursuant to the provisions of section 5(3) of Article VI of the Colorado state Constitution and Colo. Rev. Stat., §13-4-104.5, while receiving service retirement benefits, Colo. Rev. Stat., §24-51-1105. Upon written agreement with the chief justice of the supreme court prior to retirement, a member of the judicial division may, during retirement, perform assigned judicial duties without pay for between sixty and ninety days each year and shall receive a benefits increase of twenty to thirty percent of the current monthly salary of judges serving in the same position as that held by the retiree at the time of retirement. Such agreement shall be for a period not to exceed three years and may be renewed for successive three-year terms, the aggregate of which shall not exceed twelve years, Colo. Rev. Stat., §24-51-1105(1)(b). Within five years after retirement, a retiree who did not enter into such agreement prior to retirement may do so within thirty days prior to each anniversary date of retirement, Colo. Rev. Stat., §24-51-1105(2). The retirement benefit of a retiree who, having agreed to be assigned to temporary duty, refuses without cause to accept a temporary assignment is reduced by the amount of the increase above referred to, Colo. Rev. Stat., §24-51-1105(3).

Upon agreement of all parties to a civil action that a specific retired judge be assigned to hear the action, and upon agreement that one or more of the parties shall pay the agreed upon salary of the selected judge, together with all other expenses incurred, the chief justice may assign any retired judge who consents temporarily to perform judicial duties for such action, Colo. Rev. Stat., §13-3-111. Rule 260 of Colorado Rules of Court Procedure requires "all judges" to complete forty-five units of continuing legal education within the three-year compliance period, but Rule 260.5 excepts from that requirement the years following the judge's sixty-fifth birthday.

PAY AND EMOLUMENTS

For each day of temporary service a retired judge shall receive as compensation an amount equal to one-twentieth of the monthly salary then currently applicable to the judicial position in which the temporary service is rendered, Colorado Constitution, Art. VI, §5(3), Colo. Rev. Stat., §13-3-110(4). He or she also receives actual and necessary expenses as prescribed by rule of the supreme court, together with mileage at the rate prescribed for state officers and employees for each mile in traveling to and returning from the place where he or she is serving, *id.*

CONNECTICUT

Pursuant to the Connecticut Constitution, no judge shall be eligible to hold his office after he has reached age seventy, except that a chief justice or judge of the supreme court, a judge of the superior court, or a judge of the court of common pleas, who has attained the age of seventy and has become a state referee may exercise, as shall be prescribed by law, the powers of the superior court or court of common pleas on matters referred to him as a state referee, Connecticut Constitution, Article 5, §6.

Any judge who becomes so permanently incapacitated as to be unable to fulfill adequately the duties of his office may be retired by the Judicial Review Council, upon application by him or upon its own motion, Conn. Gen. Stat., §51-49(a). The procedure for such removal is set forth in Conn. Gen. Stat., §§51-51j through 51-51r. If the judge is found by the Judicial Review Council to be permanently incapacitated from adequately fulfilling his duties, he shall be retired and shall receive as retirement pay, annually, two-thirds the salary of the office which he held at the time of his retirement, Conn. Gen. Stat., §§51-49(b), 51-50.

RETIREMENT PROVISIONS RE PARTICULAR COURTS

None.

OPTIONAL PROVISIONS FOR RETIREMENT

Any judge may elect to retire after he reaches the age of sixty-five or has twenty years of service as a judge, or has thirty years of state service credit, provided not less than ten years of such state service was served as a judge, Conn. Gen. Stat., §§51-50, 51-50a(a). Such judge is entitled to retirement benefits of two-thirds of the salary of the office held at the time of retirement, Conn. Gen. Stat., §§51-50, 51-50a(b), and such benefits are increased annually on the basis of the Consumer Price Index for Urban Wage Earners and Clerical Workers, not however to exceed three percent cumulatively, Conn. Gen. Stat., §51-49b.

A person who, at the time of appointment as a judge, has at least ten years of state service in the state employees retirement system may elect to remain in, or if he or she has withdrawn from that system to be reinstated in it, and if he or she does so and makes contributions to that system, will receive credit under the system for services as a judge, Conn. Gen. Stat., §5-166a.

Voluntary retirement for any judge for disability is provided for by Conn. Gen. Stat. §51-49(a), discussed in Mandatory Retirement Provisions, above.

SERVICE AFTER RETIREMENT

Any judge who retires from fulltime active service before he is seventy years old and who is an elector and resident of the state shall be a senior judge of the court of which he is a member for the remainder of the term of office for which he was appointed and is eligible for reappointment to succeeding terms as senior judge, Conn. Gen. Stat, §51-50i(a). Any senior judge of the supreme court may be assigned by the chief justice or chief court administrator to perform such judicial duties in the supreme court, or by the chief court administrator to perform such judicial duties in the superior court as he is willing to undertake, Conn. Gen. Stat., §51-50c(a). Any senior judge of the superior court may be assigned by the chief court administrator to perform such judicial duties in the superior court as he is willing to undertake, Conn. Gen. Stat., §51-50c(b).

A senior judge may participate in an alternative dispute resolution program approved by STA-FED ADR, Inc. in any year commencing July 1, provided such judge performed the duties of a senior judge for at least seventy-five days during the preceding year, except that a senior judge may participate in said alternative dispute resolution program from the date such judge assumes the status of a senior judge, through the completion of the year commencing July 1 following such date, without having satisfied the seventy-five day requirement, Conn. Gen. Stat., §51-50c(g).

Each judge or senior judge who ceases to hold office because he has turned seventy and is retired, except for disability, shall be a state referee for the remainder of his term of office as a judge, and is eligible for appointment as a state referee during the remainder of his or her life, Conn. Gen. Stat., §51-501(a), §52-434 (which sets out the procedures for appointing and hearing cases before state referees). A retired judge acting as a state referee after attaining the age of seventy shall have the power of a judge of the superior court on matters referred to him from the superior court, Conn. Gen. Stat., §51-50f. A retired judge of the court of common pleas or superior court may act as a state referee in small claims matters, Conn. Gen. Stat., §51-50h. Any case that may be referred to a state referee may be referred to a senior judge or panel thereof by the chief court administrator, Conn. Gen. Stat., §52-434b(a).

A retired judge or justice assigned to perform judicial duties shall not engage in the practice of law, but participation in alternative dispute resolution with STA-FED shall not be considered the practice of law, Conn. Gen. Stat., §51-50k, see also Conn. Gen. Stat., §51-50c, §52-454(g) and Code of Judicial Conduct Canon 5, subds. E and F re such participation by senior judges or trial referees.

PAY AND EMOLUMENTS

A state referee shall receive, in addition to retirement salary, the sum of $160 and expenses, including mileage, for each day he is so engaged, Conn. Gen. Stat., §52-434(f).

A senior judge shall receive during the period he shall perform judicial duties, in addition to his retirement salary, the compensation provided by law for a state referee for each day he performs either judicial duties or duties as a referee or both. Conn. Gen Stat., §51-47b(a); §52-434b(c). In no event shall his total salary, including retirement benefits, exceed the amount equal to the highest salary on which his retirement salary is based during the fiscal year, Conn. Gen Stat., §51-47b(b).

State referees and senior judges have the same basic health insurance coverage as do active judges; as to such coverage see Conn. Gen. Stat., §5-259.

DELAWARE

Delaware has no mandatory retirement provision for age. Delaware Constitution, Art. IV, §37 authorizes the Court on the Judiciary to retire a judicial officer for permanent mental or physical disability interfering with the proper performance of the duties of his or her office, if after notice and a hearing it so finds by the affirmative concurrence of not less than two-thirds of the members of the court. The filing of a certificate of permanent physical or mental incapacity constitutes, without any further act of a member of the judiciary, his or her resignation by such member, Delaware Code, Title 29, §5605(c).

Rules 1–12 of the Rules of the Court provide that if on investigation probable cause is found, the matter be referred to a Board of Examining Officers, that hearings be held by the board after notice to the judge, that its report be referred to the Court on the Judiciary, which after hearings may order retirement. If the complaint is found insufficient by the chief justice, the board, or the Court on the Judiciary, it may be dismissed.

Retirement Provisions re Particular Courts

None.

Optional Provisions for Retirement

Delaware has both a State Employees' Pension Plan, Del. Code Title 29, Chap. 55, and provisions for Pensions for State Judiciary Members (*id.*, Chap. 56). The definition of "employee" in Del. Code, §5501 is broad enough to include judges, though the chapter makes no specific reference to judges. To be noted, however, is that §5605 provides that to be covered by the State Judiciary Retirement Fund a judge must file a written declaration of acceptance or authorize deductions for contributions to the fund, and that any declaration filed or authorization made shall be irrevocable. The analysis which follows deals with the Judiciary Retirement System in effect after June 30, 1980 (see §5601[6]), except to note that some provisions of the State Employees' Plan are specifically made applicable to the Judiciary Retirement System, while others are not.

Del. Code, §5612(a) provides that a judge is eligible for a pension who has: (a) completed twelve years of service and has reached the age of sixty-two; (b) completed twenty-four years of service as a judge; or (c) been involuntarily retired after having served twenty-two years as a judge. Involuntary retirement is defined by Del. Code, §5604, as failure to be reappointed or confirmed after expiration of the judge's term of office, unless he or she declined reappointment.

An active judge who becomes permanently disabled, physically or mentally, is eligible for a pension for the remainder of his lifetime, Del. Code, §5612(c), after the board of trustees has considered a certificate, signed by the chief justice of the supreme court, indicating that the judge is permanently physically or mentally incapacitated to perform the duties of the office. If the chief justice be the subject of the certificate, it must be signed by the senior justice of the supreme court and by three duly licensed physicians designated by the trustees. (As to eligibility for disability pension of members of the State Employees' Pension Plan, see Del. Code, Title 29, 5524.)

Del. Code, §5526 requires that a disability pensioner who has not attained age sixty report to the board by April 30 each year his or her total earnings from any gainful occupation or business during the preceding year, and provides that the excess of such earnings over one-half the annual rate of compensation received before the pensioner became disabled adjusted for any increase in the total "Median Usual Weekly Earnings published by the U.S. Department of Labor" be deducted in a manner determined by the board from the disability pension during the twelve months beginning in July of the calendar year following that for which the earnings were reported.

Del. Code, §5615 provides that benefits under the State Judiciary Retirement Plan shall be adjusted in the same manner as benefits under Chapter 55 of Title 29. Section 5532 authorizes increases in service or disability pensions up to various stated maximums, depending on when the pension became effective.

Del. Code, Title 29, §5503 provides that except for orders of the Delaware family court for a sum certain payable on a periodic basis, the benefits provided under the State Employees' Retirement Plan are not subject to attachment or execution and are not subject to assignment or transfer, but no similar provision with respect to benefits under the Judiciary Retirement provisions of Title 29, Chap. 56, has been found.

SERVICE AFTER RETIREMENT

Any retired state judge or retired justice of the supreme court who assents to active judicial duty and who is not engaged in the practice of law is authorized, upon designation of the chief justice of the supreme court, to sit temporarily in the court from which he retired or in any other court to which he could be designated under the constitution and statutes of the state if he still held the judicial position from which he retired, Delaware Constitution, Art. IV, §38; Del. Code, §5610.

There is a proposed amendment to the Delaware Constitution, regarding senior judges, which has been initially approved but which as of December 1996 had not yet been adopted. Article IV, §39 provides that any eligible senior judge must perform at least three months of judicial work each year to continue as a senior judge in the following year, that such senior judge shall receive all pension benefits he would have received had he retired and be paid one-fourth of the current salary of an active judge on the court from which he retired, and that he may be designated to sit on any court to which he could be designated under the constitution or statutes of the state during active service as a judge.

Delaware Continuing Legal Education Rules 4(A) and 4(A)(4) require that judges complete thirty hours of continuing education courses for each two-year period, but provides for the granting of exemption upon review of a petition seeking exemption. The rule does not specifically mention retired judges serving after retirement, but appears broad enough to include them.

PAY AND EMOLUMENTS

Delaware Constitution, Art. IV, §38 provides that the General Assembly shall prescribe the compensation for retired judges acting on temporary assignment. Delaware Code §5610(b) provides that any retired judge accepting active duty shall be compensated on a per diem basis of $150 per day; but in no event shall the total compensation received on a per diem basis, when added to his retirement pay, exceed the then current annual salary of the judicial position from which such judge has retired. In addition, each retired judge shall receive reimbursement for expenses for travel or secretarial services necessarily incurred for the performance of such active duty. *Id.*

DISTRICT OF COLUMBIA

MANDATORY RETIREMENT PROVISIONS APPLICABLE GENERALLY

Judges are required to retire at age seventy-four, District Charter, §431(c); D.C. Stat., §11-1502.

The District of Columbia Commission on Judicial Disabilities and Tenure has the power to retire a judge, District Charter, §431(c); D.C. Stat., §11-1521. A judge shall be involuntarily retired when (1) the Commission determines that the judge suffers from a mental or physical disability (including habitual intemperance) which is, or is likely to become, permanent and which prevents, or seriously interferes with, the proper performance of the judge's judicial duties, and (2) the commission files in the D.C. court of appeals an order of involuntary retirement and the order is affirmed on appeal or the time for appeal has expired, District Charter, §432(c); D.C. Stat., §11-1526(b). The eligibility of a judge involuntarily retired for disability is not conditioned upon prior service, D.C. Stat., §11-1562(d). The procedure before the commission is spelled out in D.C. Stat., §11-1527 and District of Columbia Register, §§2010-2022.9.

D.C. Stat., §11-1526(c)(2) permits suspension of the judge upon filing with the commission, with the concurrence of three members, an order of involuntary retirement, subject to reinstatement and recovery of salary less retirement received by the judge if the order is set aside. Note, however, that D.C. Stat., §11-1527(a)(2) requires concurrence of *four* members after notice and hearing for adoption of an order of involuntary retirement, and that such an order is subject to judicial review by a special court of three judges appointed by the chief justice of the U.S. Supreme Court from among the active and retired federal judges of the U.S. Court of Appeals and the U.S. District Court for the District of Columbia, D.C. Stat., §11-1529.

RETIREMENT PROVISIONS RE PARTICULAR COURTS

For retirement provisions relating to judges of the tax court see D.C. Stat., §47-3302.

OPTIONAL PROVISIONS FOR RETIREMENT

A judge is eligible for retirement when the judge has completed ten years of judicial service, whether continuous or not. The retirement salary of a judge shall commence as follows: (1) with twenty years of service at age fifty; (2) with less than twenty years of service at age sixty, unless the judge elects to receive a reduced salary beginning at age fifty-five or at the date of retirement if subsequent to that age, D.C. Stat., §11-1562(a), (b).

A judge with five years of creditable service may voluntarily retire for a mental or physical disability which is, or is likely to become, permanent and which prevents, or seriously interferes with, the proper performance of judicial duties, D.C. Stat., §11-1562(c). As to the procedure on retirement for disability see D.C. Reg., §2038.1-2038.5.

The retirement salary of any judge receiving such a salary on the effective date of any increase payable under U.S.C. Title 5, §8340(b) shall be increased on the effective date of the §8340(b) increase by a percentage equal to the percentage of increase under §8340, D. C. Stat., §11-1571. Section 8340 provides for a cost of living adjustment based on the Consumer Price Index.

Monies in the retirement fund or payable from it are not assignable or subject to execution, levy, attachment, garnishment, or other legal process, D.C. Stat., §11-1570(d).

SERVICE AFTER RETIREMENT

A judge, retired for reasons other than disability, willing to perform judicial duties may request an appointment as a senior judge from the District of Columbia Commission on Judicial Disabilities and Tenure. A judge seeking appointment or reappointment as a senior judge must submit the report of a physician who examined him or her, attesting to the judge's physical or mental fitness to perform the duties of the office, and, when requested by the commission, must submit to a physical or mental examination by a physician appointed by the commission, D.C. Reg., §2038.1-2038.5. The commission submits a written report of its recommendations and findings to the appropriate chief judge who must decide within thirty days after receipt of the commission report whether to recommend appointment, D.C. Stat., §11-1504(b)(2), (3). The decision of the chief judge is final, §11-1504(b)(3). A senior judge so appointed is subject to such review every four years unless the senior judge has reached the age of seventy-four, whereupon review shall be at least every two years, D.C. Stat., §11-1504.

The District of Columbia Retirement Board includes one senior judge and an alternate senior judge appointed by the Joint Committee on Judicial Administration of the District of Columbia. D.C. Stat., §1-711(b)(1)(A)(vii).

PAY AND EMOLUMENTS

A senior judge shall be entitled, during the period for which he or she serves, to receive the same daily rate of pay as a judge on the court in which he or she performs such duties. The cumulative daily earnings of a senior judge, in any single year, when added to the annual retirement salary, may not exceed the current annual salary of a judge of the court in which he or she performs duties, D.C. Stat., §11-1565. However, performance of such service does not affect the retirement benefits to which the judge or his or her survivors are entitled (*id*).

FLORIDA

Article V, Section 8, of the Florida Constitution provides that no justice or judge shall serve after age seventy, except upon temporary assignment or to complete a term one-half of which he or she has served. Art. V, §20(e)(2) makes a further exception for a justice or judge who held office on July 1, 1957, but in Greenbaum v. Firestone, 455 So.2d 368 it was held that that exception only applies if the justice or judge still holds the same office when he or she reaches seventy as he or she held on July 1, 1957. See also, State Ex. Rel. Judicial Qualifications Commission v. Rose, 286 So.2d 562.

Judges may also be retired involuntarily for disability (as to voluntary disability retirement, see Optional Provisions for Retirement, below). To be noted, however, is that Florida has two retirement systems for judges. Prior to July 1, 1972 there existed only the Judicial Retirement System, which covered supreme court justices, district court of appeals judges, and circuit judges, and was provided for in Florida Statutes Annotated, Chapter 123; but effective on that date any person elected or appointed to such a judgeship, who was not already a member of the Judicial Retirement System when appointed or elected, was eligible for membership only in the Florida Retirement System, into which the Judicial Retirement System was merged, F.S.A., §121.046. The rights of members of the system established by Chapter 123 were, however, preserved unless such a member elected prior to June 30, 1973 to transfer to the Florida Retirement System, F.S.A., §123.046(3).

Involuntary disability retirement is provided for by Const., Art. V, 12(f), F.S.A., §§ 121.091(4) and 123.17, and Rule 14 of the Rules of the Judicial Qualification Commission. F.S.A., §121.091(4) provides that a member of the Florida Retirement System may be retired for total and permanent disability if, in the opinion of the administrator, he or she is prevented, by reason of a medically determined physical or mental impairment, from rendering useful and efficient service, unless the disability results from an intentional self-inflicted injury or an injury sustained while committing an act of violence, or a felony, or after termination of employment. Proof of such disability must include the certificate of two licensed physicians and such other evidence as the administrator may require. To receive a disability benefit the member, unless disabled in the line of duty, must have completed five years of creditable service, or, if on July 1, 1980, he or she had less than five years of service or became a member of the system on or after July 1, 1980, must have completed ten years of creditable service. The benefit continues for life unless, prior to the judge's normal retirement date, the administrator finds him or her no longer disabled.

With respect to the Judicial Retirement System, the constitution and statutory provisions above referred to authorize the Judicial Qualification Commission to order the judge to submit to a mental or physical examination, and if he or she fails to do so, to suspend the judge without compensation until the judge complies with the order, and after notice and hearing, to retire a justice or judge for disability if it certifies to the Division of Retirement that he or she suffers from "any permanent disability that seriously interferes with the performance of his [or her] duties." Section 123.17 requires the commission to specify the retirement plan chosen by the retiree or by the commission if the disability renders the retiree incapable of making a selection of the alternative retirement plans he or she is to be retired under. Section 123.19 authorizes the commission to retire for disability a judge or justice who disappears or has been absent without explanation for 180 days.

In Re Nelson, 288 So.2d 218, applied the involuntary retirement provisions of F.S.A., §121.091(4)(d) and Falk v. Kennedy, 322 So.2d 329, held a circuit judge who had elected the Florida Retirement System, who was involuntarily retired for disability, to be entitled to the retirement benefits of the Judicial Retirement System.

RETIREMENT PROVISIONS RE PARTICULAR COURTS

None.

OPTIONAL PROVISIONS FOR RETIREMENT

With respect to the Florida Retirement System, F.S.A. §121.021(29) provides that the "normal retirement date" means the first day of the month following the member's attaining age sixty-two with ten or more years of creditable service, or thirty years service regardless of age, but for a judge who is a member of the Elected State and County Officials Class (ESCOC) of the Florida Retirement System, normal retirement means eight years of ESCOC creditable service and sixty-two years of age. Judges of the supreme court, the district court of appeals, or circuit court who assumed office on or after July 1, 1972, and county court judges who assumed office on or after July 1, 1977, are members of ESCOC unless they opt out, F.S.A., §121.052(2) and (3).

With respect to the Judicial Retirement System, there are a number of relevant provisions. F.A.S., §123.04(1) provides that any supreme court justice, district court of appeals judge, or circuit judge electing the benefits of the Judicial Retirement System may retire if he or she has attained sixty years and has served as such for at least ten years in the aggregate, F.S.A., §123.04(1). But see §123.40(1)(a), which appears to change the age required to sixty-five years. Any such person who was serving in an elected term as supreme court justice or circuit judge on July 1, 1955 and thereafter completed at least twenty years of service in the aggregate may, without regard to his or her age, retire, F.S.A., §123.04(1). Any such person who has attained age fifty-five or more, but less than sixty years, and has accumulated at least ten years of service in the aggregate, and who has contributed to the Judicial Retirement Trust Fund for a least five years of creditable service, may elect to retire at a reduced benefit, F.S.A., §123.04(3); see also §123.40(1)(b). Moreover, F.S.A., §123.051, entitled "Special retirement," permits any person who has served as a supreme court justice, district court of appeals judge, or circuit judge for five years, but less than ten years, to retire without retirement benefit to himself or herself, his or her contributions to the retirement trust fund to be paid on his or her death to the heirs, legatees, beneficiaries, or personal representative of the deceased judge or justice.

To be noted also are F.S.A. §§25.101, 25.112 and §38.14. Section 25.101 provides that a justice of the supreme court may retire at or after age sixty-five with twenty years service on that court at the full pay of a justice of that court; and §25.112 permits a supreme court justice who served twenty years or more on the circuit and supreme courts to retire at two-thirds of the salary of a judge of the supreme court. F.S.A. §38.14, which deals with voluntary retirement of circuit judges, provides that any circuit judge who has served as such for twelve years or more, continuously or otherwise, and has reached age sixty, or has served for twenty years or more, continuously or otherwise, may voluntarily retire and shall thereafter be paid two-thirds of the compensation being paid to him or her at the time of retirement.

Voluntary retirement for disability is governed by statutes relating to the Florida Retirement System (F.S.A. §121.091 ff), the Judicial Retirement System (F.S.A. §123.08 ff), and to circuit judges (F.S.A. §38.15).

F.S.A., §121.091(4), deals with disability retirement of justices and judges who are members of the Florida Retirement System. That section requires proof, including that of two licensed physicians, of total and permanent disability, but excludes disability sustained while participating in an act of violence or through intentional self-inflicted injury. It covers disability incurred in the line of duty, but otherwise requires, in order to be entitled to a disability benefit, that the person have completed five years of creditable service or ten years of such service if the person became a member of the Florida Retirement System after July 1, 1980. Periodic reexaminations of a disability retiree may be required, and if he or she is found no longer disabled, disability benefits are terminated and the retiree may reenter judicial service.

Disability retirement of justices and judges who remain members of the Judicial Retirement System is dealt with in F.S.A., §§123.08, 123.17 and 123.19. Section 123.08 permits a supreme court justice or circuit judge[2] who has served for not less than ten years, the last five of which are continuous unbroken service, and who is regularly contributing to the Judicial Retirement Trust Fund, who becomes permanently and totally disabled, physically or mentally, from rendering useful and efficient service to retire and receive a retirement benefit, provided he or she has been examined by a physician or surgeon or board of physicians and surgeons appointed by the governor and found to be so disabled. Periodically thereafter such retiree is examined by a physician or surgeon or board of physicians and surgeons appointed by the governor; and if found to be fully recovered, his or her retirement benefits cease.

F.S.A. §38.15 provides that a circuit judge who has served as such for ten years or more, continuously or otherwise, who while holding office becomes totally and permanently disabled, physically or mentally, or both, from rendering useful and efficient service may voluntarily resign or retire and will thereafter receive one-half the compensation paid to such judge at the time of retirement or resignation.

---

[2] Note, however, that no mention is made in the section of a judge of a district court of appeals.

Service After Retirement

Const. Art. V, §2(b), empowers the chief justice of the supreme court to assign consenting retired judges to temporary judicial duty in any court for which the judge is qualified; see also Art. V, §8, and Judicial Administration Rules, Rule 2.030(3).The form of such consent is set forth in Supreme Court Rule, reported in 236 So.2d 769 and 239 So.2d 254; but note that the thirty-day limitation on such service in paragraph 3 of the Rule has been extended by F.S.A., §25.073(2)(a) referred to below.

F.S.A., §121.011, provides that any justice or judge who transfers to the Florida Retirement System and retires under its provisions is eligible for judicial service if he or she has had no less than five years of judicial service at the time of retirement. But as to a justice or judge in the Judicial Retirement System, F.S.A., §123.051(2)(a) limits assignment to temporary duty of any such person to one who has served for a period of five, but less than ten, years or has at least five, but less than ten, years of creditable service.

For purposes of assignment to temporary duty, "retired justice" or "retired judge" means one who has not been defeated for reelection to, or failed to be retained in seeking retention in, his or her last judicial office and who is not engaged in the practice of law, F.S.A., §§25.073, 121.046(4), or if he or she has been so engaged but ceased such practice, upon approval by the supreme court of an application to so serve, stating how long he or she has not engaged in the practice of law, Rules of Supreme Court 2.030(a)(3)(A), (B) and (C).

A retired justice or judge assigned to temporary duty by the chief justice may not, however, serve more than sixty days in any one year without the approval of the chief justice, F.S.A., §25.073(2)(a). Rule 2.150(b) of Florida's Rules of Judicial Administration requires retired judges who have been approved for assignment to temporary active duty to complete a minimum of thirty credit hours of continuing judicial education programs every three years.

A retired justice or judge may also be appointed referee to try disciplinary cases, Rules of Discipline Procedures, §3-7.6 and may serve as a mediator, Code of Judicial Conduct, §B. F.S.A. §38.13 permits the parties, when the judge of a circuit or county court is disqualified, to agree upon an attorney-at-law as judge ad litem to preside over the case. The section makes no mention of retired judges, but a retired judge engaged in the practice of law would appear to be within its provisions.

PAY AND EMOLUMENTS

Any retired justice of the supreme court, or judge of a district court of appeals or circuit or county court, assigned to temporary duty pursuant to Article V of the Constitution shall be paid not less than $200 for each day or portion of a day he or she is assigned to temporary duty, as well as necessary travel expenses, F.S.A., §25.073, §2(a) and (b). A retired justice or judge serving as a certified mediator is paid $125 an hour.

A justice or judge who reaches seventy before he or she has served half the term to which elected may purchase credit for service as a temporary judge if the temporary assignment follows immediately the last full term of office served and the purchase is limited to the number of months' service needed to vest retirement benefits, F.S.A., §121.052(4)(d)(2).

GEORGIA

Mandatory Retirement Provisions Applicable Generally

None, but there are mandatory provisions as to particular courts (see next section).

Retirement Provisions re Particular Courts

A judge of the court of appeals or a justice of the supreme court may retire under either the Employee Retirement System or under the optional system established by Ga Code §47-2-244, provided he or she files a notice of election to do so as required by subdivision (c) of that section. By that notice the judge waives any benefit otherwise available to him or her and waives the right to appointment to, and the holding of, any emeritus office and agrees to resign from office as an appellate court judge on or before the day he or she reaches seventy-five years of age or on the last day of the term in which he or she is serving when he or she attains age seventy, whichever is later (*id*, subds. b and c), but a judge who fails to retire at such time receives no retirement benefit and forfeits all contributions, (*id*, subd. l). The retirement benefit that an appellate judge is entitled to receive after ten years of service during his or her life is equivalent to seventy-five percent of the salary of an appellate judge then serving in the office from which such judge retired, (*id*, subd. f). However, no benefit is payable to an appellate court judge under this section until the judge reaches sixty-five years of age, except for incapacity (*id*, subd. m).

A superior court judge who fails to retire effective on the first day of the calendar month next succeeding that in which he or she reaches seventy-five forfeits all retirement benefits, provided that a judge who held office as a judge of the superior court on July 1, 1976 is not required to retire, regardless of age, until he or she obtains ten years of creditable service, Ga Code §§47-9-70(a)(1); 47-9-71, or, if the judge was reelected in the 1988 retention election, until completion of the term of office to which he or she was then reelected, Ga Code, §47-9-70(a)(2), (a)(3), (f).

A trial judge, other than one who held office as a juvenile court judge or a judge or solicitor of the inferior courts on July 1, 1980, is required to retire on the first day of the calendar month following that in which he or she reached seventy, failing which the judge forfeits all retirement benefits. Judges within the above exception are not required to retire at any age, Ga Code, §47-10-100(a).

A judge of the probate court, who has applied for membership in the Probate Courts Retirement Fund and otherwise complied with Ga Code, §47-11-40, may retire after at least four years service as a regularly qualified and commissioned probate judge, upon having attained sixty years of age and filed an application with, and approval of the application by, the Board of the Probate Courts Retirement Fund, Ga Code, §47-11-70. A probate judge who has completed four years of creditable service may, regardless of age, upon determination by the board of trustees that he or she has become totally and permanently disabled to perform the duties of office, retire, Ga Code, §47-11-73.

Concerning the mandatory provisions of the above statutes, see Smith v. Miller, 261 Ga 560, 407 SE2d 727, in which a supreme court judge and an appellate judge were prohibited from completing their terms of office because they would have attained age seventy-five and forfeited retirement benefits. The court upheld Ga Code, §47-2-244(c) and required the judges to retire at age seventy-five.

Optional Provisions for Retirement

After ten years of service as an appellate judge, the judge may retire at any age and still be entitled at age sixty-five to receive for the rest of his life retirement benefits of seventy-five percent of the salary of an appellate judge then serving in the office from which he retired, 1971 Op. Atty. Gen. No. 71-203, and proportionately for any increase thereafter granted, 1978 Op. Atty. Gen. No. U78-5.

A judge of the superior court who has served as such for at least ten years, who becomes disabled from continuing such service, who has attained sixty-two years of age, and whose retirement for disability the board of trustees recommends, may retire for disability, Ga Code, §§47-8-41(b)(2); 47-9-22(a)(8); 47-9-60(a)(1), or, if a majority of the board so determines, may without regard to his or her age, be appointed a senior judge, Ga Code, §47-8-40(c).

Trial judges are entitled to retire after sixteen years of creditable service upon reaching age sixty, Ga Code, §47-10-100(b), but no member can accumulate more than twenty-two years of creditable service for the purposes of maximum retirement benefits, 1980 Op. Atty. Gen. No. 80-155. Such benefit is not payable until the judge reaches age sixty-five and makes written application for such benefit, 1975 Op. Atty. Gen. No. 75-104. After ten years of creditable service, a trial judge may retire at a lesser benefit at age sixty, Ga Code, §47-10-101.

A trial judge who becomes totally and permanently disabled to perform the duties of office and who has attained a minimum of ten years of creditable service may, regardless of age, upon determination of the board of trustees that he or she is so disabled, retire, Ga Code, §47-1-103, but cannot thereafter be appointed a senior judge, §47-10-130(d).

Service After Retirement

After retiring any state court judge, juvenile court judge, or superior court judge who has served for ten years or more on any combination of such courts may be appointed a senior judge of the type of court from which the judge retired, Ga Code, §§47-8-60, 47-9-60, 47-10-130(a), upon applying for such status to the governor and receiving appointment by the governor as such, *id.* 47-8-60, 47-10-131(b). A senior judge may be called upon to serve as a judge or justice of any court of the state, Constitution Art. 6, Sec. 1, paragraph III; Ga Code, §47-10-131(a). He or she holds office as a senior judge for life (*id.* 47-8-61), but prior to July 1, 1994 was precluded from practicing law in any state court (*id.*) and even now remains ineligible for election or appointment to any other office or to practice law without resigning from office as a senior judge (47-10-131[c]), but may be reappointed a senior judge upon ceasing to hold such office or to practice law (*id.*). The practice of law by a retired judge does not, however, deprive the retired judge of his or her retirement benefits, State v. McMillan, 253 Ga 154, 165; 319 S.E.2d 1.

It is the duty of a senior judge to consult with justices of the supreme court and judges of the court of appeals with respect to revision of their rules of practice and in handling administrative duties and to consult with the attorney general when so requested; Ga Code, §47-8-63.

PAY AND EMOLUMENTS

When called back into service as a senior judge, a retired judge receives $165 per day, plus expenses incurred, Ga Code, §15-1-9.2(d) (see also, as to trial judges, §47-10-132), in addition to his or her retirement benefits. Note, however, that Ga Code, §47-8-62 provides that a judge of the superior court appointed as a senior judge receives from the state an annual salary equal to two-thirds of the salary paid to a judge of the superior court at the time of appointment as a senior judge, and receives from the counties of the circuit in which he or she serves two-thirds of the amount paid to him or her as a judge by those counties at the time of such appointment.

HAWAII

Mandatory Retirement Provisions Applicable Generally

Constitution Art.VI, §3 provides that justices and judges of the supreme court, intermediate appellate court, circuit court, district court, and district family court shall be retired upon attaining the age of seventy years. A judge who terminates his or her membership in the retirement system pursuant to H.R.S.A., Title 7, Chap. 88, §88-61(c) may not serve after age sixty-five, unless the judge was in office and sixty-five or over on May 24, 1971.

Constitution Art. VI, §5 and Supreme Court Rules 8.13 and 8.14 provide that the supreme court, on recommendation of the Commission on Judicial Conduct, may retire a judge for disability that is found, after hearing, to seriously interfere with the performance of his or her duties and is, or is likely to become, permanent, but that a judge or justice so retired shall be considered to have retired voluntarily.

Retirement Provisions re Particular Courts

None.

Optional Provisions for Retirement

A judge who has at least five years of credited service and has attained age fifty-five, or who has at least twenty-five years of credited service, or at least ten years of credited service as a judge or in enumerated nonjudicial positions, may retire upon written application stating the date the member wishes to be retired, H.R.S.A. Title 7, Chap. 88, §88-73(1). A judge who elects to retire may continue in active service but receives no retirement allowance until termination of active service. Upon leaving active service, however, he or she receives a retirement allowance, plus a postretirement allowance computed as though the judge had left active service on the date of the election, *id*, §88-73(3).

Upon application of a member of the retirement system who has had ten or more years of credited service, he or she may be retired if the medical board certifies, after examination, that the member is mentally or physically incapacitated from further performance of duty, the incapacity is likely to be permanent and the member should be retired, H.R.S.A., Title 7, Chap. 88, §88-75, and receives a retirement allowance computed as provided in §88-76. If, however, the disability is the natural and proximate result of an accident occurring in the performance of duty and not through willful negligence on the member's part, and those facts are certified to the retirement board by the head of the agency (chief justice or judge of the court on which he or she served), and the medical board certifies that the member is incapacitated for gainful employment and that the incapacity is likely to be permanent, the judge receives an annuity, plus a pension of two-thirds of the member's average final compensation, *id*, §§88-77. 88-78. As to retirement of district court judges for disability, see also H.R.S.A., Div. 4, Title 32, Chap. 604, §604.2.

SERVICE AFTER RETIREMENT

Retired judges of the supreme court may serve temporarily on the supreme court; retired judges of the intermediate appellate court, the circuit court, the district courts, and the district family courts may serve temporarily on the intermediate appellate court, on any circuit court, on any district court, and on any district family court, respectively, Const. Art. VI, §2. When a vacancy in the supreme court occurs by reason of termination of a justice's term, disqualification, recusal, or other cause, the vacancy may be temporarily filled by a circuit judge designated by the chief justice or appointment of a retired supreme court justice, but such retired justice shall not be actively engaged in the practice of law, H.R.S.A. Div. 4, Title 32, Chap. 602, §602-10. When because of vacancy or disqualification available intermediate appellate judges are insufficient to make up a panel of three judges, the chief justice of the supreme court may designate retired supreme court justices or retired intermediate appellate judges to fill such need temporarily, but a judge so serving shall not be actively engaged in the practice of law, *id*, §602-55. A retired circuit judge may be assigned by the chief justice of the supreme court to hear matters in any circuit when it is advisable to do so because of disqualification or inability of a circuit judge, a vacancy in office, or for any other reason, but a judge so serving temporarily shall not be actively engaged in the practice of law, *id,* §603-41.

Const. Art. VI, §3, authorizes the chief justice to appoint per diem district court judges as provided by law. H.R.S.A., Div. 4, Title 32, Chap. 604, §604.2, which provides for such appointments, does not mention retired judges, but it would appear to permit the chief justice to appoint a retired judge as a per diem district court judge on his or her consent. A per diem district court judge may engage in the private practice of law during his or her term of service.

Pay and Emoluments

Retired justices of the supreme court, judges of the intermediate appellate court, circuit judges, and district court judges are compensated per diem at a rate of pay equivalent to that of associate justices or judges of the court on which he or she is serving, *id,* §§602-10, 602-55, 603-41. They do not receive retirement pay while so serving, *id,* §88-73(3), but receive credit for the period of such active service in the determination of his or her retirement allowance, *id.*

A per diem district court judge receives compensation for the days on which actual service is rendered based on the monthly rate of compensation of a district court judge, a month being deemed to consist of twenty-one days, H.R.S.A., Div. 4, Title 32, Chap. 604, §604.2.

IDAHO

Under the Idaho State Constitution, the retirement, discipline, and removal from office of justices and judges shall be provided by law, Idaho Const. Art. V, §28. The "Age Limit" requirement of Idaho Code, §1-2007 was repealed in 1984. Idaho Code, §1-2103 and 1-2103A provide that a judge or magistrate may be retired for disability seriously interfering with the performance of his duties, which is, or is likely to become, of a permanent character; and §1-2404(3) provides that a judge of the court of appeals is subject to removal or retirement pursuant to §1-2103. The standard of proof in a retirement or removal proceeding is clear and convincing evidence, Idaho Judicial Council v. Becker, 122 Idaho 238, 834 P.2d 290.

Retirement Provisions re Particular Courts

None.

Optional Provisions for Retirement

Idaho has both a Judges Retirement System (Idaho Code, §2001 ff.) and a Public Employees' Retirement System ("PERS") (Idaho Code, §59-1301 ff.). While the PERS definition of "employee" is broad enough to include justices and judges, the chapter makes no specific reference to justices or judges. In the following sections of this report, therefore, notations of PERS provisions are included when there are no parallel provisions in the statutes relating to the Judicial Retirement System.

The Idaho Code provides that any supreme court justice or any district court judge upon reaching the age of sixty-five with at least four years of service on the bench, or who has an aggregate of twenty years or more of service, continuous or otherwise, may retire or resign, and receive retirement compensation based upon his or her years of service, but not exceeding 62.5 percent of the current annual compensation of the office from which he or she retired, Idaho Code, §1-2001.

A judge may retire by reason of disability preventing further performance of the duties of the office, after service of four years or more, and receive retirement compensation similarly computed, Idaho Code, §12001(4). Note, however, that the words "which is or is likely to become of a permanent character" that are contained in §1-2103 and 1-2103A do not limit optional retirement for disability under §1-2001(4). A judge who has served less than four years is entitled to the refund of all contributions made by him or her to the judges retirement fund, with interest, Idaho Code, §1-2001(5).

The PERS defines "disabled" in Idaho Code, §59-1302(12) to mean that the member is prevented from engaging in any occupation or employment for remuneration or profit as a result of bodily injury or disease, either occupational or nonoccupational, that did not result from service in the armed forces of any country or from an intentionally self-inflicted injury, from which the member will likely remain so disabled permanently and continuously during the remainder of his or her life.

Idaho Code, §59-1355 provides for increase of the retirement allowance of a PERS retiree on the basis of the U.S. Department of Labor Consumer Price Index for all urban consumers as determined by the board, subject to a concurrent resolution of the legislature rejecting the proposed adjustment. No similar provision with respect to the Judicial Retirement System has been found, the only provision of that system dealing with increased retirement compensation being Idaho Code, §1-2001a, the effect of which is limited to a justice or judge who retired or resigned before July 1, 1967.

Retirement benefits under the Public Employees' Retirement System are not assignable, nor are they subject to execution, garnishment, attachment, or the operation of any bankruptcy or insolvency law, except for enforcement of an order for the support of a minor child, Idaho Code, §59-1317. No similar provision with respect to benefits payable pursuant to the Judicial Retirement System has been found, and, it should be noted, the PERS provision is expressly limited to "benefits under this chapter."

SERVICE AFTER RETIREMENT

Any retired judge or justice while he or she remains capable may sit as a judge of the district court or as a magistrate in any county upon the request and order of the chief justice, and when any such request is made or approved by the chief justice, it shall be his duty to do so, Idaho Code, §1-2005. Any retired justice or district judge may sit with the supreme court and exercise the authority of a member thereof in any cause in which he is requested by that court so to do, and when requested by the chief justice shall perform such other duties pertaining to the judicial department of government as directed, Idaho Code, §1-2005. Any justice or judge who voluntarily leaves full-time judicial employment prior to eligibility for retirement under Idaho Code, §1-2001 may, while he or she remains capable, sit with the supreme court or as a judge of the court of appeals, or district court, or as a magistrate in any county upon the request and order of the Chief Justice, Idaho Code §1-2005.

Commencing July 1, 1981, until funds have been appropriated for, and the governor has filled by appointment three positions on the Idaho court of appeals, and continuing thereafter as needed, the supreme court may provide for the assignment of active and retired district judges or retired justices of the Supreme and appellate courts to serve on a panel of the court of appeals, Idaho Code, §1-2405(1). Compensation for retired judges serving on the court of appeals shall be paid in the same manner provided for such temporary service on the supreme court, Idaho Code, §1-2405(3).

Any retired magistrate, while he or she remains capable, may hold court in the magistrate division of any district court of any county at the request of the administrative judge of the district in which the court is located and upon approval of the chief justice of the supreme court, Idaho Code, §1-2221.

Time served shall not be computed for additional retirement benefits, nor shall any deduction be made from such compensation for retirement benefits, Idaho Code §§1-2005, 1-2221.

Constitution Article V, §12 provides that a cause in the district court may be tried by a judge pro tempore. Neither that section nor Rule 4 of Idaho Court Administrative Rules dealing with judges pro tempore mentions a retired judge, but nothing in the rule excludes retired judges from such an appointment, the only requirement being that the parties agree in writing upon the person designated and that the person be a member of the bar in good standing, meet all constitutional and statutory qualifications as a district judge or lawyer magistrate, and execute the oath required of judges, requirements which a retired judge, if designated by the parties, could meet. A judge pro tempore acts solely as a trial judge and does not have any of the inherent powers of a district judge. A judge pro tempore receives compensation as agreed upon by the parties and is paid directly by the parties.

PAY AND EMOLUMENTS

Compensation for service shall be as provided by the legislature, Const. Art V, §12. During the period that any retired justice, judge, or magistrate is serving and holding court pursuant to Idaho Code §1-2005 or §1-2221, he shall be entitled to receive all of his retirement benefits under the judges' retirement fund together, with an additional sum as compensation for his services sufficient to amount to an aggregate sum of retirement benefits and additional compensation so as to be equal to the current salary of the judicial office from which such justice, judge, or magistrate has retired, Idaho Code, §§1-2005, 1-2221. When serving outside his county of residence, such retired judge, justice, or magistrate shall be paid his necessary traveling and subsistence expenses, Idaho Code §1-2005.

ILLINOIS

Constitution Art. 6 §15(a) authorizes the legislature to fix the age at which judges must retire. The Compulsory Retirement of Judges Act (705 ILCS 55/1) makes its automatic retirement provision applicable to all supreme court, appellate, circuit, and associate judges. The act, which presently fixes the age as seventy-five (previously seventy), requires all such judges to retire at the expiration of the term during which they reach seventy-five, 705 ILCS 55/1. In Trafelet v. Thompson, 594 F.2d 623, cert. den. 444 U.S. 906, mandatory retirement at age seventy was held rationally related to the state's purpose of competency of its judiciary and, therefore, not unconstitutional; and in U.S. Equal Employment Opportunity Commission v. State of Illinois, 721 F.Supp. 156 it was held not in conflict with the Age Discrimination in Employment Act as to *appointed* state judges, although that statute (29 U.S.C. §680([f]) expressly excluded from its protection only *elected* officials including judges. Note, however, that in Anagnost v. Laylie 230 Ill.App.2d 109, 595 N.E.2d 109, a divided court held that a seventy-eight year old former judge was a proper candidate for reelection even though over the mandatory retirement age, since the statute imposed no bar concerning who could run for election to judicial office!

A judge who is physically or mentally unable to perform his or her duties may be suspended, with or without pay, or retired pursuant to Section 15(c) of Article 6 of the constitution. Section 15(b) creates a Judicial Inquiry Board which, if at least five members of the board believe that a reasonable basis exists to charge that a judge or associate judge is physically or mentally unable to perform his or her duties, is authorized to file a complaint with the Courts Commission, consisting of one supreme court judge, two appellate court judges, and two circuit judges. The Courts Commission may suspend or retire a judge whom it finds after notice and public hearing is physically or mentally unable to perform his or her duties. Note, however, that 40 ILCS 5/18-126 requires that the "board" (which apparently refers to the Board of Trustees of the Judges Retirement System) have received a written certificate by at least two licensed and practicing physicians appointed by it stating that the participant is disabled and that the disability occurred during employment as a judge and is likely to be permanent, and uses a slightly different definition of disability: "is of such a nature as to prevent the participant from *reasonably performing* the duties of his or her office at the time," and that 40 ILCS 5/18-143 provides for examination of a person receiving a disability annuity prior to age sixty, by one or more such physicians at least once each year during continuance of disability. 40 ILCS 5/18-126.1 also authorizes payment of fifty percent of a participant's salary as a "temporary total disability benefit" if the judge has served as a judge for at least two years, has at least two years of service credit, has been found while employed as a judge by medical examination to be mentally or physically incompetent to perform his or her duties, does not have a right to receive a salary as a judge, and is not engaged in any form of gainful occupation during disability. Such a disabled participant, however, receives service credit for the period that such temporary disability benefits are paid.

RETIREMENT PROVISIONS RE PARTICULAR COURTS

None.

OPTIONAL PROVISIONS FOR RETIREMENT

A participant in the Judges Retirement System whose employment is terminated is entitled upon written application to a retirement annuity if he or she is not receiving or entitled to receive any salary from the state or county for service as a judge currently performed, is at least fifty-five years of age or has become permanently disabled from performing the duties of his or her judgeship, or has at least ten years of service credit, or is a participant whose service terminated after June 30, 1975 with at least six years of service credit and is sixty-two years of age or older, 40 ILCS 5/18-124. But a participant who, except for disability, retires prior to age sixty with less than twenty-eight years of service is reduced by one-half of one percent for each month he or she is under age sixty at the time the annuity commences, 40 ILCS 5/18-125(c). Note, however, that a participant receiving a retirement annuity who is regularly employed by the state or county, in any capacity, is not entitled to the annuity during such employment. If he or she resumes service as a judge, the participant is entitled to credit for the additional service when he or she subsequently retires. However, temporary employment as a judge for not more than seventy-five working days in any calendar year is not deemed regular employment for compensation or the resumption of service as a judge, 40 ILCS 5/18-127(a),(b).

As noted under Mandatory Retirement Provisions, above, a judge may be retired for disability. While the language of the provisions there considered does not clearly cover voluntary retirement for disability, it appears broad enough to cover voluntary as well as involuntary retirement.

An automatic cost of living adjustment of a retirement annuity was first enacted in 1969 and in 1980 was fixed at three percent. Effective January 1, 1990 the increase was made cumulative of all prior increases, 40 ILCS 5/18-125.1.

40 ILCS 5/18-161 protects all annuities and other benefits payable to a retired judge or his or her survivor from judgment, execution, garnishment, attachment or other seizure by process, in bankruptcy or otherwise, and provides that they shall not be assignable.

SERVICE AFTER RETIREMENT

Any retired judge, with his or her consent, may be assigned by the supreme court to service after retirement, but only as an associate judge, Const. Art. 6 §15(a).

PAY AND EMOLUMENTS

Retired judges assigned to service after retirement receive the compensation applicable to the office to which assigned, in lieu of retirement benefits, Const. Art. 6 §15(a). They are also entitled to health benefits reduced as to retirees sixty-five years old or older who are entitled to Social Security or Railroad Retirement benefits or Medicare, 51 ILCS 375/6 and to group life insurance coverage based on salary immediately prior to retirement; but at age sixty coverage is reduced to $5,000, 5 ILCS 375/7(a)(2).

INDIANA

MANDATORY RETIREMENT PROVISIONS APPLICABLE GENERALLY

Article 7, §11 of the Indiana Constitution provides that every justice of the supreme court and judge of the court of appeals shall retire at the age specified by statute at the commencement of his or her current term; and Code §33-2.1-5-1 provides that justices and judges of the court of appeals and supreme court shall retire at age seventy-five, but empowers the supreme court to authorize retired justices and judges, without limitation as to age, to perform temporary judicial duties in any court of the state.

Constitution Article 7, §11, also authorizes the supreme court, on recommendation of the Commission on Judicial Qualifications and after a hearing by the supreme court, to retire a justice of the supreme court or judge of the court of appeals for disability that seriously interferes with the performance of his or her duties and is likely to become permanent, but specifies that a justice or judge so retired shall be considered to have retired voluntarily. Note, however, that Code §§33-13-9.1-5, 33-13-10.1-6 and 33-13-10.1-8, which as phrased appear to govern both voluntary and involuntary retirement for disability, are, arguably, phrased more restrictively: "total incapacity by reason of physical or mental infirmities from earning a livelihood and the condition is likely to be permanent."

RETIREMENT PROVISIONS RE PARTICULAR COURTS

There is no mandatory retirement age for trial judges, but Code §33-10.5-6-1 provides that a person may not run for judge of a county court if he or she will be seventy years of age or older before he or she begins the term of office, and Code §§33-5-4.5-2, 33-5-10.7-2, 33-5-25.7-2 and 33-5-48-2 contain similar provisions with respect to judges of the superior courts of Adams, Decatur, Jay, and Wayne counties. Implicit in those statutes is that a judge may serve until the end of the term if he or she was elected prior to his or her seventieth birthday.

Optional Provisions for Retirement

Code §33-13-9.1-4 provides that a participant in the 1977 retirement system whose employment as judge is terminated, regardless of cause, is entitled to a retirement annuity if he or she has attained at least the age of sixty-two and has served at least eight years of service credit and is not receiving salary from the state for services rendered, other than in the capacity of judge pro tempore or senior judge.

With respect to voluntary retirement for disability, see Mandatory Retirement Provisions Applicable Generally, above.

Service After Retirement

While Code §33-2.1-5-1 empowers the supreme court to authorize retired justices and judges to perform temporary judicial duties in any court of the state, that statute does not permit the appointment of a "special judge" to sit as a member of the supreme court, since the composition of that court is fixed by Constitution Art. 7, §1, State ex rel Mass Transportation Authority v. Indiana Revenue Board, 254 N.E.2d 1.

Indiana's governing provisions permit service after retirement as a special judge, a judge pro tempore or temporary judge, a senior judge, or a private judge.

Under Criminal Rule 13 or Trial Rules 53.1, 53.2, 60.5 or 79, upon agreement of the parties or by the supreme court upon request to it, a "special judge" may be appointed when circumstances warrant, as when the judge to whom a cause is assigned fails to rule on a motion or to enter judgment after trial before him or her within the periods specified in those rules. A senior judge may be appointed as a special judge under either set of rules. A special judge retains jurisdiction of the matter until judgment and with respect to post-judgment applications.

Code §33-10.5-6-1 permits the chief justice of the state to authorize a judge retired for age to perform temporary judicial duties in a county court, and §33-13-16-1 empowers the judge of a circuit, superior, or county court to appoint temporary judges. Such an appointee must be a competent attorney admitted in Indiana and a resident of the judicial district, a description which does not expressly cover retired judges but is broad enough to include them. A temporary judge appointed under the latter provision continues in office until removed by the appointing judge. Note, however, that §33-13-16-6 permits the appointing judge to specifically determine the duties of the temporary judge or otherwise limit the rights or powers of such judge as specified in the statute, and that §33-13-16-10 limits the service performed by such a judge to sixty calendar days in the aggregate during a calendar year, except for certain temporary juvenile law judges and for temporary judges appointed by a court located in a county having a population of more than 200,000 but less than 300,000. Note, further, that Indiana's supreme court has distinguished between a judge pro tempore referred to in Code §33-13-16-7 and a temporary judge, holding in State ex rel Peacock v. Marion Superior Court, 490 N.E.2d 1094, that a temporary judge is more in the nature of a referee functioning under the jurisdiction of the judge presiding, whereas a judge pro tempore is appointed to act in place of the regular judge and becomes a judge of that court for all purposes during the period he or she sits as a judge pro tempore.

A senior judge is appointed upon application to the circuit court or superior court of the need for such an appointment, stating the estimated duration of the need for a senior judge, Code §33-4-8-1. A person who desires to serve as a senior judge must apply to the Judicial Nominating Commission for certification that he or she has served as a justice or judge of a court of record in Indiana and is available to serve as a senior judge for the duration specified in the circuit court or superior court application, and that the combination of the compensation as a senior judge and the retirement benefit he or she is receiving or is entitled to receive does not exceed the minimum compensation of a judge of the circuit court, or if it does that he or she has elected to forego retirement benefits during the period of service as a senior judge, the Judicial Nominating Commission having verified that such an election is available to him or her, Code §33-2.1-4-17. Appointment of a judge so certified by the commission is made by the supreme court, Code §33-4-1-8, for the duration specified in the circuit court or superior court application, Code §33-4-8-2, and the appointee exercises the jurisdiction granted to the court on which he or she is serving, Code §33-4-8-3; and at the pleasure of the supreme court (*id*). However, the supreme court may not require a senior judge to accept such an assignment, Code §33-4-8-4.

A private judge is a person who has been but currently is not a judge of the circuit, superior, criminal, probate, municipal, or county court for at least four consecutive years, is a resident of Indiana and admitted to practice there. Such a person may act as the judge of a case only if the parties to the case file a written petition with the state court administration consenting to the case being heard by a private judge and naming the person they wish to have serve as such, the case is one over which the court in which the former judge served would have had subject matter and monetary jurisdiction and is founded exclusively on contract or tort or a combination thereof, and does not involve a utility, Code §§33-13-15-2, 33-13-15-3. The written petition of the parties, together with the written consent of the person to serve as private judge, must be presented to the regular or presiding judge at or after the action has been filed, (*id.*). The proceedings before such a judge are of record and are governed by Indiana's rules of trial procedure, except that they must be conducted without a jury. The judge has the same powers as a judge of the circuit court, and appeal from the judgment in such a proceeding is taken in the same manner as an appeal from the circuit court of the county where the case is filed, Code §33-13-15-4.

PAY AND EMOLUMENTS

A special judge appointed pursuant to Criminal Rule 13 receives no compensation for cases assigned or reassigned to him or her within his or her county. When assigned outside of his or her county, he or she will be paid twenty-five dollars per day, plus mileage and reasonable expenses; see also Trial Rule 79(P).

Note, however, that Code §34-1-13-4 provides that when a practicing attorney is called upon to preside in place of the regular judge as a judge pro tempore, either at a regular or an adjourned term, the attorney shall be allowed twenty dollars per day for each day or part thereof actually served, plus mileage, and if the judge pro tempore is a resident of another county he or she shall be paid an additional twenty dollars per day, for a total of forty dollars per day.

A temporary judge is, likewise, entitled to compensation of twenty-five dollars for each day served, Code §33-13-16-9, but if he or she serves as a judge pro tempore or special judge of the court is not entitled to additional compensation for that service.

A senior judge is entitled to a per diem of fifty dollars for each day served as such, plus reimbursement for reasonable expenses, including but not limited to meals and lodging, incurred in performing service as a senior judge, but may not be compensated as a senior judge for more than one-hundred calendar days in the aggregate during a calendar year, Code §33-4-8-5 (cf Adm. Rule 5[2], which states that, when circumstances warrant, a senior judge shall be allowed to retain jurisdiction of a case for longer than 100 days).

A private judge is compensated by the parties in an amount and subject to the terms and conditions agreed to by the judge and the parties to the case, Code §33-13-15-8.

IOWA

Iowa Constitution, Article 5, §18 provides that the General Assembly shall prescribe mandatory retirement for judges of the supreme court and district court at a specified age. 40 I.C.A., §602.1610 provides that the mandatory retirement age for supreme court justices and district judges is seventy-five for judges holding office on July 1, 1965, and seventy-two for all judges appointed after July 1, 1965. The mandatory retirement age is seventy-two for all district associate judges and judicial magistrates (*id*). A district court judge who has held office continually since before July 1, 1965, who might thereafter be appointed to the supreme court, must retire at age seventy-two, even though if he remained on the district court bench he would not have to retire until age seventy-five. Op. Atty. Gen (Bradley), Oct. 21, 1969.

Iowa Constitution, Article 5, §19 states that the supreme court shall have power to retire judges for disability and to discipline or remove them for good cause, upon application by the Commission on Judicial Qualifications. The General Assembly by 40 I.C.A., §602.2101 et seq. created the Commission on Judicial Qualifications, which after a hearing (40 I.C.A., §602.2106[1]) may petition the Iowa Supreme Court to retire a judge for a permanent mental or physical disability that substantially interferes with the performance of his judicial duties, 40 I.C.A., §602.2106(3)(a). A judge adjudicated permanently disabled, either physically or mentally, is entitled to the same retirement benefits as are provided for voluntary retirement, 40 I.C.A., §602.9113. 40 I.C.A., §602.9207(2) provides that a senior judge is also subject to retirement for disability, pursuant to §2106(3)(a).

None.

Iowa has both a Public Employees' Retirement System (PERS), 7 I.C.A., §97B.1 ff. and a Judicial Retirement System, 40 I.C.A., §602.9101 ff.

Section 97B.69, which provided that every person who becomes a member of the Judicial Retirement System shall have his or her membership in the PERS terminated, was repealed in 1984; and I.C.A., §602.11115, which was enacted in 1984, provides that a district associate judge who became such prior to June 30, 1984 could be a member of both systems, receiving retirement allowances from each based on the credited service to each. No similar provision with respect to judges of other courts has been found. Only the retirement provisions of the Judicial Retirement System are set forth in this section.

Judges who are at least sixty-five, with an aggregate of at least six years of service, or who have completed twenty-five consecutive years of judicial service, are entitled to a retirement annuity, 40 I.C.A., §602.9106. Any judge who is fifty-five years old or older, and who has served at least twenty consecutive years as a judge, is entitled to a decreased annuity, §602.9107A. (See 40 I.C.A., §602.11115 for rules relating to district associate judges' retirement.)

Any judge who has served on one or more courts for at least six years, and who believes he or she has become permanently incapacitated, physically or mentally, to perform the duties of the judge's office may personally, or by the judge's next friend or guardian, file with the court administrator a written application for retirement, 40 I.C.A., §602.9112. If after investigation by the attorney general the chief justice finds on the basis of the attorney general's report that the judge is permanently incapacitated, the chief justice declares the judge retired, and the judge is entitled to a retirement annuity as though he or she had retired pursuant to §602.9106. See §§602.9112 and 602.9113.

I.C.A., §§97B-49 and 97B-50 spell out for PERS members increases in normal retirement and early retirement allowances based on stated percentages and/or years of service in various retirement systems and on date of retirement. No similar provision with respect to retired justices or judges has been found.

I.C.A., §97B-39 provides that PERS benefits are not assignable or transferable, nor are they subject to execution, levy attachment, garnishment, or other legal process or to the operation of any bankruptcy or insolvency law, except for a marital property order requiring selection of a particular option or for the purpose of enforcing child, spousal, or medical support obligations not in excess of the amount specified in 15 U.S.C., §1673(b). No similar provision with respect to retired justices or judges has been found.

SERVICE AFTER RETIREMENT

Iowa Constitution, Article 5, §18 provides that retired judges may be subject to special assignment to temporary judicial duties by the supreme court, as provided by law. Justices and judges retired by reason of age, or who are drawing benefits under §602.9106, and senior judges who have retired under §602.9207, or who have relinquished senior judgeship under §602.9208, subsection 1, may with their consent be assigned by the supreme court to temporary judicial duties on a court in the state if the assignment is deemed necessary by the supreme court or to expedite the administration of justice, 40 I.C.A., §602.1612(1). If a retired judge elects to practice law, he must file such election with the clerk of the supreme court and is thereafter ineligible for assignment to temporary judicial duties at any time, 40 I.C.A., §601.1612(2). Iowa Rules of Court, Rule 375 provides that the supreme court through the chief justice may recall eligible retired judges as one way to provide a sufficient number of judges to handle the judicial business in all districts promptly and efficiently.

40 I.C.A., §602.9201 et seq. sets out the Senior and Retired Judges Act. Judges who are at least sixty-five with at least six years of service, or who have completed twenty-five consecutive years of judicial service, are eligible to become senior judges. Senior judges are appointed at the discretion of the supreme court for a two-year term. Senior judges are assigned to work a minimum of thirteen weeks in each twelve-month period. They may agree to work additional time, 40 I.C.A., §602.9203 but may not practice law, 40 I.C.A., §602.9205. Senior judges are required to retire at the end of the twelve-month period during which they attain seventy-eight years of age, I.C.A., §602.9207; and Iowa Rules of Court, Rule 215 mandates that no retired judge or retired senior judge shall be eligible for temporary service under the provision of Iowa Code, section 602.1612 after reaching the age of seventy-eight.

Iowa Code §602.9206 provides that §602.1612 does not apply to a senior judge but does apply to a senior judge who is retired. During the tenure of a senior judge, if the judge is able to serve, the judge may be assigned by the supreme court to temporary judicial duties on courts of this state without salary for an aggregate of thirteen weeks out of each twelve-month period, and for additional weeks with the judge's consent. A senior judge shall not be assigned to judicial duties on the supreme court unless the judge has been appointed to serve on the supreme court prior to retirement, 40 I.C.A., §602.9206. A senior judge also shall be available to serve in the capacity of administrative law judge under chapter 17A upon the request of an agency, and the supreme court may assign a senior judge for temporary duties as an administrative law judge, 40 I.C.A., §602.9206.

Supreme Court Rule 119 establishes the Code of Judicial Conduct, which provides in Canon 7 that a senior or retired judge may act as an arbitrator or mediator but shall not do so when assigned to judicial service or when to do so would interfere with an assignment to judicial service, and he shall not use the title senior judge or judge while so acting.

Supreme Court Rules 123.3, 123.7 and 123.8 require every person licensed to practice law in Iowa to complete fifteen hours of continuing legal education per year, except for persons not engaged in the practice of law, but contains no specific provision relating to judges.

PAY AND EMOLUMENTS

While serving under temporary assignment, a retired justice or judge shall be paid the compensation and expense reimbursement provided by law for all justices or judges on the court to which assigned, but shall not receive annuity payments under the judicial retirement system; and a district associate judge covered under chapter 97B shall receive monthly benefits under that chapter only if the district associate judge has attained the age of seventy years, Iowa Code Annotated, §602.1612(3). A retired justice or judge may be authorized by the order of assignment to appoint a temporary court reporter, who shall receive the compensation and expense reimbursement provided by law for a regular court reporter in the court to which the justice or judge is to serve, Iowa Code, §602.1612(4).

While serving on temporary assignment, a senior judge shall not be paid a salary but shall continue to be paid the judge's annuity as senior judge, shall be reimbursed for the judge's actual expenses to the extent expenses of a district judge are reimbursable under §602.1509, may, if permitted by the assignment order, appoint a temporary court reporter, and, if assigned to the court of appeals or the supreme court, shall be given the assistance of a law clerk and a secretary, I.C.A., §602.9206.

KANSAS

Kansas Statutes Annotated, Chap. 20, Art. 26, §20-2601 defines "judge" to mean an elected or appointed justice of the supreme court, judge of the court of appeals or any district court; and Const. Art. 3, §16 and K.S.A., §20-2608(a) provide that any judge upon reaching the age of seventy shall retire, except that when any incumbent judge attains the age of seventy, such judge may, if he or she so desires, finish serving the term during which said judge attains the age of seventy. Apparently, the exception applies only to a judge "incumbent" when the section was enacted, but no case so holding has been found.

Constitution Art. 3, §15, provides that supreme court justices may be retired, after appropriate hearing by the supreme court nominating commission, upon certification to the governor that such justice is so incapacitated as to be unable to perform adequately his or her duties. It also provides that other judges shall be subject to retirement for incapacity by the supreme court after appropriate hearing.

Retirement Provisions re Particular Courts

Any district magistrate judge may, by filing his or her written election, become a member of the retirement system, K.S.A., §§20-2601(c), 20-2620.

Optional Provisions for Retirement

Any judge age sixty-two with ten years of credited service, or the total of whose age and years of service equals or exceeds eighty-five, may retire upon application, K.S.A., §20-2608(a), or if otherwise eligible to retire may retire upon application on reaching age sixty and having not less than ten years of service, *id* §20-2608(b), or may retire with a reduced retirement annuity at age fifty-five after not less than ten years of service, *id* §20-2608(c). Membership in another retirement system is credited in determining eligibility for service or disability retirement, unless the member retired under the other system or withdrew his or her contributions to it, K.S.A., §74-4988.

K.S.A., §20-2609 states that a justice or judge permanently mentally or physically disabled and not entitled to retire pursuant to §20-2608 may, upon being found disabled by the supreme court, retire, that the court may require examination by a doctor appointed by the court and such other evidence as it deems necessary, and that a recipient of an annuity when so retired may, on reaching age sixty-five, and making application, terminate retirement under §20-2609 and be placed on §20-2608 retirement. A disability retiree may be required to submit to reexamination not more often than every six months and, if found able to serve, his or her retirement annuity ceases, K.S.A., §20-2612. As to total and permanent disability which is the natural and proximate result of an accident causing personal injury or disease, independent of all other causes and arising out of and in the course of the member's actual performance of duties, not the result of a wilfully negligent or intentional act of the member, see K.S.A., §74-4916(c).

Retirement benefits are exempt from state and local taxes, may not be assigned, and are not subject to execution or garnishment, K.S.A., §20-2618.

Service After Retirement

Three separate statutes authorize such service. K.S.A., §20-310b provides that upon stipulation of the parties to an action the court may order the action heard and determined by a temporary judge who is a retired justice of the supreme court, retired judge of the court of appeals, or retired judge of the district court and shall fix the compensation to be paid for his or her service as such.

K.S.A. Section 20-2616(a) provides that any retired judge of the supreme court, retired judge of the court of appeals, retired district court judge, or retired associate district judge may be assigned to perform such services and duties as he or she is willing to undertake, that such assignment in connection with a matter pending in the supreme court shall be made by that court, and that assignment in a matter pending in any other court shall be made by the chief justice of the supreme court. Such service includes preparation and other out-of-court judicial service for hearings or in deciding the matter assigned, and is subject to revocation by the supreme court which, or the chief justice who, made the assignment, K.S.A., §20-2616(a).

K.S.A., §20-2622, effective July 1, 1995, provides that a retiree, other than a district magistrate judge, may return to temporary judicial service for not more than 104 days or forty percent of each year while receiving retirement benefits, provided that, with the approval of a majority of the justices of that court, a written agreement is entered into with the supreme court prior to retirement, or if not then, within thirty days prior to any anniversary date of retirement that is within five years after retirement. Such agreement may not be for a period of more than two years, but a retiree may enter into subsequent agreements, provided the aggregate of such agreements does not exceed twelve years. Such an agreement terminates, however, if the retiree refuses to accept a temporary assignment without cause.

No member of the retirement system shall receive service credit for services after the date of retirement, K.S.A., §20-2603(d).

PAY AND EMOLUMENTS

A retired justice or judge assigned to service is entitled to per diem compensation at the same rate as that received by legislators, until the per diem amount, plus the retirement annuity payable to that justice or judge for the fiscal year, becomes equal to or more than the current annual salary of a district judge paid by the state. He or she is also entitled to actual and necessary expenses for other than subsistence or travel, including necessary stenographic assistance incurred in performing such duties. A retired justice or judge whose per diem compensation equals or exceeds the current annual salary of a district judge is, however, entitled to subsistence allowance, mileage allowance, and actual and necessary expenses, notwithstanding that his per diem compensation equals or exceeds that of a district court judge, K.S.A., §20-2616(c); §46-137a.

Notwithstanding the retirement provisions in effect on the date he or she retired, a §20-2622 retiree receives a monthly stipend equal to twenty-five percent of the current monthly salary of justices or judges serving in the same position as that of the retiree at the time of retirement.

If the assignment given a §20-2622 retiree will require that the 104-day limitation on stipend be exceeded, the retiree shall be compensated in accordance with K.S.A., §20-2616.

KENTUCKY

Mandatory Retirement Provisions Applicable Generally

Neither the Kentucky Constitution nor any statute mandates retirement at a particular age, but §121 of the constitution empowers the Judicial Retirement and Removal Commission, after notice and hearing and subject to Rules of the Supreme Court, to retire any justice of the supreme court or judge of the court of appeals, circuit court, or district court for disability.

The statutes and Supreme Court Rules relating to disability retirement are K.R.S., §§21.410 and 21.415 and Supreme Court Rules 4.020 and 4.270. Rule 4.020 authorizes the Judicial Retirement and Removal Commission to order temporary or permanent retirement of any judge found to be suffering from a mental or physical disability that seriously interferes with performance of duties, and Rule 4.270 provides that a judge retired for permanent disability thereupon becomes eligible for retirement benefits.

K.R.S., §21.410, discussed in the Optional Retirement section below, apparently applies to involuntary as well as voluntary retirement for disability. K.R.S., §21.415, states that as to a judge or justice retired by the Judicial Retirement and Removal Commission under Const., §121, the Retirement Board shall exercise no function with respect to determining the existence or continuance of disability.

Retirement Provisions re Particular Courts

None.

Optional Provisions for Retirement

Kentucky Revised Statutes, §21.380(1) provides that the normal retirement age of a member of the retirement system shall be his or her sixty-fifth birthday, reduced, however, by one year, but no more than five years total for each five years of service in the plan and each year of service credit the member has earned beyond that needed to receive a retirement benefit of 100% of final compensation. However, subdivision 2 of that section expressly states that the statutes concerning judicial retirement "do not require that a member retire at the normal retirement date", and K.R.S., §21.345(1) states that "retirement" means a voluntary resignation or a failure of reelection, but not removal for cause. However, §21.370(1) makes clear that, except for retirement for disability, a member receives no benefit unless he or she has completed eight years of service, including service before becoming a member. Note also that K.R.S., §21.400 provides for reduction of benefit when a judge takes early retirement and that §21.405 authorizes cost of living increases in retirement benefits.

K.R.S., §21.410, provides that a member under normal retirement age may retire for disability if upon examination it is certified that the member is so physically or mentally disabled as to be incapacitated for further performance of duty and that such incapacity is likely to be permanent. A member so retiring is entitled immediately to a disability allowance even though he or she has not completed eight years of service. The board may require such a retiree to undergo periodic examination concerning continuation of the disability; and if it is certified to the board that the member is no longer incapacitated or he or she refuses to submit to examination, the disability allowance is terminated and the member becomes entitled to such rights as he or she would have been entitled to had he or she voluntarily retired on the date he or she was retired for disability. Then, upon reaching normal retirement age, he or she may apply for and receive, in lieu of the disability allowance, the service allowance he or she would have received at normal retirement age had he or she voluntarily retired on the date he or she was retired for disability.

Retirement benefits are not subject to reduction or impairment except as to a judge convicted of a felony, K.R.S., §§21.480 and 6.696. Retirement benefits are exempt from garnishment, K.R.S., §21.470 and until December 31, 1997 were exempt from state, county, or municipal tax (*id*); but after January 1, 1998 benefits are only partially exempt from tax, *id* and §141.010.

SERVICE AFTER RETIREMENT

Constitution, §110(5)(b) authorizes the chief justice of the supreme court to assign any justice or judge, active or retired, to sit in any court other than the supreme court when he deems it necessary for the prompt disposition of causes. K.R.S., §26A.020(1) states that when from any cause a judge in the circuit or district court cannot preside, or is sought to be recused by a party, the circuit court clerk must so certify to the chief justice who shall, as to a recusal motion, review the facts to determine whether to designate a regular or retired justice or judge as special judge, and in all other cases shall immediately make such a designation. The special judge so appointed has all the powers and responsibilities of a regular judge of the court.

As to supreme court vacancies, Const., §110(3) provides that if two or more justices decline or are unable to sit on any cause, the chief justice shall certify that fact to the governor who shall appoint to hear the particular cause a sufficient number of justices to constitute a full court as to that cause. K.R.S., §21A.120(1) provides that a person so appointed by the governor "shall possess the qualifications of a Supreme Court Justice", which permits appointment by the governor of any retired justice or judge who possesses such qualifications; cf K.R.S., §21A.120(2) which with respect to the salary of a special judge appointed to the supreme court refers to "a retired justice or judge."

Although Const., §123, bars a judge from practicing law during his or her term of office, that provision is inapplicable to a special judge pro tempore. The supreme court so held in Regency Pheasant Run Ltd. v. Karem, 860 S.W.2d 755, 757, reasoning that because such a special judge holds office not for a "term of office" but at the pleasure of the chief justice, the prohibition does not apply to such special judges, and stating that

> The purpose of the use of special judges, acting pro tempore, is to expedite the handling of litigation, whenever and wherever needed. The use of such experienced, retired judges not only retains the quality of the men and women who preside at trial, but obviates the necessity for regular full-time judges to delay their own work by "filling in" the many vacancies that demand special judges. This use of retired judges, whether practicing law or not, is clearly authorized by the Kentucky Constitution, the Kentucky Revised Statutes and is in the best interest of the operation of the Kentucky Court of Justice.

PAY AND EMOLUMENTS

A retired justice or judge appointed to the supreme court by the governor and a retired justice or judge assigned to active service pursuant to Const.,

§110(5)(b) receives for each day of service the difference, if any, between 1/250th of annual retirement benefits and 1/250th of the annual salary for the judicial office in which he performs the duties of a special judge, but not less than the retirement benefits if the applicable salary would be less than the retirement benefits, K.R.S., §§21A.110(1), 21A.120(2). He or she also receives necessary expenses incidental to performance of the duties to which assigned, upon approval thereof by the chief justice or his or her designee, *id.*, §§21A.110(2), 21A.120(3).

LOUISIANA

Article V, Section 23(B), of the 1974 Constitution provides that, except as otherwise provided in Section 23, a judge shall not remain in office beyond his or her seventieth birthday. (See also Revised Statutes, §13:30[B]). The exception is contained in subdivision A of Section 23, which authorized the legislature within two years after the effective date of the constitution to adopt a retirement system in which judges in office at the time may elect to become a member, and also provided that the judicial service rights of a judge in office or retired on the effective date of the constitution shall not be diminished.

Under Article VII, Section 8(b), of the 1921 constitution the retirement age was seventy-five, and in Giepert v. Wingerter, 529 So.2d 1389 (1985) the Fourth Circuit Court of Appeals held that a judge's services could not be diminished indirectly by his reelection in 1976 and 1982 after the effective date of the 1974 constitution because "Article 5, Section 23, affords the same treatment to all judges *who were in office* when the 1974 Constitution became effective" (emphasis in original); see also In Re Levy, 427 So.2d 844 (Sup.Ct. 1980),which held that "[a] judge's willful retention of office beyond his mandatory retirement age is ground for removal by this Court." Accord: Small v. Guste, 383 So.2d 1011 (Sup.Ct. 1980).

The Retirement Plan for Judges, enacted by Rev. Stat. §13:11 and following, in §13:14 granted a judge in office on October 1, 1976, the effective date of the plan, the option, to be exercised within 120 days after that date, to become a member of the Louisiana State Employees' Retirement System, and granted each judge who thereafter assumed office the same option to be exercised within 120 days after taking the oath of office. However, a judge in office on October 1, 1976 who did not exercise the option in a timely fashion, and who was over the age of seventy on December 31, 1974, was permitted by Rev. Stat. §13:30(B), accord Rev. Stat. §11:1352(A)(2), to remain in service until he or she had served twenty years or until the age of eighty years, whichever first occurred.

A judge who was in office on October 2, 1976, and did not on a timely basis exercise the option to become a member of the State Employees' Retirement System was barred by Rev. Stat. 11:413(9) from becoming a member of the system; but a judge who took office after July 1, 1983, becomes a member of that system pursuant to Rev. Stat. §11:551 "notwithstanding anything in R.S. 11:413 to the contrary." As to judges who were in office on August 2, 1976, and failed to timely exercise the option to become a member of the State Employees' Retirement System, see 11:552(A); as to a judge who took office after August 2, 1976, but prior to July 1, 1983, and failed to exercise the option to become a member of the system, see §§11:552(B) and 11:554; as to a judge in office on September 9, 1979, and who failed to exercise such option, see Rev. Stat. §11:555; and as to a judge in office on September 6, 1985, who failed to exercise such option, see Rev. Stat. §11:556.

Finally to be noted as to mandatory retirement for age are two proposed constitutional revisions that would have returned the mandatory age to seventy-five as to judges who did not opt to become members of the Louisiana State Employees' Retirement System. Rev. Stat. §11:1351 and following deal with the Judges Non-contributory Plan (also referred to in §13:5.7 as the unfunded judges retirement plan), and §11:1352A provides for mandatory retirement at age seventy. However, in 1995 the legislature adopted Act #321, which provided that Const. Art. V, Sec. 23(B) was amended to age seventy-five, provided the amendment was *adopted* by the electors in the 1995 gubernatorial primary election. It was adopted on October 18, 1995. But Act #1317, containing a similar amendment to Section 23(B), was *rejected* by the electors on October 21, 1995. It is, therefore, unclear whether the mandatory retirement age under the Non-contributory Plan is seventy or seventy-five.

Physical or mental incapacity to perform his or her duties is a basis for involuntary retirement from office. As to members of the Judicial Retirement System who sit on multi-judge courts, Rev. Stat. §13:30(C) requires that the certificate of incapacity be executed by a majority of the other members of the court of which he or she is a member. As to other judges, the certificate must be signed by two competent physicians and approved by a majority of the supreme court. The certificate is filed with the governor and the secretary of state (*id.*) and is effective when the certificate is filed with the secretary of state, Rev. Stat. §13:30(E)(3). As to a judge who opts to become a member of the State Employees' Retirement System and thereafter becomes physically or mentally incapacitated to perform his or her duties, Rev. Stat. §§11:561 and 13:19 provide that the judge "shall be retired." Supreme Court Rule XXIII establishes the Judiciary Commission and requires that body, upon receipt of a complaint that a judge has a disability that seriously interferes with the performance of his or her duties and is or is likely to be permanent, to conduct an investigation to which the judge may make a presentation, to hold a hearing if the investigation warrants its doing so, on notice to the judge of the charges, and to file its report with the supreme court, which then receives briefs and hears arguments on the charge.

RETIREMENT PROVISIONS RE PARTICULAR COURTS

None.

OPTIONAL PROVISIONS FOR RETIREMENT

Rev. Stat. §13:30(B) provides that any judge who was in office on October 1, 1976 and did not timely exercise the option to become a member of the State Employees' Retirement System may retire on two-thirds pay, irrespective of his or her attained age upon completing more than twenty-three years of service as a judge of a court of record, or when he or she has served for twenty years and shall have reached the age of sixty-five years. It also permits an appellate judge to retire at full pay for life if he or she has served continuously as a judge for twenty-five years. Retirement is effective on the date specified in the notice of retirement given to the governor and secretary of state, Rev. Stat. 13:30(E)(2).

A judge who elected to become a member of the State Employees' Retirement System who, prior to application for retirement, had accumulated at least eighteen years of creditable service as a judge or court officer is entitled to retire without regard to attained age, Rev. Stat. §§11:558 and 13:16(A)(1). Upon attaining a total of twenty years creditable service, at least twelve of which were as a judge or court officer, a person is entitled to retire if he or she has attained fifty years, Rev. Stat. §§11:558 and 13:16(A)(2). Upon attaining at least twelve years of creditable service as a judge or court officer, a person is entitled to retire when he or she has attained fifty-five years, Rev. Stat §§11:558 and 13:16(A)(3), and upon attaining the age of seventy years is entitled to retire without regard to the number of years of creditable service as a judge or court officer, Rev. Stat. §§11:558 and 13:16(A)(4).

To be noted also is that Rev. Stat. §13:26 makes applicable to a person covered by the Retirement Plan for Judges the provisions of Chapter 10 of Title 42 of Revised Statutes of 1950, and that Rev. Stat. §42:571 permits retirement at any age after service of thirty years, at age fifty-five after service of twenty-five years, and at age sixty after service of twenty years.

Voluntary retirement for disability is covered by Rev. Stat. §§11:218 and 42:702(M) and by Supreme Court Rule XXI. Section 11:218 authorizes a member of the State Employees' Retirement System to apply to its board for disability retirement, provides that the member then be examined by a doctor of the board's choosing, who submits his or her report to the State Medical Disability Board to determine whether the judge is totally incapacitated for further performance of his or her duty, and whether the incapacity is likely to be permanent. If the physician's report is contested, a second physician is appointed, and if they disagree, a third physician is appointed, in which case the determination of a majority of the physicians governs. Rev. Stat. §11:221(C) requires a disability retiree annually to submit a notarized statement of income earned, and provides that if he or she fails to do so, the disability allowance is discontinued; and if he or she fails during the balance of the year to do so, the allowance shall be revoked. Section 11:221(B) provides that the disability allowance is increased annually based on the increase in the Consumer Price Index.

Note, however, that Rev. Stat. §42:702(M), which concerns judges who are members of the State Employees' Retirement System, provides that a member who is not eligible for regular retirement may file for disability while in service, and if after examination is found to be totally disabled is eligible for disability retirement under §42:581(B), if the State Medical Disability Board officially certifies that he or she is disabled, provided he or she has at least ten years of creditable service and the disability was incurred while he or she was in active service; but that if the application is not filed while the member is in service, it is presumed that the disability was not incurred in service. The presumption can be overcome only by "clear, competent and convincing evidence."

Supreme Court Rule XXI deals with a judge who is or becomes physically or mentally incapacitated to perform his or her duties and applies to the supreme court for approval of voluntary retirement under the provisions of Rev. Stat §13:30 (discussed above under Mandatory Retirement). Under the rule the judge must attach to the application a certificate signed by two competent physicians, the court may require a written report by a qualified physician appointed by it and may request such additional evidence as it deems necessary, and if the application is approved by a majority of the court, it shall order a certificate of incapacity to be filed with the governor and the secretary of state.

Supplemental retirement pay is provided for in Rev. Stat. §13:7 for any judge who retired under Article VII, Section 8(c), of the 1921 constitution, who thereafter before attaining age seventy, shall have been assigned by order of the supreme court under Section 8(h) of that Article to serve as a judge of another court or courts and who shall have served as a judge by assignment continuously for not less than five years and in the aggregate not less than thirty years. Upon termination of assignment, such judge receives supplemental retirement pay, to equate his or her salary at the time of termination of assignment, of two-thirds of the supplemental pay provided in Article VII, Section 8(h) of the 1921 constitution.

Retirement benefits are "exempt from seizure under any writ, mandate or process whatsoever" pursuant to Rev. Stat. §13:3881(D), which "exempts from all liability for any debt except alimony and child support: all pensions"; see also Rev. Stat. §13:5.7, which also exempts "retirement pay paid to any judge or the surviving spouse of any judge under the unfunded judicial retirement plan from any state or municipal income tax."

SERVICE AFTER RETIREMENT

Louisiana Constitution Article V, Section 5(A) permits the supreme court to assign a retired judge to any court, and Rev. Stat. §13:9.2 provides that the supreme court may assign a retired judge to a court on a contractual or per diem basis.

PAY AND EMOLUMENTS

A member of the Retirement Plan for Judges, who after retirement is assigned to sit as a judge of a court of record for a specified time, continues to receive the retirement pay being paid to him or her at the time of assignment, but the retirement pay for any month must be deducted from the salary payable to the judge as an assigned judge, Rev. Stat. §13:22. A judge who was in office on October 1, 1976, who did not timely exercise the option to become a member of the State Employees' Retirement System, and who after retirement was assigned by the supreme court to a court, is entitled to receive compensation, including his or her regular retirement pay, not less than that of a judge of the court to which he or she is assigned, and to the payment of reasonable expenses during the period of such assignment, Rev. Stat. §13:30(A) and (G). Note, however, that Rev. Stat. §13:9.2(A) provides that in lieu of the compensation for assigned retired judges established by §§13:22 and 13:30, a retired judge assigned to a court on a contractual or per diem basis is entitled to compensation, in addition to retirement pay, equal to one-twentieth the monthly salary of a judge of the court to which he or she is assigned for each day of the assignment, not to exceed 120 working days in a fiscal year, and to reimbursement of reasonable and necessary expenses incurred in the performance of the assigned service.

The travel and office expenses of judges of the courts of appeals and district courts are, pursuant to Rev. Stat. §13:694, reimbursable under the conditions defined by the supreme court. Those conditions are set forth in S.C.R. 13:694.1, which in subdivision (f) directs that a retired judge assigned to serve on any court by order of the supreme court shall submit his or her claim for reimbursement to the judicial administrator.

MAINE

Although Constitution Art. 6, §4 speaks of a judicial officer "who has reached mandatory retirement age, as provided by statute" holding over for not more than six months or until his or her successor is appointed, whichever first occurs, Maine Revised States Annotated Title 5, §4575(1) prohibits public sector employers from requiring employees to retire at a specified age or after completion of a specified number of years of service.

Based on the wording of M.R.S.A., Title 4, §1353(1), it covers both involuntary and voluntary retirement for disability. That subdivision provides that "any member disabled while in service *may receive* a disability retirement allowance *upon order of at least five Justices of the Supreme Judicial Court or upon written application* to the executive director", examination by a qualified physician, and after report by the medical board and approval of the application by at least five justices of the supreme court, if the member is shown by medical examination or tests to be so mentally or physically incapacitated that it is impossible for the member to perform his or her duties as a judge and the incapacity is expected to be permanent. A judge retired for disability may be required to undergo annual medical examinations and tests for the purpose of determining whether he or she is incapacitated, M.R.S.A., Title 4, §1353(4)(C). The allowance continues, during the first five years, as long as the retiree is unable to perform the duties of a judge, *id.*, §(5)(C), but after that period only if the retiree is unable to engage in any substantially gainful activities for which he or she is qualified, *id.*, §(4)(D), (5), but may be terminated if he or she continues to refuse for a period of one year to submit to medical examination or tests, *id.*, §(4)(C).

Retirement Provisions re Particular Courts

None.

OPTIONAL PROVISIONS FOR RETIREMENT

A justice of the Supreme Judicial Court or the superior court, a judge of the district court, an administrative judge or associate administrative court judge, actively serving on December 1, 1984, or appointed subsequent to that date, unless appointed as an active retired judge (as to which see Service After Retirement below) is required, as a condition of employment, to be a member of the Maine Judicial Retirement System, M.R.S.A., Title 4, §§1201(12), 1301. Any member who chooses to retire may retire if he or she meets any of the various age and years of service requirements of M.R.S.A., Title 4, §1351.

As to voluntary retirement for disability, see Mandatory Retirement Provisions Applicable Generally above.

SERVICE AFTER RETIREMENT

A retired justice of the Supreme Judicial Court, retired for other than disability, may be appointed by the governor, subject to review by the joint standing committee of the legislature and confirmation by the legislature, as an active retired justice of that court for a term of seven years and may be reappointed for a like term. When so appointed, he or she has the same jurisdiction as before retirement, except that he or she shall act only in matters and hold court at the terms and times as directed by the Chief Justice, M.R.S.A., Ch.1, Title 4, §6. He or she may also be assigned by the chief justice to sit in the superior court in any county with the same authority as if he or she were a regular justice of the superior court, M.R.S.A., Ch.1, Title 4, §6A.

Subject to like provisions as above set forth re judges of the Supreme Judicial Court, a justice of the superior court may be appointed an active retired justice of the superior court for a term of seven years and may be reappointed for a like term, M.R.S.A., Title 4, §104. An active retired justice of the superior court may be directed by the chief justice to hold a term of the superior court in any county, and, when so directed, he or she has the same jurisdiction as though he or she were the regular justice of that court, M.R.S.A., Title 4, §104.

Subject to like provisions as set forth re justices of the Supreme Judicial Court, a judge of the district court may be appointed an active retired judge of the district court for a term of seven years and may be reappointed for a like term, M.R.S.A., Title 4, §157-B. An active retired judge of the district court or administrative court may also be assigned to sit in the superior court of any county, and, when so directed, he or she has the same jurisdiction as though he or she were a regular justice of the superior court, M.R.S.A., Title 4, §157-C.

PAY AND EMOLUMENTS

Each of the active retired justices or judges referred to in the preceding section re service after retirement is compensated for his or her services at the rate of $150 per day or $90 per half day, provided that the total per diem compensation and retirement pension received by the justice or judge in any calendar year does not exceed the annual salary of a justice or judge of the court from which he or she retired, M.R.S.A., Title 4, §6-B as to active retired justices of the Supreme Judicial Court; M.R.S.A., Title 4, §104-A as to active retired justices of the superior court; and M.R.S.A., Title 4, §157-D as to active retired judges of the district court. Note, however, that while M.R.S.A., Title 4, §157-B as to appointment of active retired judges of the district court provides that such a judge shall receive reimbursement for expenses actually and reasonably incurred in the performance of his or her duties, no similar provision is contained in Title 4, §6 as to active retired justices of the supreme court, or in Title 4, §104, as to active retired justices of the superior court.

The state also pays all or a proportionate part of the premium for the group health plan that it maintains for state employees, depending on the date of employment and the years of participation in the plan, M.R.S.A., Title 5, §§285(1)(A), (1)(B) and (7).

MARYLAND

Judges of the court of appeals, court of special appeals, circuit court, district court, and orphans' court must retire at age seventy, Const., Art. IV, §3; Art. IV, §5A(f); Art. IV, §41D. A 1994 proposed constitutional amendment changing the mandatory retirement age to seventy-five was not approved by the voters.

A judge may be involuntarily retired by vote of two-thirds of the members of each house of the General Assembly and with the approval of the governor, in case of his or her inability to discharge his or her duties with efficiency by reason of continued sickness or of physical or mental disability, Const., Art. IV, §3; see also Maryland Code Annotated (MCA), Courts and Judicial Proceedings (CJP) §1-402. Alternatively, upon recommendation of the Commission on Judicial Disabilities after hearing, to the court of appeals and after hearing by that court, the court may retire a judge from office upon a finding of mental or physical disability which is, or is likely to become, permanent and which seriously interferes with the performance of his or her duties, Const., Art. IV, §4B subds. (b) and (c); see also CJP §1-402 and Commission on Judicial Disabilities Rule 1227. A judge retired under §4B has the rights and privileges prescribed by law for other retired judges, Const., Art. IV, §4B, subd.(b)(3).

RETIREMENT PROVISIONS RE PARTICULAR COURTS

None.

OPTIONAL PROVISIONS FOR RETIREMENT

A judge who is at least sixty years old and who has at least sixteen years of service is entitled to retire, MCA, State Personnel and Pensions (SPP)

§§27-101(b)(2), 27-101(bb) and 27-407, or prior to sixteen years of service at a reduced retirement allowance, *id.*, §§27-101(b)(3) and 27-402(c).

A judge may voluntarily resign or retire because of disability, SPP, §§27-101(b)(3), 27-401(2), 27-402(d)(1), but must have at least three years of service credit as a member of the judicial retirement system to be entitled to a retirement allowance, *id.*, §27-402(d)(2).

There is no statute expressly providing for a cost of living adjustment of retirement benefits, but SPP §27-402(a) provides that a retiree is entitled to a retirement allowance that equals two-thirds of the salary payable in that fiscal year to a member holding the same level judicial position as that held by the retiree on termination of service.

Money in the retirement fund and retirement benefits, both current and future, are not subject to attachment, execution, garnishment, or other seizure, except pursuant to an order or decree in a matrimonial or child support action ordering assignment, or a court-approved property settlement, SPP §21-502.

SERVICE AFTER RETIREMENT

Const., Art.IV, §3A, provides that any former judge, except a former judge of the orphans' court, may be assigned by the chief judge of the court of appeals, upon approval of a majority of that court, to sit temporarily in any court of the state, except an orphans' court, as provided by law, and expressly states that the provisions of the section apply, notwithstanding provisions in the same article of the constitution pertaining to retirement of judges upon attaining age seventy.

CJP §1-302(a) defines "former judge" to mean a judge who previously served in a court. A judge retired voluntarily or involuntarily for disability may not, however, be recalled for temporary assignment, *id.*, subd.(c), nor may a judge whose most recent service as a judge terminated by defeat for election or rejection of confirmation by the Senate, or who was censured by the court of appeals, or is engaged in the practice of law (*id*). Moreover, to be temporarily assigned, a former judge must have served an aggregate of at least two years as a judge, or in Baltimore City and Charles, Prince George's, and Harford Counties an aggregate of at least three years as a judge, been approved for assignment by a majority of the members of the court of appeals, met any additional standards established by the court of appeals, and consented to the assignment, CJP §1-302(b).

A judge so recalled may not be temporarily assigned for more than 180 working days in any calendar year, except that the period may be extended at the end of the 180-day period until conclusion of a case being heard by the former judge, CJP §1-302(d). Preference must be given to retired judges from the circuit in which the temporary assignment is to take place (*id.*, subd.[g]). A temporarily assigned judge has all the power and authority of a judge of the court to which he or she is assigned (*id.*, subd.[e]). However, such service does not provide additional service for retirement credit purposes (*id.*, subd.[f][2]), unless the retiree was assigned under the authority of Const. Art.IV, §3A, such a judge being so assigned not being a member of the Judges' Retirement System, SPP, §27-201(b). A retired judge may not serve as a member of the Commission on Judicial Disabilities, Const., Art.IV, §4A(c)(3).

PAY AND EMOLUMENTS

A former judge temporarily assigned receives per diem compensation for each day actually engaged in judicial duties, based on the current annual salary of the court in which he served immediately prior to resignation or retirement, the per diem being computed on the basis of 246 working days a year, CJP, §1-302(f)(1). However, if the sum of per diem payments to a former judge in a calendar year, when added to his or her retirement allowance for that calendar year, equals the annual salary of a judge of the court in which the former judge served immediately prior to termination of his or her active service, no further per diem is payable to the former judge in that calendar year (*id*). In addition to the per diem, the judge is reimbursed for reasonable expenses actually incurred by reason of assignment, CJP §1-302(f)(3).

MASSACHUSETTS

MANDATORY RETIREMENT PROVISIONS APPLICABLE GENERALLY

Const., Part 2, Chap. III, Art. I provides that "upon attaining seventy years of age [all judicial officers] shall be retired." In Kingston v. McLaughlin 359 F.Supp. 25, affd. Mem. 411 U.S. 923, that provision was held not in violation of the contract clause of the federal Constitution, and both the Supreme Judicial Court, in Apkin v. Treasurer and Receiver General, 401 Mass. 427, 517 N.E.2d 141, and the court of appeals for the First Circuit, in Equal Employment Opportunity Comm. v. Commonwealth, 858 F.2d 52, have held it not preempted by the Federal Age Discrimination in Employment Act, notwithstanding that that statute referred to elected officials and did not explicitly cover appointed officials, even though, as stated at page 54 of the latter decision, all Massachusetts judges are appointed.

The governor may, with the consent of the council, retire a judicial officer, after notice and hearing, because of advanced age or mental or physical disability, Const., Part 2, Chap. III, Article I; Commonwealth v. Harriman, 134 Mass. 314.

RETIREMENT PROVISIONS RE PARTICULAR COURTS

No distinction drawn, but note that General Laws, Chap. 32, §65A recognizes the right of a judge to resign before his or her term of office expires; see Opinion of the Justices, 360 Mass. 907, 277 N.E.2d 293.

OPTIONAL PROVISIONS FOR RETIREMENT

A chief justice or associate justice of the Supreme Judicial Court and a chief justice or associate justice of the appeals court appointed prior to January 2, 1975 may retire after serving at least fifteen years continuously, at or after attaining age sixty-five, General Laws, Chap. 32, §65A. A chief justice, associate justice of the appeals court, or any justice of a trial court appointed on or after January 2, 1975 who is retired under Article LVIII of the Amendments to the Constitution (i.e. Chap. III as it read prior to November 15, 1918), or who has served for at least fifteen years continuously and attained age sixty-five but not seventy is entitled to a retirement allowance, General Laws, Chap. 32, §65(D)(c). A special justice of a district court or of a juvenile court retired under *id*, §65B and Article LVIII of the Amendments to the Constitution (*supra*), or who resigns after having served for at least ten years and at or after age sixty-five, is entitled to a pension, as also is a special justice of a district court, or of a juvenile court, or a special judge of probate and insolvency retired under *id*, §65B and Article XCVIII of the Amendments to the Constitution (i.e. Chap. III, Art. I, as it read prior to January 7, 1972) who retires at age seventy after having served three years or more but less than ten years.

Any member in service who becomes totally and permanently incapacitated from further duty before attaining age sixty-five and after completing fifteen or more years of creditable service, upon his or her written application and certification after examination by a medical panel, which the member and his or her counsel and counsel for the employer may attend, that he or she is so disabled, shall be retired for ordinary disability, General Laws, Chap. 32, §6. Similar provisions are contained in Chap. 32, §7 with respect to retirement for accidental disability of a member who becomes totally and permanently incapacitated from further duty by reason of a personal injury sustained or hazard undergone as a result of, and while in performance of, his or her duties at some definite time and place, without serious and willful misconduct on the member's part, provided such injury or hazard was undergone within two years prior to the filing of his or her application, unless written notice thereof was filed within ninety days after its occurrence.

SERVICE AFTER RETIREMENT

A chief justice or any associate justice of the Supreme Judicial Court or an appeals court who is retired may notify the chief justice of the Supreme Judicial Court in writing that he wishes his name to be placed on the list of retired justices of the appeals court, and upon his or her name being so placed, is eligible for a term of two years and for succeeding two-year terms, upon his request and with the reapproval of the chief judge of the Supreme Judicial court, to serve as an associate judge of the appeals court or a judge of a lower court, but no single assignment shall be of a term longer than ninety days, General Laws, Chap. 32, §§65E and F and Title I, Chap. 211, §24, and Chap. 211B, §16. Like provisions with respect to service by a retired chief justice or associate justice of the appeals court or of any lower court are contained in General Laws, Chap. 211A, §16 and with respect to retired trial justices serving on trial courts are contained in General Laws, Chap. 32, §65G(b) and Title I, Chap. 211 B, §14. Note, however, that §§65E, F and G provide that no such retired judge, while eligible to perform judicial duties, shall engage in the practice of law, directly or indirectly, nor may he or she hold any office which is incompatible with holding the office of judge of the court of which he or she is on the retired list.

PAY AND EMOLUMENTS

In general, but subject to exceptions concerning time of appointment and length of service, retired justices or judges of appeals and trial courts are entitled to a pension of three-fourths of the salary paid to him or her at the time of retirement, General Laws, Chap. 32, §65A. For purposes of that section, any chief justice, judge, or justice appointed to the superior court, the land court, a housing court, the Boston Municipal Court, a juvenile court, a probate court, or a district court who held office on July 1, 1978 is deemed to have been appointed to the trial court. See also §65B relating to special justices of the juvenile court or of the court of probate and insolvency as to computation of the salary of such justices, and see §65D as to the retirement allowance of any chief justice or associate justice of the appeals court or any justice of the trial court appointed on or after January 2, 1975 and who is not included under §§65A or 65B by way of previous appointment to judicial office.

The pay for services that a retired chief justice or associate justice of an appeals court or a retired justice of the trial court receives, in addition to the pension received, is a per diem differential compensation equivalent to $1/220$th of the balance remaining after deducting the pension received from the current annual salary such justice would receive if not retired, General Laws, Title I, Chap. 211, §24 and Chap. 211B, §§14(c) and 16(c), and he or she is entitled to all other benefits of an incumbent of the appeals or trial court on which he or she is serving and to be reimbursed for expenses incurred while so serving at any place other than his or her place of residence. (*id*). Upon retirement, a judge or justice will continue to receive $5,000 life insurance, $5,000 in accidental death and dismemberment insurance, and hospital, surgical, medical, dental, and vision insurance under the same conditions as if he or she were still actively serving. See Title IV, Ch. 32A, §§6, 8, 10, 17. Generally, the state pays for seventy-five percent of the premiums with the remainder paid by the employee or retiree. §8.

MICHIGAN

Mandatory Retirement Provisions Applicable Generally

Constitution, Article 6, Section 19, provides that "[n]o person shall be appointed to a judicial office after reaching the age of 70 years." That provision is construed to apply to all judicial offices, whether designated as a court of record or not, and to permit a judge elected or appointed before his or her seventieth birthday to serve until the end of the term to which he or she has been elected, Ball v. Thomas, 1 Mich.App. 1, 133 N.W.2d 218; Hackett v. Kress, 1 Mich.App. 6, 133 N.W.2d 221, Op. Atty. Gen. 1955–56, No. 2735, p.636.

Constitution, Article 6, Section 30(2) provides that upon recommendation of the Judicial Tenure Commission the supreme court may retire a judge for "physical or mental disability which prevents the performance of judicial duties . . . or habitual intemperance." In Matter of Mikesell, 396 Mich. 517, 243 N.W.2d 86, it was held that habitual intemperance refers only to abuse of alcohol.

Retirement Provisions re Particular Courts

No distinction made; see the *Ball* and *Hackett* cases cited above.

Optional Provisions for Retirement

Comp. Laws Annot. §38.2501 provides that a member or vested former member of the retirement system with four or more years of membership service may retire by filing a written application and will be entitled to a retirement allowance if he or she meets one or more of the following requirements: (a) is sixty years of age or older and has eight or more years of service, (b) is fifty-five years of age or older and has eighteen or more years of credited service of which the last six are continuous, (c) has twenty-five or more years of service of which the last six are continuous, (d) is fifty-five years of age or older, but less than sixty, and has twelve or more, but less than eighteen, years of service of which the last six are continuous.

Comp. Laws Annot. §38.2507 authorizes a member who has eight or more years of credited service and who is physically or mentally totally disabled to perform his or her duties to make written application to retire. If the medical adviser after examination certifies that the disability is likely to be permanent and that the member should be retired due to disability, that determination may be appealed to a medical committee, which certifies its findings to the retirement board. A member who refuses for ninety days or more to submit to examination, or who fails to retire before the end of sixty days after notice from the retirement board of its determination, forfeits all rights to retirement benefits.

SERVICE AFTER RETIREMENT

Constitution, Article 6, Section 23 provides that the supreme court may authorize persons who have been elected and served as judges to perform judicial services for limited periods or specific assignments. Only the supreme court may authorize a retired judge to perform judicial duties, for a limited period or for specific assignments, even though the parties to a proceeding have agreed to such appointment by a circuit court judge, Brockman v. Brockman, 113 Mich. App. 233, 317 NW2d 327; See Const., Art. 6, §27; Comp. Laws Annot. 600.226. There is no age restriction on such an appointment, People v. Booker, 308 Mich. App. 163, 527 N.W.2d 42, app. den. 538 N.W.2d 581.

Note, however, that pursuant to Comp. Laws Annot. §§600.226(3) and 600.557 in any nonjury civil action pending in any court, the parties may stipulate for trial before a "senior judge," as defined in subd.(1) of that section, and deposit funds to cover fees and expenses of trial, and upon approval of the stipulation by the chief judge of the court in which the action is pending and by order of the supreme court or state court administrator assigning the judge named in the stipulation, the trial may proceed before that judge. However, such a stipulation may be withdrawn by any party or with the consent of the senior judge, §600.557(13), (14). While the order, decision, or judgment of the senior judge is enforceable to the same extent as an order, decision, or judgment of the court in which the action was pending, no appeal is permitted from the order, decision, or judgment of the senior judge, §600.557(12).

PAY AND EMOLUMENTS

A retired judge authorized by the supreme court to perform judicial duties is credited with service for each thirty days in which he or she performed services on at least twenty days, Comp. Laws Annot. §38.2402(4). The per diem salary of a retired judge appointed to serve after retirement is the greater of either (a) $100 per day or part of a day spent in the discharge of his or her duties, or (b) the difference between $1/250$th of the annual salary paid to a judge of the court in which the retired judge is sitting and $1/250$th of the retirement allowance paid to the retired judge during the time the retired judge serves pursuant to such appointment, Comp. Laws Annot. §600.226(c). Necessary expenses incidental to the performance of the duties required by the assignment, including travel, meals, and lodging, are paid by the state in accordance with provisions established for state officials and upon approval of the court administrator, Comp. Laws Annot. §600.226(d). A retired judge is also entitled to hospitalization insurance, but a judge who has hospitalization insurance as a result of prior service as a police officer is not entitled to hospitalization insurance as a retired judge, Moore v. Marshall, 141 Mich.App. 167, 366 NW2d 26.

MINNESOTA

Mandatory Retirement Provisions Applicable Generally

The Minnesota Constitution, Article 6, §9 empowers the legislature to provide by law for retirement of all judges, including retirement or removal of any judge who is disabled.

Minnesota Statutes Annotated (MSA), §490.121(12) defines mandatory retirement date to mean the last day of the month in which a judge has attained sixty years of age, and 490.125(1) requires, except as to judges whose term has been extended by the governor (see second paragraph under Optional Provisions below), each judge to retire on the judge's mandatory retirement date. Any judge in office on December 31, 1973 who shall have attained seventy years of age on or prior to such date shall retire upon the expiration of the term of office of such judge. MSA, §490.125(2).

On recommendation of the Board on Judicial Standards, the supreme court may retire a judge of any court for disability that seriously interferes with the performance of duties and is, or is likely to become, permanent, MSA, §§490.16(3), 490.121(3). Compare, however, MSA, 490.025(1) as to the retirement of a justice of the supreme court who "becomes incapacitated." A judge retired by the supreme court shall be considered to have retired voluntarily, MSA, §490.16(4). A judge retired for disability continues to receive full salary for a period of up to one full year but in no event beyond the judge's mandatory retirement date, during which year the judge earns additional service credit, after which the judge receives a disability retirement annuity of not less than twenty-five percent of his or her final average compensation, MSA, §490.124(4).

Retirement Provisions re Particular Courts

Upon the retirement of any judge of the municipal court of Hennepin County, the judge may, with the judge's consent, be appointed and assigned, by the then chief judge upon authorization of a majority of the municipal court judges, to hear any cause properly assignable to a judge of the municipal court of Hennepin county and act thereon with full powers of such a judge. When such retired judge undertakes such service, the retired judge shall be provided at the expense of the county a courtroom or hearing room for the purpose of holding court or hearings, and shall be paid in addition to a retirement compensation an additional sum of fifty dollars per diem, together with travel pay in the sum of twelve cents per mile and the retired judge's actual expenses incurred in such service, MSA, §488A.021(9).

With respect to retirement of a district court judge, a judge of the municipal court of Hennepin County, and judges of the probate court, see Optional Provisions for Retirement below.

OPTIONAL PROVISIONS FOR RETIREMENT

Minnesota has twelve different retirement plans, including the Judicial Retirement Plan, the provisions of which are contained in MSA, §§490.121-490.132 and in the sections of MSA Chapter 487 through 490. See also Chapter 356 dealing with "Retirement Systems Generally," which in MSA, §356.30(1) permits a covered person to receive an annuity from each fund in which the person has at least six months allowable service, and in §356.302 permits receipt of a disability benefit from both. To be noted are the provisions of §356.20, subd.2(11), and §356.30, subd.3(15) and §356.302, subd. 7(12), each of which expressly refer to the Judges Retirement Plan.

Minnesota Constitution, Article 6, §9 authorizes the legislature to provide by law for the extension of the term of any judge who becomes eligible for retirement within three years after expiration of the term for which he is selected. If a judge of the district court who is within three years of being eligible to retire when his or her term would expire applies to the governor for extension of the term stating his or her intention to retire when eligible, the governor shall extend the term for three years or such part thereof as necessary for eligibility to retire, MSA, §490.101(4). A similar provision with respect to a judge of any court who was in office on December 31, 1973 is contained in MSA, §490.124(2). As to the application of those provisions, see Page v. Carlson, n.o.r., 488 N.W.2d 274.

When a justice of the supreme court, having served at least one term, arrives at the age of seventy years, or having served at least two full terms or the equivalent thereof, becomes incapacitated for the performance of official duties to the extent that the public service suffers therefrom, and makes written application to the governor for retirement, the governor shall direct the justice's retirement, MSA, §490.025(1). If a justice of the supreme court serves for two full terms and during this period attains the age of seventy, the justice, upon the completion of this period, may apply for, and be entitled to receive, the equivalent of the retirement annuity granted to retiring justices of the supreme court pursuant to subdivision 2; or if a justice serves a minimum of twelve years on the supreme court and attains the age of sixty-five, the justice may be entitled to apply for, and receive, the equivalent of the retirement annuity payable pursuant to subdivision 2 to a retired justice whose final elective term has expired, MSA, §490.025(3).

A judge of the district court who has served for not less than fifteen years as such judge, or as such judge and as judge of a court of record, and arrives at the age of seventy years may make a written application to the governor for retirement, MSA, §490.101(1)(a). A judge of the district court who has served for at least twenty-four years and is at least sixty-five years old may make written application to the governor for retirement, MSA, §490.101(1)(b).

If a district court judge becomes mentally or physically incapacitated from performing official duties, and the governor has determined that the judge shall be retired on the application of either the judge or of the legally appointed guardian of the judge, he or she shall be entitled to a disability benefit, MSA, §490.101(2).

A judge retired for disability continues to receive full salary for a period of up to one full year but in no event beyond the judge's mandatory retirement date, MSA, §490.124(4). During the year the judge earns additional service credit, and the salary earned is subject to retirement deductions and will be included in computing final average compensation. After the year a retirement annuity of not less than twenty-five percent of the judge's final average compensation, not exceeding sixty-five percent of that sum, shall be paid, *id.* and §490.124(1).

A probate judge who has attained age seventy and has served as such judge or as judge of a court of record or as such judge and as a probate referee for twenty years, or has attained age sixty-five and served as such judge or as a judge of a court of record, or as such judge and a probate referee for twenty-four years, may voluntarily retire and receive for life one-half of the compensation paid to probate judges at the time of his or her retirement, MSA, §490.12.

A probate judge who becomes incapacitated physically or mentally from performing judicial duties during the remainder of a term of office shall make written application to the governor, setting forth the nature and extent of such disability; and after such investigation as the governor deems advisable, and if the governor determines that the disability exists and that the public service is suffering and will continue to suffer by reason thereof, the governor by written order shall direct retirement of the judge for the unexpired portion of the term of office, MSA, §490.11, and he or she shall receive the compensation allotted to the office for the remainder of the term, and thereafter, if past sixty-five years of age and having served as such a judge and as a judge of a court of record, or as such judge and a referee in probate for twenty-four years, shall receive for life one-half of the compensation paid to probate judges at the time of his or her retirement, MSA, §490.12(1), reduced, however, by the full amount of any other retirement pension until the total reduction equals the amount of the other pension, plus the amount of the contribution by the state or other plan to fund the other pension, MSA, §490.12(5). For provisions applicable to certain other probate judges, see MSA, §490.12(9).

Retirement benefits increase annually, based upon the increase in the cost of living index for urban wage earners and clerical workers, MSA, §11A.18(9)(b); see also, *id.*, §490.107(4). However, they are not assignable either in law or equity, nor are they subject to execution, levy, attachment, garnishment, or other legal process, except with respect to a division of marital property or payments to a former spouse or for child support, MSA, §§490.126(5), 518.58, 518.581 and 518.611.

SERVICE AFTER RETIREMENT

Minnesota Constitution, Article 6, §10 provides that as provided by law a retired judge may be assigned to hear and decide any cause over which the court to which he is assigned has jurisdiction.

The chief justice of the supreme court may assign a retired justice of the supreme court to act as a justice of the supreme court or as a judge of any other court, MSA, §2.724(2) and (3). Upon retirement of a justice of the supreme court, the court may appoint him or her a commissioner of that court to assist in the performance of such of its duties as may be assigned with the justices's consent, MSA, §490.025(5). The chief justice may assign a retired judge of any court who is not practicing law to act as a judge of any court except the supreme court, MSA, §2.724(2) and (3). A retired judge of the district court may be appointed to hear any cause properly assignable to a judge of the district court and act thereon with full powers of a judge of the district court, pursuant to section 2.724 with the retired judge's consent, MSA, §484.61.

The presiding judge of the second or fourth judicial district may, with the consent of the parties, appoint a retired judge as a special magistrate in a case in which the amount in controversy exceeds $50,000, to preside over any pretrial and trial matters and, if there is a right to a jury trial, to conduct the jury trial. The presiding judge may adopt the rulings and findings of the special magistrate and the result of a jury trial without modification. The parties have a right to appeal therefrom. Fees and expenses are borne by the parties as determined by the presiding judge on recommendation of the special magistrate, MSA, §484.74(2a).

Rule 3 of the Rules of the Supreme Court requires continuing legal education of forty-five hours during a three-year period unless waived in individual cases, but provides that judicial officers are not eligible for waiver until they retire.

PAY AND EMOLUMENTS

A retired judge assigned by the chief justice shall receive pay and expenses in the amount and manner provided by law for judges serving on the court to which the retired judge is assigned, less the amount of retirement pay that the judge is receiving, MSA, §2.724(3)(a).

When a retired judge of the district court undertakes such service, the retired judge shall be provided with a reporter, selected by the retired judge, at the expense of the state, and with a deputy clerk, bailiff, if the judge deems a bailiff necessary, and a courtroom or hearing room, to be paid for by the county in which the service is rendered, and shall receive pay and expenses in the amount and manner provided by law for judges serving on the court to which the retired judge is assigned, less the amount of retirement pay that the judge is receiving, MSA, §484.62.

MISSISSIPPI

MANDATORY RETIREMENT PROVISIONS APPLICABLE GENERALLY

Mississippi Constitution, Article VI, §177A, mandates retirement for any justice or judge for habitual intemperance in the use of alcohol or other drugs or for physical or mental disability seriously interfering with the performance of his or her duties, which is, or is likely to become, of a permanent character, but makes no provision for mandatory retirement based on age and/or years of service, and Mississippi Code Ann., §9-3-12, (dealing with voluntary retirement) expressly states in subd. 3 that the provisions of the section "shall not in any manner be construed to require any judge to resign"; see also Miss. Code Ann., §25-11-112(e). Note also that §9-19-75 provides that a justice or judge retired by the supreme court or the seven-member tribunal (referred to below) shall be considered to have retired voluntarily.

The procedure for involuntary retirement for disability is set forth in the constitution section above referred to, which establishes a Commission on Judicial Performance, the proceedings of which are confidential and which may by a two-thirds vote recommend suspension of a justice or judge against whom formal charges are pending. A recommendation of the commission for retirement of a supreme court justice is determined by a tribunal of seven judges selected by lot from all circuit and chancery judges at a public drawing by the secretary of state (*id*). As to suspension during commission proceedings and other procedural provisions, see also Miss. Code Ann., §§9-19-13 through 9-19-23.

RETIREMENT PROVISIONS RE PARTICULAR COURTS

Any judge of the Mississippi Supreme Court who has reached the age of sixty-eight and retires as hereafter provided, may retire from active service as chief, presiding or associate justice of the supreme court. Such judge shall perform for the justices of the supreme court such service as the court may designate from time to time, but is not entitled to vote as to the decision of any case heard by the supreme court. Each such judge shall serve for a term equal to the balance of the term for which he was last elected by popular vote as a supreme court judge, provided, however, no such judge shall serve for a longer period than four years. Such judge shall receive a salary equivalent to two-thirds of the salary of an associate justice, Miss. Code Ann., §9-3-12, subds. (1) and (2).

Optional Provisions for Retirement

The Public Employees' Retirement System (PERS) defines "member" in terms broad enough to include judges and justices, see Miss. Code Ann., §§25-11-103 and 25-11-105. Retirement based on age and/or service, referred to as "superannuation retirement," is provided for in Miss. Code Ann., §§25-11-111(a) and (b). Subdivision (a) provides that any member upon withdrawal from service upon or after attainment of sixty years of age with four years of creditable service, or any member upon withdrawal from service regardless of age who shall have completed twenty-five years of creditable service, shall be entitled to receive a retirement allowance. Subdivision (b) provides that any member whose withdrawal from service occurs prior to attaining sixty years of age, who shall have completed four or more years of creditable service and shall not have received a refund of his accumulated contributions, shall be entitled to receive a retirement allowance upon attaining sixty years of age, of the amount earned and accumulated at the date of withdrawal from service.

Voluntary retirement based on disability is dealt with in Miss. Code Ann., §25-11-113, re mental or physical incapacitation, and §25-11-114, which deals with death or disability in line of duty. Section 25-11-113 permits a member, who has at least four years of membership service credit, upon application of the member or his or her employer, to seek retirement, provided the medical board, after a medical examination, certifies that the member is mentally or physically incapacitated for further performance of duty, that such incapacity is likely to be permanent, and that the member should be retired, but also provides that the PERS board may accept a disability medical determination from the Social Security Administration in lieu of a medical board certificate. Disability is defined as not only the inability to perform the usual duties, but also the incapacity to perform such lesser duties as may be assigned without material reduction in compensation, and the employer must certify that it has complied with provisions of the Americans With Disabilities Act in affording reasonable accommodations that would allow the employee to continue employment. Subdivision 3 of the section provides for reexamination of a disability retiree once a year during the first five years following retirement and once in every three years thereafter, that the board of trustees may, and upon application of the retiree shall, require such a retiree who has not yet attained sixty years of age to undergo medical examination, and that upon refusal to submit to such examination, the retirement allowance shall be discontinued; and if the refusal continues for one year, his or her right to disability benefits shall be revoked. Further, if the medical board certifies that the member is physically and mentally able to return to the employment from which he or she retired, the board of trustees may terminate the disability allowance, whether or not he or she seeks reemployment, and if the evidence of the retiree's earned income warrants, may terminate the allowance, but the retiree may thereafter qualify for a superannuation retirement allowance.

Section 25-11-114 provides in subdivisions (1) through (5) for death benefits for the spouse or dependent children of any active member who has completed four or more years of creditable service and who dies before retirement, and, regardless of number of years in creditable service, for a death benefit for the spouse or dependent children of a member killed in line of performance of duty or who dies as a direct result of an accident occurring in line of performance of duty. It also provides in subdivision (6) that regardless of the number of years of creditable service, upon application of the member or employer, any active member who becomes disabled as a direct result of an accident or traumatic event resulting in a physical injury occurring in line of performance of duty, may be retired by the board of trustees, provided the medical board or the designated governmental agency after a medical examination certifies that the member is mentally or physically incapacitated for further performance of duty and such incapacity is likely to be permanent.

Mississippi's Government Employee Deferred Compensation Plan Law (Miss. Code Ann., §25-14-1.ff.) permits an employee who has agreement with his or her employer agency to defer compensation without reducing any benefit of the Public Employees' Retirement System, Miss. Code Ann., §§25-14-11, and specifically states that any compensation deferred shall be considered part of an employee's compensation for purposes of any other employee retirement, pension, or benefit program, *id.* §25-14-13.

Cost of living adjustment of retirement benefits is provided for in Miss. Code Ann., §25-14-112. Subdivision 1 of that section provides that persons receiving retirement benefits shall receive in one additional payment an amount equal to a cumulative percentage of: 2.5 percent of the annual retirement allowance for each full fiscal year of retirement through June 30, 1984; for the period after June 30, 1984, and through June 30, 1993, the annual percentage increase in the Consumer Price Index set by the U.S. government (CPI) in each fiscal year, not exceeding 2.5 percent for any fiscal year; for each full fiscal year of retirement after June 30, 1993, the annual percentage increase in the CPI for the calendar year ending during each fiscal year, not exceeding 2.5 percent for any fiscal year, times the annual rate of retirement allowance. Subdivision 2 of that section provides that in addition they may receive a payment as determined by the board, calculated in increments of one-fourth of one percent, not to exceed 1.5 percent of the annual retirement allowance for each full fiscal year of retirement, provided that any such payment shall be contingent upon the reserve for annuities in force for retired members and beneficiaries providing sufficient investment gains in excess of the accrued actuarial liabilities for the previous fiscal year as certified by the actuary and determined by the board.

The right of any person to an annuity, a retirement allowance or benefit, or to the return of contributions, as well as to monies in the retirement system, is exempt from any state, county, or municipal ad valorem taxes, income taxes, premium taxes, privilege taxes, property taxes, sales and use taxes, or other taxes not so named, and exempt from levy and sale, garnishment, attachment, or any other process whatsoever, except as specifically otherwise provided in Articles 1 and 3 of Chapter 25, Miss. Code Ann., §25-11-129; see also as to income tax exemption §27-7-15.

SERVICE AFTER RETIREMENT

Whenever any judicial officer is unwilling or unable to hear a case or unable to hold or attend any of the courts at the time and place required by law by reason of physical disability or sickness, absence from the state, or disqualification of the judicial officer, the chief justice of the Mississippi Supreme Court, with the advice and consent of the majority of other members of the supreme court, may appoint a special judge to hear the case or attend and hold a court. Upon request of the chief judge of the court of appeals or the senior judge of a chancery or circuit court district, the chief justice of the Mississippi Supreme Court, with the advice and consent of the majority of other members of the supreme court, may appoint a special judge to serve on an emergency basis in a circuit or chancery court. During the period specified in the order of appointment, "a special judge shall assist the court to which he is assigned in the disposition of pending cases. A person appointed to serve as a special judge may be . . . [a] retired chancery, circuit or county court judge, court of appeals judge or Supreme Court justice . . . provided, however, that a judge or justice who was retired from service at the polls shall not be eligible for appointment as a special judge in the district in which he served prior to his defeat," Miss. Code Ann., §§9-1-105(1), (2), (6) and (8), 9-3-6. Note, however, that a retired supreme court justice recalled to assist the court is not entitled to vote on the decision of any case heard by the supreme court, Miss. Code Ann., §9-3-6(2). Note also that when a judge of the youth court is unable to serve from illness or absence, he or she may appoint a special judge to act in his or her stead, and in the order of appointment fixes the compensation of the appointee, Miss. Code Ann., §43-21-113. The section makes no mention of retired judges and, therefore, appears not to exclude them.

A retired chancery, circuit, or county court judge or retired supreme court justice, who is at least sixty-two years of age, who has served as a judge for at least eight years, who desires to serve as a senior judge, may file with the supreme court a certificate for designation as such, and by the filing of the certificate becomes a senior judge, Miss. Code Ann., §9-1-107(1). The service and tenure of senior judges is governed by supreme court rule, but §9-1-107(3) expressly provides that the supreme court may remove from senior status any judge who, without good cause, refuses appointment as a special judge under §9-1-105.

During tenure as a senior judge, a senior judge is required to satisfy the requirements of continuing judicial education, Miss. Code Ann., §9-1-107(5).

PAY AND EMOLUMENTS

Any retired judge or justice appointed as a special judge shall, for the period of his service, receive compensation from the state for each day's service a sum equal to 1/260th of the current salary in effect for the judicial office; provided, however, that no retired chancery, circuit, or county court judge, retired court of appeals judge, or any retired supreme court justice appointed as a special judge may, during any fiscal year, receive compensation in excess of twenty-five percent of the current salary in effect for a chancery or circuit court judge. Travel expenses incurred in the performance of official duties are to be reimbursed in the same manner as other public officials and employees, Miss. Code Ann., §9-1-105(10); see also §9-1-107(4) re service by a senior judge as a special judge under §9-1-105.

MISSOURI

Constitution, Article V, §26(1) requires that, with an exception that is no longer pertinent, all judges, other than municipal judges, retire at age seventy; see also Vernon Annotated Missouri Statutes §476.520. Under Art. V, §25, of the 1972 Constitution (no longer in effect, see V.A.M.S., §476.451[1]) judges of the supreme court and courts of appeals were required to retire upon attaining seventy-five years of age. In Gregory v. Ashcroft, 501 U.S. 452, the U.S. Supreme Court held that that provision violated neither the equal protection provision of the United States Constitution, nor the federal Age Discrimination in Employment Act. Apparently municipal judges were excepted because such courts were abolished, Const. Art V, §27(2), subject to municipal judges then in office completing the term to which elected or appointed.

Another exception, contained in Const. Art. V, §27(24), is no longer pertinent. While it permitted some judges to petition for continuance in office beyond age seventy, the period of continuation was at most twelve years, which, since it was measured from the August 3, 1976 adoption date of the section, has long since expired. Any judge who becomes eligible after August 13, 1988 for annual compensation, salary or retirement compensation who fails to retire on or before his or her seventieth birthday automatically waives all such annual compensation, salary, and retirement compensation, V.A.M.S., §476.683. Note, however, the exception contained in V.A.M.S., §476.510 for a judge retiring under the provisions of §476.450 to 476.510 who is under the age of seventy-six, if he or she makes himself or herself available to serve as appointed defense counsel for indigent persons facing a criminal charge, and for judges seventy-six or older who retire or are retired under those provisions who may practice law without serving as such defense counsel. Similar exceptions are contained in V.A.M.S., §476.565 for judges who receive retirement compensation under the provisions of §§476.515 to 476.570.

Const., Art. V, § 24(1), (2) and (6) deal with retirement for disability.

They provide that any judge or member of a judicial commission may be retired by the supreme court *en banc*, if after notice and hearing before the commission on retirement, removal, and discipline, he or she is found unable to discharge the duties of the office with efficiency because of permanent sickness or physical or mental infirmity. Rule 12.05 of the Supreme Court Rules requires the commission to investigate any request or suggestion for the retirement for disability of a judge, and if at least four members find probable cause to believe the judge disabled, to conduct a hearing, after which if at least four members find the judge disabled, retirement of the judge is recommended to the supreme court.

V.A.M.S., §104.110(4) and (6) provide that a medical examination of a disabled member may be required, and if the board finds that the member is able to perform duties of his or her former position, or if the member refuses to submit to such examination, it shall discontinue his or her retirement benefits. To be noted, however, is that the section relates to the State Employees' Retirement System, which is separate from the statutes dealing with retirement of judges (V.A.M.S., §476.450 *et seq.*), and no provision similar to §104.110 in the statutes relating to retired judges has been found, nor is there any cross-reference in the section to judges' retirement as there is, for example, in §§104.515, 104.516, 104.517 and 104.518.

RETIREMENT PROVISIONS RE PARTICULAR COURTS

None.

OPTIONAL PROVISIONS FOR RETIREMENT

V.A.M.S., §476.450 and V.A.M.S., §476.520 both deal with a judge who has ceased to hold office by reason of "voluntary resignation or retirement" by reason of specified provisions of the Constitution. To be noted, however, is that §476.520 contains a comma after the word "resignation" while §476.450 does not. Under both provisions, however, the former judge is entitled to retirement compensation. It is submitted, therefore, that both are to be read to equate "voluntary resignation" with retirement and not limited by reference to the constitution provisions referred to. The inference arising from the provisions of V.A.M.S., §§476.450 through 476.510 and 476.515 to 476.570, which establish separate systems for calculating retirement compensation based on age and years of service as variously specified in those sections, is that voluntary retirement may occur as early as age sixty; see V.A.M.S., §§476.450, 476.455, 476.520 and 476.545. Note, however, that a judge eligible to retire who elects not to do so shall have added to the retirement compensation when he or she does retire or die all annual cost of living increases that he or she received between the time he or she became eligible to retire and the year the judge actually retires or dies, not, however, to exceed sixty-five percent of the retirement compensation at the time of retirement or death, V.A.M.S., §476.690.

Const. Article V, §24(1), requires the Commission on Retirement Removal and Discipline of Judges to "investigate all requests and suggestions for retirement for disability," and Rule 12.05 of the Supreme Court Rules uses the same language. It is, therefore, clear that the procedures set forth in the Mandatory Retirement section above apply as well to a judge's voluntary retirement for disability.

A retired judge serving as a consultant to the board of the State Employees' Retirement System receives, in addition to all other compensation, an increase in compensation each year over the prior year equal to eighty percent of the increase in the Consumer Price Index, not, however, to exceed in total sixty-five percent of the initial benefit received, V.A.M.S., §476.601.

The compensation of a retired judge serving as a senior judge or special commissioner is neither subject to legal process or claim nor assignable, V.A.M.S., §476.688, except as provided in §104.312 relating to marital property.

SERVICE AFTER RETIREMENT

Const., Art. V, §26(3) provides that any retired judge, associate circuit judge, or commissioner, may, with his or her consent, be assigned by the supreme court to any court in the state as a senior judge or commissioner. For appointment as a senior judge application must be made to the supreme court, detailing the judge's legal and judicial experience and relevant medical and health records. If the application is approved by the supreme court, the appointment is valid for one year, but may be extended for additional one-year periods. A senior judge may be appointed by the supreme court to serve on any district court of appeals or circuit court, Const., Art V, §26(3), V.A.M.S., §476.681; Sup. Ct. Rule 11.07, 11.08, to serve as a special commissioner to hear and report in a case commenced by original writ, Rule 11.08, or to serve in a circuit court or court of common pleas as a referee to hear and report, or serve as a special commissioner to take depositions, Rule 11.08. Under Const., Art. V, §26(3), a retiree serving as a senior judge has the same powers as an active judge.

Under the provisions of V.A.M.S., §§476.450 through 476.510 a judge or commissioner of specified courts, including the supreme court, who so elects and accepts the provisions of those sections (see V.A.M.S., §476.500), who having reached age sixty-five and served an aggregate of twelve years continuously or otherwise, who ceased to hold office by reason of expiration of his or her term, or who voluntarily resigns or retires under Const., Art V, §25 by reason of having reached age seventy-five, may be appointed a special commissioner or referee, for and during the remainder of his or her life. V.A.M.S., §476.451(1) states that the Section 25 of Const. Art V referred to is that which was part of the Constitution prior to January 1, 1972. A retired judge who is appointed a special commissioner or referee pursuant to V.A.M.S., §476.450 is then subject to call by the supreme court for temporary duty in any court of the state to render such duties as directed by the Supreme court or as prescribed by law, V.A.M.S., §476.460.

A retired judge upon application to the board of trustees of the Missouri State Employees' Retirement System becomes a special consultant to the board on retirement, aging, and other state matters for the remainder of the person's life, and, upon request of the board or the court from which the person retired gives opinions as requested, V.A.M.S., §476.601.

A retired judge of the court of appeals or circuit court may also be appointed as a special investigator for the Missouri Ethics Commission, V.A.M.S., §105.961(16), and one member of the Citizen's Commission on Compensation for Elected Officials must be a retired judge, appointed by the supreme court, *en banc*, Const., Art. XIII, §3(2).

PAY AND EMOLUMENTS

A retired judge assigned as a senior judge receives for each day of service one hundred percent of the current annual salary of the office from which he or she retired attributable to one day of service. For purposes of that calculation, one year equals 235 days, V.A.M.S., §476.682(1). He or she is also reimbursed for travel and other actual and necessary expenses for service outside the county in which he or she resides, V.A.M.S., §476.682(2);

and, for the purpose of determining whether the judge is entitled to retirement benefit based on twelve years of judicial service, is also credited with one year of judicial service for each 235 days of service as a senior judge, V.A.M.S., §476.682(4).

A retired judge serving as special commissioner or referee receives, while he or she remains a resident of Missouri, during the remainder of his or her life, depending upon age and time of service, either one-half the salary or compensation provided for by law on January 1, 1989 for the office from which he or she retired, or, if he or she elected prior to June 30, 1988 to become a special commissioner or referee, one-half the compensation provided for at the time of such election for the office from which he or she retired, V.A.M.S., §476.450. He or she also receives actual expenses for service outside the county of his or her residence, V.A.M.S., §476.490.

Members of the judicial retirement system are also entitled to medical, life, and disability insurance, the cost of which is borne in part by the state and in part by the judge, V.A.M.S., §§476.590, 104.515-104.518.

A retired judge serving as special investigator for the Ethics Commission receives the same compensation as does a senior judge, plus expenses incurred, V.A.M.S., §105.961(16).

The retired judge who serves as a member of the Citizens Commission on Compensation receives no compensation for services, but is reimbursed for actual and necessary expenses incurred in performing such duties, Const., Art. XIII, §3(7).

MONTANA

Neither the Montana Constitution nor Montana Code Annotated makes any provision for mandatory retirement for age or years of service. Article VII, Section 11 of the Montana Constitution establishes a Judicial Standards Commission and provides that upon recommendation of the commission, the supreme court may retire any justice or judge for disability that seriously interferes with the performance of his or her duties and is or may become permanent.

Mont. Code Ann., §§3-1-1105 through 3-1-1107 provide that proceedings before the commission are confidential, that notice must be given the judicial officer involved, that if after investigation by the commission it finds good cause, it may either order a hearing before itself or request the supreme court to appoint one or more special masters who are judges of courts of record to hear and report to the commission, and if the commission finds the charges true, it recommend disability retirement of the judicial officer to the supreme court which then reviews the record and either rejects the recommendation or orders retirement of the judicial officer. Any hearing before the supreme court and the papers pertaining to the commission's recommendation are accessible to the public. Note that the procedure for disability retirement before the commission is to be distinguished from the procedure before the Public Employees' Retirement System (PERS) Board (discussed under Optional Provisions for Retirement, below), when a judge or someone on his or her behalf applies for disability retirement. Note also that §3-1-1117(1) provides that upon an order for retirement the judicial officer shall be retired with the same rights and privileges as if retired pursuant to statute.

RETIREMENT PROVISIONS RE PARTICULAR COURTS

None.

OPTIONAL PROVISIONS FOR RETIREMENT

Montana has both a Judges' Retirement System, Mont. Code Ann., §§19-5-101 through 19-5-901, (JRS) and a Public Employees' Retirement System, Mont. Code Ann., §§19-2-301 through 19-2-1101 and 19-3-101 through 19-3-1605 (PERS). Except for a judge or justice who elected on or before October 7, 1985 to remain a member of PERS, a judge of the district court, a justice of the supreme court, and the chief water judge must be a member of the judges' retirement system.

The JRS provides for service retirement, involuntary retirement, and disability retirement. Service retirement permits any member who has at least five years of membership service and has reached the age of sixty-five to retire and receive a retirement benefit computed as provided in §19-5-502, and benefits may not be withheld for receiving compensation as a judge pro tempore, Mont. Code Ann., §19-5-501. Involuntary retirement is defined in §19-5-101 as a retirement not for cause and before retirement age, and §19-5-503 provides that a member who is involuntarily discontinued from service before reaching retirement age receives a retirement allowance depending on the number of membership service years he or she has completed. Disability as defined in §19-2-303(15) means total disability to perform the member's duties by reason of physical or mental incapacity incurred while the member is an active member and of permanent duration or of extended and uncertain duration as determined by the PERS board on the basis of competent medical opinion. Under Section 19-5-612 the board may require the recipient of a disability retirement benefit to undergo a medical examination by a physician or surgeon at the board's expense, on the basis of which the board determines whether the recipient can perform the essential elements of the position held when he or she was retired. If the board determines the recipient is not incapacitated or if he or she refuses to submit to a medical examination, the disability retirement benefit must be canceled.

A judge or justice who is a member of PERS, who has attained the age of sixty and has five years of membership service is eligible for service retirement, as also is a member who has attained age sixty-five while employed in a position covered by PERS, regardless of the number of years of membership service, and as is a member who has thirty years or more of membership service regardless of age, Mont. Code Ann., §19-3-901. A member who is not eligible for service retirement and who has attained age fifty and has five years of membership service, or who has completed twenty-five or more years of membership service, is eligible for early retirement at a reduced benefit, Mont. Code Ann. §§19-3-902 and 19-3-906.

Cost of living adjustments for JRS members are provided for in Mont. Code Ann., §19-5-901, which dictates an annual increase of 1.5% if the recipient is not an active member of PERS, the benefit's initiation date is at least thirty-six months prior to January 1 of the year in which the adjustment is to be made, that the member or benefit recipient first become an active member on or after July 1, 1997 or, prior to January 1, 1998 filed an irrevocable voluntary election to be covered under the section.

Mont. Code Ann., §19-2-1101 provides cost-of-living adjustments for PERS benefit recipients in identical language, except for subdivision(c) of §19-5-901 relating to contingent annuitant recipients. See also, §19-3-1008, which in subd. (3) provides that a disability retirement benefit as calculated prior to February 24, 1991 is subject to any postretirement or cost of living increases granted by the legislature.

The right of any person to any benefit or payment from the retirement systems and the money in the pension trust fund is not subject to execution, garnishment, attachment, or other process, Mont. Code Ann., §19-2-1004(1), except pursuant to a court order reviewed and approved by the PERS board for child or parental support, spousal maintenance, or marital property right, Mont. Code Ann., §§19-2-907, 19-2-909; nor is it assignable, except for a rollover allowed by the U.S. Internal Revenue Code, Mont. Code Ann., §19-2-602(2), or in payment of an employer's employment related claim against the member who terminates membership, id., subd. (4), or with respect to a group insurance premium which the retiree has elected to have withheld, Mont. Code Ann., §9-2-904. Nor is the right to such benefit or payment subject to state, county, or municipal taxes, except for (a) a benefit or annuity received in excess of $3,600 or adjusted by an amount determined pursuant to Mont. Code Ann., §15-30-111(2)(c)(ii) or (b) a refund of a member's regular contributions picked up by the employer after June 30, 1985 as provided in §§19-3-315 or 19-5-402, Mont. Code Ann., §§15-30-101(13) and 15-30-111(2)(c).

SERVICE AFTER RETIREMENT

Every judge or justice who has voluntarily retired after eight years of service shall, if physically and mentally able, be subject to recall by the supreme court or the chief justice to aid and assist the supreme court, any district court, or any water court under such directions as the supreme court may give, including the examination of the facts, cases and authorities cited, and the preparation of opinions for and on behalf of the supreme court, district court, or water court, or to serve as water judge. The opinions, when and if and to the extent approved by the court, may be ordered by the court to constitute the opinion of the court. The court and the retired judge or justice may, subject to any rule that the supreme court may adopt, perform any and all duties preliminary to the final disposition of cases that are not inconsistent with the constitution of the state, Mont. Code Ann., §19-5-103(1).

One of the six members of the PERS Board is a retired public employee who is an inactive member of the Public Employees' Retirement System, Mont. Code Ann., §2-15-1009(2)(b).

The only statute relating to judicial education found is Mont. Code Ann., §3-11-204 which deals with education of city judges, but makes no reference to retired judges.

PAY AND EMOLUMENTS

A retired judge or justice, when called to duty, must be reimbursed for actual expenses, if any, in responding to the call. In addition, for each day of duty a retired judge or justice is entitled to receive compensation in an amount equal to one-twentieth of the monthly salary then currently applicable to the judicial position in which the duty is rendered, minus an amount equal to one-twentieth of the monthly retirement benefit the retired justice or judge is receiving, if any, for each day of duty rendered, Mont. Code Ann., §19-5-103(2).

NEBRASKA

Mandatory Retirement Provisions Applicable Generally

Neither the Nebraska Constitution nor statutes prescribe a mandatory retirement age.

A justice or judge of any court may be retired by the Commission on Judicial Qualifications for physical or mental disability seriously interfering with the performance of his or her duties if after hearing such disability is determined to be permanent or reasonably likely to become permanent, Nebraska Constitution, Article V, §30, Neb. Rev. Stat., §24-709. Such judge shall be retired with the same rights and privileges as a judge who retired pursuant to statute, *Id.*

A judge retired pursuant to §24-709 by the commission or at his or her own request may be required by the commission to submit to a physical examination, or upon his or her application to the commission, not more often than once every six months, has the right to re-examination. If the commission finds that the permanent disability no longer exists, annuity payments are discontinued unless the judge has in the meantime qualified for retirement because of age. If a judge refuses to submit to reexamination, the commission shall immediately terminate the annuity, Neb. Rev. Stat., §24-712.

Retirement Provisions re Particular Courts

None.

Optional Provisions for Retirement

Any judge may retire when he or she reaches the age of sixty-five, Neb. Rev. Stat., §24-708. A judge may retire when he or she reaches the age of fifty-five and receive a reduced monthly income. *Id.*

Neb. Rev. Stat., §24-709 permits a judge to retire for physical or mental disability upon application to the Commission on Judicial Qualifications, and subject to the same procedures and determination outlined in the second paragraph under Mandatory Retirement above.

The benefits of a member who ceased employment on or after April 10, 1996, beginning with the first payment of the sixth year after his or her initial benefit, are increased annually by thirty hundredths of one percent, Neb. Rev. Stat., §24-710.08. Note, however, that as to a judge who retired prior to June 30, 1992, Neb. Rev. Stat., §24.710(4) authorized a one-time increase based on cost of living or wage level between the effective date of retirement and June 30, 1992, not, however, to exceed three percent per year, and the total increase not to exceed $250 per month.

A retired judge's retirement benefits are not subject to garnishment, attachment, levy, the operation of bankruptcy or insolvency laws, or any other legal process, and shall not be assignable except as they are subject to a qualified domestic relations order, Neb. Rev. Stat., §24-710.02.

SERVICE AFTER RETIREMENT

Any retired supreme court, appellate court, or district court judge may be called upon for temporary duty by the supreme court, Nebraska Constitution, Article V, §§2, 12. Such supreme court, appellate court, or district court judge who has not been retired for disability may, with his or her consent, be called upon to serve in any court in the state to relieve congested dockets or to prevent the docket from becoming congested, or sit for an absent judge, Neb. Rev. Stat., §24-729. Retired judges of the separate juvenile court, municipal court, county court, or worker's compensation court, who have not been retired for disability, may be assigned to temporary duty in a court having the same jurisdiction as the one in which such judge served. *Id.*

PAY AND EMOLUMENTS

A retired judge on temporary assignment shall receive, in addition to his or her retirement benefits, for each day of temporary duty an amount established by the supreme court. Such amount, when taken together with one-twentieth of the judge's monthly retirement benefits, shall not exceed one-twentieth of the monthly salary he or she would receive if he or she were an active judge of that court, Neb. Rev. Stat., §24-730. A retired judge on temporary duty is not required to contribute to the retirement fund, nor are his or her benefits increased or decreased for such services, Neb. Rev. Stat., §24-732.

A retired judge on temporary assignment shall be reimbursed for his or her expenses at the same rate as provided for state employees, Neb. Rev. Stat., §24-731, but is required to submit within fifteen days following completion of the assignment an application to the chief justice of the supreme court for payment for services or reimbursement of expenses incurred, Neb. Rev. Stat., §24-733.

NEVADA

Mandatory Retirement Provisions Applicable Generally

The Nevada Constitution and statutes do not prescribe a mandatory retirement age. The constitution does, however, provide in Article 6, §21 that a justice of the supreme court, a district judge, a justice of the peace or a municipal judge may be retired by the Commission on Judicial Discipline for advanced age which interferes with the proper performance of his or her judicial duties, or for mental or physical disability which prevents the proper performance of judicial duties and which is likely to be permanent in nature. The commission's findings must be based on clear and convincing evidence, see Goldman v. Commission on Judicial Discipline, 108 Nev. 251, 830 P.2d 107, 116. Its decision is final unless the justice or judge appeals to the supreme court, *id.* 830 P.2d at 117, 118. Review by the supreme court concerns whether there was clear and convincing evidence before the commission which supported its findings, *id.* A judge who is so retired receives for the rest of his or her life the same pension he or she would have received based on years of service, but without regard to age, Nev. Rev. Stat., §3.092(2).

The formal statement of charges must be under oath and demonstrate clearly and convincingly that the judge has been performing official duties in a manner inconsistent with any reasonable view of judicial process, Judicial Discipline Rule 33. Unless the justice or judge has retained counsel at his or her own expense, the commission must authorize an attorney to represent him or her at public expense, *id.* Rule 34. Denial by the judge of the charges is deemed consent to a physical or mental examination by a qualified medical practitioner designated by the commission, *id.* Rule 35. The judge is, however, permitted to have counsel and a medical expert of his or her own choosing present at all phases of the examination, *id.* Rule 36. A judge who retires during pendency of an involuntary retirement hearing is deemed to have retired voluntarily, *id.* Rule 37.

RETIREMENT PROVISIONS RE PARTICULAR COURTS

Any district court judge who retired in good standing may sign any records left unsigned at the time of his retirement during the twelve months following his departure from office, Nev. Rev. Stat., §3.081(1).

OPTIONAL PROVISIONS FOR RETIREMENT

Nevada has a judicial retirement system and a public employees' retirement system. Nev. Rev. Stat. §286.305(1) provides that a supreme court justice or district judge who became a member of the public employees' system before July 1, 1997 may remain a member of that system, but provides in §286.297(6) that such a justice or judge first elected or appointed after July 1, 1997, who is not enrolled in that system at the time of election or appointment, is not eligible to become a member of the system. Nev. Rev. Stat. §286.305(3) authorizes a justice or judge who qualifies under the judicial retirement system to withdraw from the public employees' system the amount credited to his or her account, and provides that no justice or judge may receive benefits under both systems.

Any justice of the supreme court or district court judge who has served in the courts for twenty-two years is, after reaching the age of sixty, entitled to receive a pension equal to two-thirds the sum received as a salary during the last year of his judicial service, Nev. Rev. Stat., §§2.060, 3.090. Any judge who has served in any one or more of those courts for a period aggregating five years is, after reaching the age of sixty, entitled to receive a pension equal to 4.1666 percent of the sum received as a salary during the last year of his judicial service. *Id.* Such judge receives an additional 4.1666 percent of the sum received as a salary in his last year of judicial service for each year between five and twenty-two, *Id.* A judge with the required years of service, but who has not reached the required age, is entitled to benefits but they are actuarially reduced, *id.*

A judge who has served as a district judge or justice of the supreme court for a period aggregating five years or more and who becomes permanently incapacitated, physically or mentally, to perform the duties of his office may retire regardless of age, Nev. Rev. Stat., §§2.065(1), 3.092(1) and will receive the same pension he or she would receive based on years of service, but without regard to age, Nev. Rev. Stat., §§2.065(2), 3.092(2).

Postretirement increases under the public employees' retirement system are provided for in a number of sections of Nev. Rev. Stat. Chap. 286: §§286.575, 286.5756, 286.5765, 286.577, 286.5775, 286.578, 286.5785, 286.579, each of which deals with different dates on which the member began receiving benefits, most of which specify the percentage increase in retirement benefits referred to, but one of which permits the use of the U.S. Department of Labor Cost of Living Index for retired employees (§286.5756[4]) and another of which provides that its listed percentage increases may not exceed the percentage increase for "All Items Consumer Price Index" for the preceding year.

As to justices of the supreme court and judges of the district court, Nev. Rev. Stat. §§2060(6) and 3090(6) respectively provide in identical wording that any such justice or judge receiving a pension under the provisions of the section is entitled to receive postretirement increases equal to those provided for persons retired under the public employees' retirement system.

Exemption of a person's right to a pension, annuity, retirement allowance, or return of contributions, or of the pension, annuity, or allowance itself, are exempt from all state, county, and municipal taxes, are not subject to execution, garnishment, attachment, or any other process, nor to the operation of any bankruptcy or insolvency law, and are unassignable and exempt from assessment for insolvency of any life or health insurance company, except for money owed the Public Employees' Retirement System or for matrimonial or child support decrees, Nev. Rev. Stat. §286.670. To be noted, however, is that the section appears in the chapter dealing with the Public Employees' Retirement System and is limited to rights "accrued or accruing under the provisions of this chapter." No similar provision relating to benefits under the Judicial Retirement System has been found.

Service After Retirement

Any justice or judge eligible for retirement under Nev. Rev. Stat. §§2.060, 3.090, or 286.290 et seq., and who was not retired for cause or defeated for retention in office, may apply to become a senior judge of the Nevada Court System, Nevada Supreme Court Rules, Part II, Rule 10(1). If the supreme court determines that he or she is capable of performing valuable judicial service on a continuing basis, he or she receives a commission and becomes ineligible to practice in any court of the state unless he or she relinquishes status as a senior judge, (*id*). A senior judge, with his or her consent, is eligible for temporary assignment to any state court at or below the level of the court in which he or she was serving at the time of retirement. If designated by the governor, at the request of the chief justice, a senior judge may also hear specific cases in the supreme court upon disqualification of a justice thereof. The chief judge may also assign a senior judge to act as a settlement judge in any state court designated by the chief judge, *id*, Rule 10 (2). In order to serve as a settlement judge, a judge must take a course in alternative dispute resolution offered by the National Judicial College or its equivalent. Such course is paid for by the court. *Id*. The chief justice when making temporary assignments should accord preference to those judges who have declared their continuing availability as senior justices and judges, Nevada Supreme Court Rules, Part II, Rule 11(5). A senior judge may perform weddings and administer oaths, *id.,* 10(3).

Any former justice or judge who is not a senior judge and who retired in good standing may be recalled to temporary service as a judge pro tempore, Nevada Supreme Court Rules, Part II, Rule 11 (1). The chief justice may recall to active service any retired judge or justice of the court system who consents to such recall and who has not been removed or retired for cause or defeated for retention in office, and may assign him or her to appropriate temporary duty within the court system at or below the level of the court on which the former jurist qualified for retirement, Nevada Constitution, Article 6, §19; Nevada Supreme Court Rules, Part II, Rule 11(2). Upon application of the chief justice, and approval of the governor, such judge may be assigned as a judge pro tempore, to hear specific cases in the supreme court. *Id.*

A justice or judge recalled to active service is entitled to credit for the time served toward accumulating twenty-two years of service for the maximum pension, Nev. Rev. Stat., §§2.060, 3.090.

Rule 210 of Supreme Court Rules on Continuing Legal Education requires active members of the state bar, including each active member who is also a member of the judiciary, to complete a minimum of twelve hours of accredited educational activity in each calendar year unless entitled to exemption under Rule 214. Rule 214 exempts members who have attained age seventy, and authorizes the board to exempt a member for exceptional, extreme, and undue hardship unique to the member.

PAY AND EMOLUMENTS

A senior judge or judge pro tempore shall receive as compensation for each day he or she is actually engaged in the performance of duties under assignment an amount equal to five percent of the gross monthly salary of a regularly elected and qualified judge of the court on which he qualified for retirement, or one-half of that daily compensation for one-half days service or less, Nevada Supreme Court Rules, Part II, Rule 10(5); 11(5). However, a judge pro tempore who accepts an assignment as a judge in a justice's court or a municipal court, shall receive as compensation for each day actually engaged in the performance of duties under the assignment an amount equal to five percent of the gross monthly salary of a regularly elected and qualified judge of the court to which he or she is assigned, Nevada Supreme Court Rules, Part II, Rule 11(5).

If a senior judge notifies the chief judge that he or she will serve for not less than one-third of the total judicial days which a sitting judge is expected to work annually, he or she shall receive at least twenty percent of such gross salary monthly, chargeable against compensation for later assignments. However, a senior judge shall not receive for service during a calendar year a sum of money which when added to retirement pay exceeds the annual salary of a judge of the court on which he or she qualified for retirement, Nevada Supreme Court Rules, Part II, Rule 10(5).

A senior judge or judge pro tempore assigned to a court located outside the county in which he or she regularly resides shall receive traveling expenses and per diem as provided by law, Nevada Supreme Court Rules, Part II, Rules 10(6); 11(6).

NEW HAMPSHIRE

New Hampshire Constitution, Part 2, Article 78, provides that "[n]o person shall hold the office of judge of any court, or judge of probate . . . after he [or she] has attained the age of seventy years", and Revised Statutes Annotated, §493:2 states that the office held by any judge becomes vacant when the judge attains the age of seventy (see also as to probate judges R.S.A., §547.19). In Grinnell v. State, 121 N.H. 823, 435 A.2d 523 (1981) the supreme court held that the Fourteenth Amendment to the United States Constitution was not violated by the provision, it being rationally related to goals of high performance, efficiency and fitness, notwithstanding that the court recognized that mandatory retirement deprived the bench of many able jurists who are forced to retire in the height of their intellectual creativity, and that any line drawn on the basis of age will likely have that effect. In Keniston v. State, 63 N.H. 37 (1884) however, the court held Article 78 of the state constitution not applicable to justices of the peace.

Involuntary retirement because of permanent disability is authorized by R.S.A., §490:2(I) as to justices of the supreme court, which requires that the chief justice and two associate justices (or, if the chief justice is unable to perform because of permanent disability, the senior associate justice and two other associate justices) certify in writing the justice's disability to the governor and council, who shall if they find the justice, after due notice and hearing, unable to perform his or her duties because of permanent disability, order retirement of the justice from regular active duty. Similar provisions with respect to superior court justices are contained in R.S.A., §491:2(I), except that the certificate of disability is made by the chief justice or senior associate justice and two associate justices of the superior court; provisions with respect to district court judges are contained in R.S.A., §502-A:6-a, except that the certificate of disability is made by the administrative committee of the district and municipal courts; and with respect to probate judges are contained in R.S.A., §547:19-a, except that the certificate of disability is made by any three judges of the probate court.

Additionally, R.S.A., §100-A:6(I)(a) provides for involuntary retirement upon application by the Retirement System member's employer of a Group I member[2] who has ten or more years of creditable service on an ordinary disability retirement allowance, provided a physician or physicians designated by the board of trustees, after medical examination of the member, certifies, and the board finds, that he or she is mentally or physically incapacitated from further performance of duty, that such disability is likely to be permanent, and that he or she should be retired. Further, subdivision I(c) of that section provides that such a member's employer may apply to the board for the retirement of a member who has become totally and permanently incapacitated for duty as the natural and proximate result of an accident occurring while in the actual performance of duty at some definite time and place, or as the natural and proximate result of repeated trauma or gradual degeneration occurring while in actual performance of duty, or arising out of and in the course of employment of any occupational disease arising out of and in the course of employment as defined in the workers' compensation law and found to be compensable by the commissioner of labor, provided such injury was without willful negligence on his or her part, and provided the board of trustees finds that he or she is mentally or physically incapacitated for further performance of duty and that such incapacity is likely to be permanent.

R.S.A., §100-A:6(III)(a) provides that the board of trustees may, and upon his or her application shall, require a disability retiree who has not attained age sixty, once a year during the first five years following such retirement, and once in every three-year period thereafter, to undergo a medical examination by a board-designated physician. If the judge refuses to submit to such examination, the board may discontinue his or her pension; and if the refusal continues for more than one year, his or her pension rights may be revoked. Paragraph (b) of subdivision III permits the board, if it finds that a disability beneficiary is engaged in, or able to engage in, a gainful occupation, to reduce his or her pension as provided in that paragraph. If a retiree is restored to service, his or her pension ceases, he or she

---

[2] Although the definition of "employee" in R.S.A., §100:A-1(v) governing the New Hampshire Retirement System does not contain the word "judge" or "judges," it is broad enough to include judges as employees. Group I under that system includes "employees and teachers" and Group II includes policemen, firemen, R.S.A., §100:A-1(x).

again becomes a member of the Retirement System entitled to a retirement allowance computed as provided in that paragraph.

RETIREMENT PROVISIONS RE PARTICULAR COURTS

None.

OPTIONAL PROVISIONS FOR RETIREMENT

Any supreme court or superior court judge may retire at age sixty-five, but must give thirty days notice of intention to do so to the chief justice of his or her court and to the governor and council, or if the chief wishes to retire to the senior associate justice and the governor and council, R.S.A., §493:3.

A judge of probate who is not a full-time judge may, under the provisions of R.S.A., §547:I-a, retire at age sixty-five after having served in such capacity for twenty years, on a reduced pension, such payments being in lieu of his or her rights under the New Hampshire Retirement System to which the judge would otherwise be entitled, R.S.A., §547:19-d.

R.S.A., §100-A:19:b defines minimum age for any member who has completed less than twenty years of combined creditable service in both Group I and Group II as sixty years, and for a member who has completed more than twenty years of such service, sixty years, less one year for each year of creditable Group II service, but not less than forty-five years. A member who has creditable service in both groups and has attained minimum age as thus defined may retire on an allowance computed as set forth in R.S.A., §100-A:19-c; or if he or she has at least ten years of continued creditable service and is at least forty-five years old and is within ten years of the minimum age as above defined may, in accordance with R.S.A., §100-A:19-d, elect to retire at such a benefit reduced by the percentages set forth in R.S.A., §100-A:5 I(c).

Voluntary retirement because of permanent disability is provided for in R.S.A., §490:2(I) as to supreme court justices; in R.S.A., §491:2(I) as to superior court justices; in R.S.A., §502-A:(6) as to district court judges; and in R.S.A., §547:19-a as to probate judges. Additionally, R.S.A., §100-A:6 provides in subsections 1(a) and (c) that a Group I member may, upon his or her application, be retired on ordinary disability or accidental disability retirement under the same conditions set forth above in the Mandatory Retirement section.

Effective July 1, 1994, and every July 1 thereafter, any retired member of the New Hampshire Retirement System or any predecessor system, who has been retired for at least twenty-four months, is entitled to a supplemental cost of living allowance actuarially computed of from one to five percent, with increments of no less than one-half of one percent, included in the monthly annuity paid to the retired member, R.S.A., §100-A:41-a.

The rights accruing to any person under the New Hampshire Retirement System are exempt from any state, county, or municipal tax and are not subject to assignment, execution, attachment, or other process, legal or equitable, R.S.A., §100-A:26, except to the extent that such rights are subject to assignment, execution or attachment under private retirement systems, R.S.A., §100-A:26-a.

SERVICE AFTER RETIREMENT

Each justice of the supreme or superior court and each full-time justice of the district or probate courts who is retired by reason of age limitation or voluntary retirement after having served on any or any combination of said courts for an aggregate of ten or more years, and however combined, upon retirement becomes a judicial referee and may be assigned, by the chief justice of the supreme court or his or her designee, to hear and determine cases in any court, but not to preside at trials by jury or to enter judgments, R.S.A., §493-A:1.

R.S.A., §490.3(II) provides that when a vacancy exists in the supreme court by reason of retirement, disqualification, or inability to serve, the chief justice or senior associate justice may assign a retired supreme court justice to sit while the vacancy continues, or may notify the chief justice or senior associate justice of the superior court of the vacancy, who may then provide the names of two or more superior court justices, including retired justices, who are not disqualified, to the chief justice or senior associate justice of the supreme court who may assign one of the superior court justices whose names have been furnished to it temporarily on the supreme court.

R.S.A., §502-A:6-b provides that a justice of the district court retired therefrom by age limitation who has served on the court shall upon retirement become a referee empowered to act as such in the district courts.

A probate judge may appoint as a *master* in any contested case a former judge of the probate court retired therefrom by age limitation when to do so will expedite the business of the court, R.S.A., §547:37. Note, however, that R.S.A., §547:19-c provides that a judge of the probate court retired by age limitation who has served on the court shall upon retirement become a *referee* empowered to act as such in the probate courts.

PAY AND EMOLUMENTS

A judicial referee is compensated for his or her services as such and is paid an annual sum equal to three-quarters of the currently effective salary of the office from which he or she retired, R.S.A., §493-A:2, and is allowed actual expenses and office rent as provided for justices of the superior court, R.S.A., §493-A:1.

A retired justice of the district court sitting as a referee is allowed expenses and a per diem compensation fixed by the supreme court on recommendation of the judicial branch administrative council. A former probate judge sitting as master is, like the retired district court judge, allowed per diem compensation recommended by the judicial branch administrative council, plus reasonable expenses, R.S.A., §547:37(II).

NEW JERSEY

Constitution Art. 6, §6, &3 requires that justices of the supreme court and judges of the superior court retire upon attaining the age of seventy years. Chapter 6A of Title 43 of New Jersey Statutes establishes the Judicial Retirement System (JRS). New Jersey Statutes Annotated (N.J.S.A.) §43:6A-5 requires not only supreme court justices and superior court judges, but also judges of the county court, a full-time judge of the county district court, and a full-time judge of the juvenile and domestic relations court to be members of the JRS; and §43:6A-7 provides that any member of the JRS who has reached age seventy shall be retired forthwith. See also §43:6A-3(j). Note also that N.J.S.A. §43:6A-8, which is headed "Eligibility for retirement," provides that any JRS member who has "served at least 10 years as a judge of the several courts and having attained the age of 70 years shall be retired." Judges of the tax court are also subject to age seventy mandatory retirement; see N.J.S.A. §§10:3-1 and 43:6A-3(j).

New Jersey has both the Judicial Retirement System (JRS) and a Public Employees' Retirement System (PERS). N.J.S.A. §43:6A-14 provides that a judge required to be a member of JRS who has membership in any other retirement system shall cease to be a member of the latter system on the date he or she becomes a judge, but may elect to receive an annuity from the other system based on his or her own contributions, while continuing to serve as a judge; but if the judge thereafter elects to receive JRS benefits, all rights to retirement benefits are terminated. A judge receiving a retirement allowance or pension from a system other than JRS when he or she becomes a judge may, under the provisions of N.J.S.A. §43:6A-14.1, terminate his or her status in the other system or may continue to receive such allowance or pension by filing with the JRS within ninety days after appointment his irrevocable intention not to enroll in the JRS. A judge who enrolls in JRS receives credit for service in the other system (*id*). A judge who remains a member of PERS is required to retire on attaining age seventy, but under N.J.S.A. §43:15A-47 may be continued in service on an annual basis by the head of the state department or employer (presumably the chief justice of the supreme court). It has been held that a judge enrolled in the Public Employees' Retirement System, based on both nonjudicial and judicial service, is subject to the provisions of N.J.S.A. §43:15A-47(b), mandating retirement at age seventy for all members of that System, Division of Pensions v. Lindeman, 103 N.J. Supp. 375, 247 A.2d 354, affd. for the reasons stated, 53 N.J. 70, 248 A.2d 427.

Constitution, Art. 6, §6, &5 provides that any justice of the supreme court or judge of the superior court may be retired by the governor whenever the supreme court certifies to the governor, after inquiry by a three-person commission, that the justice or judge is so incapacitated as substantially to prevent performance of judicial duties.

RETIREMENT PROVISIONS RE PARTICULAR COURTS

Although the mandatory retirement provisions of N.J.S.A. §43:6A-7 earlier included judges of the county court, of the county district court, and of the juvenile and domestic relations court of any county, those offices were abolished by amendment of Constitution Art. 6, §6, &1; but a judge who was not eligible to retire at that time now may apply for retirement upon attainment of age sixty while serving as such judge, N.J.S.A. §43:6A-9.2.

OPTIONAL PROVISIONS FOR RETIREMENT

A judge may retire after fifteen years service and having attained age sixty-five, but not seventy, or after twenty years and having attained age sixty, but not sixty-five, N.J.S.A. §43:6A-8. Section 43:6A-9 provides that a judge who has served five years as a judge and a total of fifteen years in government service and attained age sixty-five may retire; §43:6A-9.1 makes similar provision for a judge who has served five years as a judge and a total of fifteen years in government service to retire at or after age sixty; and §§43:6A-9.2 and 43:15A-47 permit any judge who has attained age sixty while serving as a judge to retire upon his or her written application. See also, §43:6A-10 re retirement before age sixty after five years successive service as a judge and a total of twenty-five years in government service of a member who resigns or fails of reappointment as a judge, and

§43:6A-11 re retirement at or before age sixty after five years successively as a judge and a total of ten years in government service of a member who resigns or fails of reappointment.

Voluntary retirement for disability is permitted under N.J.S.A. §43:6A-12. It provides that a judge may be retired for disability whenever the supreme court certifies to the governor that the judge has become physically or otherwise incapacitated for full and efficient service in his or her judicial capacity. The governor then refers the disability claim to three physicians who examine the judge and report to the governor as to the disability they find existent, and whether in all reasonable probability it will continue permanently and does and will prevent the member from giving full and efficient service. If the report confirms disability and the governor approves it, "the member shall be retired not less than one month next following the date of filing of an application with the retirement system." In Matter of Yaccarino, 101 N.J. 342, 502 A.2d 3, 31, the supreme court held that a member's application for a retirement pension based on disability was not barred by removal proceedings brought against the judge.

The rights of a person to retirement allowance or other benefits are exempt from state or municipal tax and from attachment or other process arising out of any state or federal court, N.J.S.A. §43:6A-41.

SERVICE AFTER RETIREMENT

Any justice of the supreme court may, with his or her consent, be recalled for temporary service in the supreme court or elsewhere within the judicial system, and judges of the superior court, juvenile and domestic relations court, community district court, or tax court who have retired on pension or retirement allowance may, with his or her consent, be recalled for temporary service within the judicial system other than the supreme court, N.J.S.A. §43:6A-13(b).

No member of the JRS may engage in the practice of law before any New Jersey court while receiving a pension or retirement allowance, N.J.S.A. §43:6A-13(a). In Schwartz v. Judicial Retirement System, 584 F.Supp. 711 (D.N.J.) that provision was held constitutional under the rational basis test because it avoided the appearance of impropriety in the judiciary.

PAY AND EMOLUMENTS

The compensation paid for such service is a per diem salary set by the supreme court which, when added to the normal retirement and pension allowance, does not exceed the current salary of a judge or justice of the court from which he or she retired, N.J.S.A. §43:6A-13(c). In addition, recalled judges are entitled to reimbursement for reasonable expenses incurred by reason of the assignment (*id*).

Retired judges also receive a life insurance benefit of twenty-five percent of final salary with only a spouse surviving. There are additional payments made to surviving children, and children where there is no surviving spouse, N.J.S.A. §§43:6A-18, 43:6A-19. However, if a judge who retired on a disability pension dies before reaching age sixty, the beneficiary receives one-and-one-half times the final salary, N.J.S.A. §43:6A-20.

NEW MEXICO

Neither the New Mexico Constitution nor New Mexico Statutes Annotated (NMSA) mandate retirement based on age or years of service.

Involuntary retirement for disability seriously interfering with the performance of the duties of a justice, judge, or magistrate of any court which is, or is likely to become, of a permanent character is, however, provided for by Const. Art. VI, §32. That section provides for a Judicial Standards Commission, and empowers it, after investigation, to order a hearing before it or to appoint three masters who are justices or judges of courts of record to hear evidence and report their findings to the commission. After hearing or after considering the findings and report of the masters, the commission, if it finds good cause, recommends to the supreme court retirement of the justice, judge, or magistrate. The supreme court reviews the record on the law and the facts and may permit introduction of additional evidence. It then either orders retirement or wholly rejects the recommendation. If retirement is ordered, the justice, judge, or magistrate participating in a statutory retirement program is retired with the same rights as if he or she had retired pursuant to the retirement program. See also NMSA, §34-10-1, which creates the Judicial Standards Commission and sets forth the procedure for determining involuntary retirement for disability in essentially the same language as that of Constitution Art. VI, §32.

The Constitution section also provides for removal for misconduct of a justice, judge, or magistrate, and in Matter of Martinez, 99 N.M. 198, 686 P.2d 861, it was held that the standard of proof in a removal proceeding is clear and convincing evidence. No case dealing with the standard of proof with respect to retirement, as distinct from removal, has been found.

RETIREMENT PROVISIONS RE PARTICULAR COURTS

There is a Judicial Retirement Act (JRA) (NMSA, §§10-12B-1 through 10-12B-19), a Magistrates Retirement Act (MRA) (NMSA, §§10-12C-1 through 10-12C-18), a Public Employees Retirement Act (PERA) (NMSA, §§10-11-1 through 10-11-141), and a separate article entitled Public Employees Retirement Reciprocity Act (NMSA, §§10-13A-1 through 10-13A-18). Rather than discuss the Magistrates Retirement provisions here, all of the foregoing statutes are discussed under Optional Provisions for Retirement, below.

OPTIONAL PROVISIONS FOR RETIREMENT

NMSA, §10-19B-2(J) defines judge to mean judge of the district court or court of appeals, and 2(L) defines justice to mean justice of the supreme court. NMSA, §10-12B-4, provides that every judge or justice upon taking office is subject to the provision of the JRA, except for one who has previously retired pursuant to the provisions of any state system (defined by NMSA, §10-13A-2(N) as the JRA, MRA or PERA or the educational retirement system), unless he or she filed with the Public Employees Retirement Association a written application for exemption from JRA membership within ninety days of taking office. However, the application may be revoked, in which case membership commences on the first day of the first pay period following the date the application for membership was received by the Public Employees Retirement Association. Thus, a judge or justice or magistrate who acquired service credit under the PERA prior to becoming a judge can seek retirement under that act using total eligible reciprocal credit under all state systems to satisfy the service credit requirement for normal retirement from the state system from which he or she retires (NMSA, §10-13A-4[A]) but must terminate employment under all state systems before receiving a pension; and in no case can a member retire from more than one state system, NMSA, §10-13A-4(B)(3) and 4(F).

The Judicial Retirement Act in NMSA, §10-12B-8, provides in subd. A that a member age sixty-four or older who has five or more years of service credit, or who is age sixty or older and has fifteen or more years of service credit may retire, and in subd. B that if a member leaves office before reaching the above age and service requirement and leaves his or her contributions to the plan, the member may apply for retirement benefits when he or she meets the above age and service requirements or provisions of the Public Employees Retirement Reciprocity Act. JRA, §10-12B-12, authorizes early retirement by a member with at least eighteen years of service credit at any time between age fifty and age sixty at a lesser pension.

The Magistrates Retirement Act defines magistrate to mean a magistrate or a metropolitan court judge. It contains in §10-12C-4, in language identical to §10-12B-4, discussed above, provision for exemption from membership, and in NMSA, §10-12C-8(A) and (B) wording identical with that of §10-12B-8(A) and (B), except that it adds to subd. A provision for retirement at any age with twenty-four or more years of service credit. However, it does not authorize early retirement.

The Public Employees Retirement Act provides in NMSA, §10-11-8 for normal retirement, depending on the coverage plan of which the retiree is a member, at varying ages from sixty to sixty-five, and years of service from twenty or more for age sixty to five or more for age sixty-five, and at any age with twenty-five years of service.

Voluntary retirement for disability is dealt with by all three Acts. The JRA provides in NMSA, §10-12B-13(A) that a judge or justice with at least five years of service credit accrued pursuant to the provisions of the Act who becomes unable to carry out the duties of that office due to physical or mental disability shall, upon determination of the disability and relinquishment of office, receive a pension so long as the disability continues. However, subd. (C) states that the five-year service credit requirement is waived if the board finds that disability was the direct and proximate result of causes arising solely and exclusively out of and in the course of the member's performance of duty as a judge or justice; and the amount of the pension shall be computed as if the member had five years of service credit as a judge or justice. The MRA contains in NMSA, §10-12C-12 (A) and (B) wording identical with that of §10-12B-13(A) and (B). And both Acts, the JRA in §10-12B-13A, and the MRA in §10-12C-12A, provide that disability shall be determined by the board in accordance with the provisions of the Public Employees Retirement Act and rules promulgated thereunder.

The Public Employees Retirement Act provisions with respect to procedure are contained in NMSA, §10-11-10.1. It creates a disability review committee of the Public Employees Retirement Board which reviews the application filed by the member or his or her employer, establishing that the member was a member when the disability was incurred, has five or more years of service credit, or the disability was the natural and proximate cause arising solely and exclusively out of and in the course of the member's performance of duty with the employer. If the review committee finds that the member is currently employed by a public employer and is totally incapacitated for continued employment with such employer, or, if not

currently employed by a public employer, that the member is totally incapacitated for any gainful employment, and in either case that the incapacity is likely to be permanent, the member is paid a disability retirement
pension for a period of one year. At the end of the first year the member's
condition is reevaluated to determine eligibility for continuation of the
pension, unless the federal Social Security Administration has finally determined that the member qualifies for federal disability benefits based on the
same condition. The state disability provision is discontinued if the review
committee finds the member capable of gainful employment. Each disabil-
ity-retired member is required to submit to the association annually prior
to July 1 a statement of earnings from gainful employment during the
preceding calendar year, on the basis of which, or for failure to submit
which, the disability pension may be discontinued; and when the member
meets minimum age and service credit requirements, the pension becomes
a normal retirement pension and no further determination of eligibility for
continuation of disability pension shall be made. Moreover, if the review
committee finds the disability to have resulted from causes arising out of
the member's public employment, service credit continues to accrue during
disability retirement as though the member were actually employed.

Cost of living adjustment of retirement benefits is provided for in
NMSA, §10-12B-15 of the JRA and §10-12C-14 of the MRA, both of
which provide for yearly cost of living adjustment of pensions payable
under the respective acts as provided in the PERA. NMSA, §10-11-118 of
the latter act authorizes an increase of three percent each July 1 cumulatively for (i) a normal retirement member who has been retired for at least
two years from the date of the latest retirement prior to July 1 of the year
in which the pension is being adjusted, (ii) a normal retirement member
who has reached age sixty-five and been retired for one full calendar year
from such date, or (iii) a disability retiree who has been retired for one full
year prior to such date, but a qualified pension recipient may decline such
an increase by giving written notice of the decision to decline.

In a provision found in the governing law of no other jurisdiction, the
JRA (§10-12B-18), the MRA (§10-12C-17) and the PERA (§10-11-
118.1) provide in identically worded provisions for a reduction in the payment of a pension or other retirement benefit if such payment would cause
a decrease in the amount of the monetary payment due a payee from
another governmental department or agency of the federal government or
of any other state.

Retirement pensions or other benefits are not assignable, nor are they subject to execution, levy, attachment, garnishment, or other legal process, except with respect to division of community property in a divorce proceeding or a court order with respect to child support. Identically worded sections so providing are contained in the JRA (§(10-12B-7), the MRA (§10-12C-7), and the PERA (§§10-11-135, 136 and 136.1).

There was provision in New Mexico statutes for exemption of retirement benefits from taxation, but after the U.S. Supreme Court in Davis v. Michigan Department of the Treasury, 489 U.S. 803, 103 L.Ed.2d 891, found the failure to grant exemption to federal retirees discriminated in favor of state retirees and against federal retirees in violation of intergovernmental tax immunity, the New Mexico statute was repealed. See Pierce v. State, 121 N.M. 212, 910 P.2d 288.

SERVICE AFTER RETIREMENT

Const. Art. VI, §15(C) provides that if any district judge is disqualified from hearing any cause or is unable expeditiously to dispose of any cause in the district, the chief justice of the supreme court may designate any retired New Mexico district judge, court of appeals judge, or supreme court judge, with the designee's consent, to hear and determine the cause and to act as district judge pro tempore for such cause. No similar provision authorizing a retired judge to substitute for a disqualified judge or justice of the supreme court or court of appeals has been found.

PAY AND EMOLUMENTS

No provision relating to compensation and expenses of a retired district judge serving as a district judge pro tempore has been found.

NEW YORK

Constitution, Art. VI, §25(b) requires that each judge of the court of appeals, justice of the supreme court, judge of the court of claims, judge of the county court, judge of the surrogate's court, judge of the family court, judge of a court of the City of New York and judge of the district court retire on the last day of December in the year in which he or she reaches the age of seventy. Judiciary Law §23 provides likewise. Those provisions have been held constitutional in Maresca v. Cuomo, 64 N.Y.2d 242, app. dismd., 474 U.S.802 and Diamond v. Cuomo, 130 A.D.2d 292, affd. 70 N.Y.2d 338, app. dismd. 486 U.S. 1028. Also to be noted is §530(c) of the Retirement and Social Security Law, which states that "[n]othing contained in this article shall be construed to prohibit mandatory retirement or separation from service on the basis of age where age is a bona fide occupational qualification reasonably necessary to the performance of the employee's public duties." Whether age is such a qualification is a question of fact, Tom Hoeve v. Board of Education, 64 N.Y.2d 1036.

RETIREMENT PROVISIONS RE PARTICULAR COURTS

Judiciary Law §23 excepts from retirement at the end of the year in which he or she becomes age seventy a justice of the peace of a town or police justice of a village, as to whom there is no constitutional or statutory provisions for retirement.

Section 16.1 of the Rules of the Chief Judge of the Court of Appeals provides that no former judge of that court or of the appellate divisions or appellate terms of the supreme court shall appear in person in the appellate court on which he or she served, or use or permit the use of his or her name on a brief filed in said court within two years after having left said court. However, the law firm with which the former appellate judge is associated may appear, and its name may be used on papers filed with the court.

OPTIONAL PROVISIONS FOR RETIREMENT

Retirement and Social Security Law (RSS) §2(18) defines "minimum retirement age" as sixty, except as to a member who has elected to contribute on the basis of retirement at age fifty-five, and RSS §70 permits retirement of any member who attains at least such an age while in service as a member.

Judiciary Law §§25 and 25-a provide that a state-paid full-time judge or justice of the unified court system or New York City civil court housing judge may apply to the appellate division of the supreme court in which he or she resides for a special disability allowance by filing a petition stating that he or she is, for reasons specified, incapacitated to perform the duties of the office, together with his or her resignation. If the appellate division finds the judge or justice incapacitated, he or she is retired and receives a special disability allowance, which does not, however, reduce or suspend any retirement allowance to which he or she is entitled, but the total of the allowances may not exceed his or her annual salary at the time of retirement from office.

RSS §63(a) provides for accidental disability retirement for a person under age sixty, physically or mentally incapacitated as the natural and proximate result of an incident not caused by his or her own willful negligence in service, and while actually a member of the retirement system, and actually in service, upon which his or her membership is based.

As to medical examination of a disability retiree and restoration to employment, see Comptroller's Regulations, 2 N.Y.C.R.R. §§336.5, 336.6, 337.5, 337.6; and as to termination of membership of such a retiree, see *id*. §338.2.

No provision for a cost of living adjustment of a judge's retirement allowance has been found, other than Retirement and Social Security Law §78, which granted to judges who retired prior to calendar year 1980 a supplemental allowance ranging from six percent for judges who retired in 1979 to 300.8 percent for those who retired in 1923.

Retirement and Social Security Law §110 exempts from state or municipal tax, except estate tax, and from execution, garnishment, attachment, or any other process whatsoever, a state pension, annuity, or retirement allowance. The section also makes such a pension, annuity, or retirement allowance unassignable; but §§110-a and 110-b permit deduction therefrom for group plan insurance or medicare premiums and employee organization membership dues.

SERVICE AFTER RETIREMENT

A retired judge of the court of appeals who has the mental and physical capacity to perform the duties of such office may be certified by the administrative board as a justice of the supreme court for a period of two years, and for additional terms of two years, if it is found that mental and physical capacity continue, but no such retired judge may serve beyond the last day of December in the year in which he or she reaches the age of seventy-six, Const., Art VI, §25(b); Judiciary Law §§114, 115. A retired judge so certified who served as a justice of any appellate division immediately preceding his or her retirement may be designated by the governor as a temporary or additional justice of the appellate division, Const., Art.VI, §25(b), and a retired judge of the court of appeals or retired justice of the supreme court so certified may be certified by the administrative board as a justice of the supreme court, with all the powers and duties of a justice of the supreme court in the district in which he or she resides when so certified, Judiciary Law §§114, 115. If a judge or justice so certified was receiving a retirement allowance, that allowance shall cease, and he or she again becomes a member of the retirement system of which he or she formerly was a member, subject to contribution to the retirement fund, but upon subsequent retirement is credited with such service and receives a retirement allowance based on accumulated contributions and additional member service credits, Retirement and Social Security Law §101(c). A judge or justice so certified is an elected official and as such is excluded from the protection of the Age Discrimination in Employment Act, EEOC v. State of New York, 907 F.2d 316 (2d Cir.).

Judges of courts, other than the a town or village court, who no longer hold judicial office, may upon application be designated by the chief administrator as a judicial hearing officer, if found after physical examination to have the mental and physical capacity, competence, character, experience, and judicial temperament necessary to perform the duties of that office, and by the hearing officer selection advisory committee to be qualified to perform the duties of such office, Judiciary Law §850, N.Y.C.R.R.,

VOL. 22(a), §122.2; and see generally Goldstein, Expanding the Role of JHOS, N.Y.L.J., September 24, 1996, p.1, col. 3. Such designation is for a term of two years, and at the end of any term the judicial hearing officer may apply for an additional two-year term, N.Y.C.R.R., *id.*, §122.3. Reference of a matter to a JHO must indicate whether he or she is to hear and determine, or hear and report, or otherwise act with respect to the matter, or as to pending appeals may assign the JHO to perform the functions of a pre-argument screening program of the appellate division, N.Y.C.R.R., Vol. 22(A), §122.6. A JHO does not have authority to conduct a jury trial and even a reference to hear and report for a nonjury trial requires consent of the parties, Civil Practice Law and Rules §4317. Nothing in the Judiciary Law or the Rules of the Chief Administrator establishes an age limit beyond which a judicial hearing officer found qualified, and to have the mental and physical capacity required, may not be designated; but §122.12 of the chief administrator's regulations provides that he may require a JHO to attend continuing education courses. However, by amendment dated January 27, 1997, adding subdivision (e) to §122.5, it is now provided that the chief administrator, in consultation with the appropriate appellate division, may remove any judicial hearing officer, after notice and a hearing if requested, for unsatisfactory performance or any conduct incompatible with service as a judicial hearing officer.

A retired judge or justice, if he or she has been certified by the chief administrator of the courts to do so pursuant to §212(k) of the Judiciary Law, may perform marriages, Domestic Relations Law §11(3).

PAY AND EMOLUMENTS

The salary of a retired judge of the court of appeals or justice of the supreme court certified as a justice of the supreme court is that of a justice of the supreme court, Judiciary Law §§114(3), 115(3). Article 6, §25(a) of the New York Constitution provides that the compensation of a retired judge shall not be diminished during his or her term of office; but that provision does not proscribe suspension of compensation by the Court on the Judiciary during suspension proceedings, Pfingst v. State, 85 Misc.2d 689, affd. 57 A.D.2d 163, 165, see also Const. Art. 13, §7 and Ginsberg v. Purcell, 51 N.Y.2d 272, 276.

The compensation of a judicial hearing officer is fixed at $250 per day or part thereof that he or she performs duties in a courtroom or other designated facility, plus actual and necessary expenses incurred in the performance of his or her duties, Judiciary Law §852, N.Y.C.R.R., Vol. 22(A), §122.8, but no compensation is paid for out-of-court work performed by the officer, N.Y.C.R.R. §122.8. However, Retirement and Social Security Law §212, which is made applicable to JHOs by Judiciary Law §852(2), imposes an earnings limitation of $11,280 if the retiree so elects, but provides that "there shall be no earnings limitations under [its provisions] on or after the calendar year in which any retired person attains age seventy."

NORTH CAROLINA

North Carolina Constitution, Art IV, §8, provides that

> The General Assembly shall provide by general law for the retirement of Justices and Judges of the General Court of Justice, and may provide for the temporary recall of any retired Justice or Judge to serve on the court or courts of the division from which he was retired. The General Assembly shall also prescribe maximum age limits for service as a Justice or Judge.

N.C. Stat., §§7A-4.20 and 135-57(b) provide that any member of the Judicial Retirement System who is a justice or judge of the general court of justice shall be automatically retired as of the first day of the calendar month next following attainment of his or her seventy-second birthday, but §7A-4.20 makes clear that justices and judges so retired may be recalled for periods of temporary service.

Upon recommendation of the Judicial Standards Commission, the supreme court may remove any judge for mental or physical incapacity interfering with the performance of his or her duties, which is, or is likely to become, permanent. A judge so retired is entitled to retirement compensation if he or she has accumulated the years of creditable service required for incapacity or disability retirement under any provision of state law (as to which see paragraphs 12 through 15 of Optional section below), but is ineligible to sit as an emergency justice or judge, N.C. Stat., §7A-376, see §7A-55.

RETIREMENT PROVISIONS RE PARTICULAR COURTS

None.

OPTIONAL PROVISIONS FOR RETIREMENT

North Carolina Statutes concerning its Judicial Department (Chapter 7A) include Article 6, dealing with retirement of justices and judges of the appellate division, and Article 8, dealing with retirement of judges of the superior court and recall to service of judges of the district court. Chapter 135 of N.C. Stat. establishes a retirement system for teachers and state employees, which includes as Article 4 the Consolidated Judicial Retirement Act, as Article 5, the Supplemental Retirement Income Act of 1984, the purpose of which is to permit participation in an I.R.S. §401K plan, which in N.C. Stat., §135-92, provides that members of the Consolidated Judicial Retirement may voluntarily enroll in the plan, which in N.C. Stat., §135-56A, permits transfer of creditable service from other specified retirement systems, and which in §135-28.1(o) permits a member eligible for benefits under both the State Employees System and the Uniform Judicial Retirement System, who became a judge after service as a teacher or state employee, which, terminated other than by retirement or death, to apply for benefits under both systems, (to similar effect, see N.C. Stat., §135-70).

Based on years of service and/or age

Any member of the Judicial Retirement System on or after January 1, 1974, who has attained his or her fiftieth birthday and five years of membership service may retire upon written application to the board of trustees setting forth the time as of the first day of a calendar month not less than one day, nor more than ninety days, subsequent to the filing of the application, he or she desires to retire, N.C. Stat., §135-57(a), provided he or she has not withdrawn his or her contributions prior to the effective date of retirement, *id*, subd.(c), and any member who was in service October 8, 1981, who had attained fifty years of age, may likewise retire upon written application, *id*, subd.(d).

Note, however, that N.C. Stat., §7A-51 makes the following provisions for retirement: Any judge of the superior court or administrative officer of the courts, who has attained the age of sixty-five and who has served for a total of fifteen years, whether consecutive or not, as a judge of the superior court, or as administrative officer of the courts combined, may retire and receive for life compensation equal to two-thirds the total annual compensation from the office from which he or she retired, N.C. Stat., §7A-51(a).

Any judge of the superior court or administrative officer of the courts who has served for twelve years, whether consecutive or not, as a judge of the superior court, and/or as administrative officer of the courts combined, may at age sixty-eight retire and receive for life compensation equal to two-thirds the total annual compensation from the office from which he retired, N.C. Stat., §7A-51(b).

Any person who has served for a total of twenty-four years, whether consecutive or not, as a judge of the superior court, and/or as administrative officer of the courts, combined, may retire regardless of age and receive for life compensation equal to two-thirds the total annual compensation from the office from which he retired, N.C. Stat., §7A-51(c).

N.C. Stat., §7A-39.12 provides that §7A-39.2 discussed in the following three paragraphs of this report applies only to justices or judges who entered into office prior to January 1, 1974, and that the extent of such application is specified in Chapter 135, Article 4, enacting the Consolidated Judicial Retirement Act.

Any justice of the supreme court or judge of the court of appeals who has attained the age of sixty-five and who has served for a total of fifteen years, whether consecutive or not, on the supreme court, court of appeals, or superior court, or as administrative officer of the courts, or any combination thereof, may retire and receive for life compensation equal to two-thirds the total annual compensation from the office from which he retired, N.C. Stat., §7A-39.2(a).

Any justice of the supreme court or judge of the court of appeals who has attained the age of sixty-five and who has served for a total of twelve consecutive years, in the appellate division, may retire and receive for life compensation equal to two-thirds the total annual compensation from the office from which he retired, N.C. Stat., §7A-39.2(b).

Any justice or judge of the appellate division who has served for a total of twenty-four years, whether consecutive or not, on the supreme court, court of appeals, or superior court, or as administrative officer of the courts, or any combination thereof, may retire regardless of age and receive for life compensation equal to two-thirds the total annual compensation from the office from which he retired, N.C. Stat., §7A-39.2(c). In determining eligibility for retirement under this subsection, time served as a district solicitor of the superior court prior to January 1, 1971, may be included, provided the person has served at least eight years as a justice, judge, or administrative officer of the courts, or in any combination of those offices, *id.*

N.C. Stat., §135-63(b) authorized a death benefit for a former judge who died in service prior to January 1, 1974, and §135-64(e) authorized an annual retirement allowance to the surviving spouse of a retired former judge equal to one-half the judge's retirement allowance. All of the other subdivisions of the two sections speak of a "former member" of the retirement system governed by Chapter 135 and presumably, therefore, do not apply to retired or former judges.

Based on disability

N.C. Stat., §135, article 4, establishes the Consolidated Judicial Retirement Act, and §135-51 states that that Act applies to judges and justices who are serving on January 1, 1974, and become such thereafter, and that the extent of such application is specified in that Act.

N.C. Stat., §135-59 provides that a justice or judge who has completed five years or more of creditable service and has not attained his or her sixty-fifth birthday may apply for retirement provided that the medical board, after a medical examination of the member, shall certify that he or she is mentally or physically incapacitated for the further performance of duty and that such incapacity was incurred at the time of active employment and has been continuous thereafter, that such incapacity is likely to be permanent and did not exist when the member first became a member of the system or is in receipt of payments on account of the same disability which existed when he or she first established membership in the system. If the medical board determines that the member is able to engage in gainful employment, the disability benefit otherwise payable is reduced.

With respect to justices or judges who entered into office prior to January 1, 1974 (see N.C. Stat., §7A-39.12), section 7A-39.11 provides that every justice of the supreme Court or judge of the court of appeals who has served for eight years or more on the supreme court, court of appeals, or the superior court, or as administrative officer of the courts, or any combination thereof, and who while in active service becomes totally and permanently disabled so as to be unable to perform efficiently the duties of the office, and who retires by reason of such disability, shall receive for life compensation equal to two-thirds the annual salary from time to time received by the occupants of the office from which he or she retired.

N.C. Stat., §7A-55 provides that every judge of the superior court or administrative officer of the courts who has served for eight years or more, in either or both offices combined, may petition for retirement due to total and permanent disability so as to be unable to perform efficiently the duties of his or her office, and is eligible to receive compensation for life equal to two-thirds of the total annual compensation of the office from which he retired. Time served as district solicitor of the superior court prior to January 1, 1971, may be included. Judges retired under this section are not eligible for recall as emergency judges. *Id.*

Article 30 of Chapter 7A establishes the Judicial Standards Commission, and §7A-376 authorizes the supreme court on recommendation of the commission to remove any judge for mental or physical incapacity interfering with the performance of his or her duties which is, or is likely to become, permanent, and provides that a judge so removed is entitled to retirement compensation if he or she has accumulated the years of creditable service required for incapacity or disability retirement under any provision of state law, but may not sit as an emergency judge. The procedures with respect to such disability retirement are contained in N.C. Stat., §7A-377, including hearings before the commission and the supreme court, a majority of whose members must concur in any order of removal. If the proceeding relates to a justice of the supreme court, however, the recommendation for removal is made to the court of appeals, which proceeds under the same authority as is granted the supreme court under §§7A-376 and 7A-377(a).

N.C. Stat., §§135-65 and 135-5(o) require postretirement adjustment of retirement allowances, based in part on the consumer price index, effective with respect to July 1 of various years and parts of years and at various percentage specified in the various subdivisions of those sections.

The right to a pension, annuity, or retirement allowance or to the return of contributions is exempt from levy and sale, garnishment, attachment, or any other process whatsoever and is unassignable, except with respect to child support and equitable distribution payments and the right of offset of overpayment of benefits by a state administered system or plan, N.C. Stat., §135-9.

SERVICE AFTER RETIREMENT

N.C. Statutes contain provisions as to both emergency judges or justices and recalled justices or judges; see, generally, §§7A-39.5 through 7A-39.15. Both require the consent of the retired justice or judge and are appointed only to fill the place of an active judge who is temporarily incapacitated, but the emergency justice or judge is one who has not yet reached mandatory retirement age, who is appointed at the request of the incapacitated active judge or on order of the chief justice based on medical proof, N.C. Stat., §§7A-39.5 and 7A-39.15, whereas recalled justices and judges are those who have been mandatorily retired, N.C. Stat., §7A-39.13. They differ also in that the emergency justice's or judge's recall is only for the period the incapacity of the disabled judge continues, whereas the recalled justice or judge is recalled for a period not in excess of six months, renewable for six months if the emergency which caused his or her recall continues.

Upon application by a retired justice of the supreme court or retired judge of the appellate court, the governor may certify such individual for temporary service as an emergency justice or judge of the court from which he or she retired, N.C. Stat., §7A-39.6.

N.C. Stat., §7A-39.14 provides that the chief justice may recall a retired justice of the supreme court or judge of the appellate court, with the retired judge's consent, in the following additional circumstances:

1. To serve on the supreme court until a vacancy is filled.
2. To serve on the court of appeals until a vacancy is filled.
3. To serve on the supreme court to fill in for a sitting judge who is temporarily unable to perform the duties of the office.
4. To serve on the court of appeals to fill in for a sitting judge who is temporarily unable to perform the duties of the office.

Any justice or judge of the appellate division of the general court of justice who retires under Article 4 of Chapter 135 of the General Statutes, or who is eligible to receive a retirement allowance under that Act and who has not reached mandatory retirement age and has served at least five years as a superior court judge or justice or judge of the appellate division, or any combination thereof, and whose judicial service has ended within the preceding ten years, may apply to the governor for appointment as an emergency special superior court judge, N.C. Stat., §7A-45.2.

Upon reaching mandatory retirement age for superior court judges, any retired judge or any emergency special superior court judge appointed pursuant to §7A-45.2 may be recalled as a recalled emergency special superior court judge to preside over any regular or special session of the superior court, if the judge consents and the chief judge so orders and finds the judge capable of efficiently and promptly discharging the duties of the office to which recalled, N.C. Stat., §§7A-45.2; 7A-57.

Judges of the district court and judges of the superior court who have not reached mandatory retirement age but who have retired, may apply to become emergency judges of the court from which they retired upon application to and approval by the governor, N.C. Stat., §7A-52; §7A-53.

Note, however, that compensation as an emergency justice or judge does not affect the retirement allowance payable to him or her, N.C. Stat., §135-71(c).

Rule I of the N.C. Rules of Continuing Judicial Education, which require thirty hours in each biennium, is specifically made applicable to retired judges and justices qualified as emergency or recalled judges or justices, but the chief justice of the supreme court is authorized by Rule V to exempt justices or judges from that requirement for undue hardship by reason of disability or other cause.

PAY AND EMOLUMENTS

In addition to the compensation or retirement allowance the judge would otherwise be entitled to receive by law, each emergency judge of the district or superior court who is assigned to temporary active service by the chief justice shall be paid by the state the judge's actual expenses, plus $200 for each day of active service rendered upon recall. No recalled retired trial judge shall receive from the state total annual compensation in excess of that received by an active judge of the bench to which he or she is recalled, N.C. Stat., §7A-52(b).

NORTH DAKOTA

MANDATORY RETIREMENT PROVISIONS APPLICABLE GENERALLY

The legislative assembly may provide for the retirement of any judge, North Dakota Constitution, Art. VI, §12.1. Although there is no explicit mandatory retirement age, retirement is encouraged by age seventy-three pursuant to North Dakota Statutes, Section 27-17-01, which provides that any judge appointed or elected after July 1, 1960 who fails to make application for benefits prior to attaining age seventy-three shall waive all retirement benefits, except that a judge who has not served at least ten years at age seventy-three does not waive retirement benefits, provided he or she retires at the expiration of his or her present term, North Dakota Statutes, §27-17-01.

Article VI, §11, of the Constitution provides that when any justice or judge is unable to sit in court because he is physically or mentally incapacitated, the chief justice, or a justice acting in his stead, shall assign a judge, or retired justice or judge, to hear the cause. Article XI, §10, makes judicial officers subject to impeachment, and Article XI, §11, provides that an officer not liable to impeachment shall be subject to removal for habitual drunkenness or gross incompetency in such manner as may be provided by law. North Dakota Stat., §27-23-02(3) and (4) provide that on recommendation of the Commission on Judicial Conduct the supreme court may retire a judge for disability that seriously interferes with the performance of his or her duties and is, or is likely to become, permanent, but that a judge so retired must be considered to have retired voluntarily.

RETIREMENT PROVISIONS RE PARTICULAR COURTS

None.

OPTIONAL PROVISIONS FOR RETIREMENT

Based on years of service and/or age

North Dakota Constitution, Art. VI, §§12 and 12.1 authorize the legislative assembly to provide for retirement of judges. The legislature has established two retirement systems for judges—one for judges appointed or elected prior to July 1, 1973, North Dakota Stat., Chapter 27-17, the second providing that judges of the supreme court or district court elected or appointed after that date are governed by the public employees' retirement system established by North Dakota Stat., §54-52-02.3.

As to retirement under the first system, North Dakota Statutes, §27-17-01 states that any judge of the supreme court or district court has a vested right to judicial retirement at the time he or she ceases to serve, regardless of age, payable upon application at any time after attaining any of the retirement ages with years of service as follows:

- sixty-five and twenty years of service, or
- sixty-six and eighteen years of service, or
- sixty-seven and sixteen years of service, or
- sixty-eight and fourteen years of service, or
- sixty-nine and twelve years of service, or
- seventy and ten years of service

and that any judge serving fewer than the prescribed years of service will receive a retirement salary in proportion to the years of service.

North Dakota Statutes, §54-52-02.3 requires that judges of the supreme court or district court elected or appointed for the first time after July 1, 1973, must be members of the public employee retirement system and are not eligible for membership in, or receipt of benefits from, the retirement program established by Chapter 27-17, and defines "for the first time" to mean a person elected or appointed, who, after July 1, 1973, does not hold office as a judge of the supreme court or the district court at the time of his or her appointment or election.

The statute governing public employees' retirement provides for normal and early retirement dates. The normal retirement date for judges is the first day of the month next following the month in which the judge attains the age of sixty-five years, or when the member has a combined total of years of service credit and years of age equal to eighty-eight and has not received a retirement benefit under the system; and early retirement date is the first day of the month next following the month in which the member attains the age of fifty-five years and has completed five years of eligible employment, North Dakota Stat., §54-52-17(3)(a) and (d).

Based on disability

If a judge who is not a member of the public employees' retirement system is unable to serve due to mental or physical disability during the remainder of the term for which he is elected or appointed, he may petition the chief justice for his retirement, North Dakota Statutes, §27-05-03.1. A judge retiring under this provision shall receive the compensation allotted the office for the remainder of the term, and thereafter judicial retirement salary, regardless of age or years of service at that time, North Dakota Statutes, §27-05-03.2.

Under the public employees' retirement statute, disability retirement date is the first day of the month after a member becomes permanently and totally disabled and has completed at least 180 days of eligible employment, but the member is entitled to receive a disability benefit only if he or she became disabled during the period of eligible employment and has applied for such benefits within twelve months after he or she terminates employment, North Dakota Stat., §54-52-17(3)(e).

For prior service retirees (i.e. who served or were employed prior to January 1, 1966, North Dakota Stat., §54-52-01[11]) receiving benefits from the Public Employees' Retirement System on July 1, 1993, North Dakota Stat., §54-52-17.9 granted an increase of two percent in benefits beginning August 1, 1993, and North Dakota Stat., §54-52-17.10 on December 31, 1993, granted an increase of one percent in benefits beginning January 1, 1994.

Retirement and disability benefits payable by, or amounts received as a return of contributions and interest from, a retirement system established pursuant to state law by the state (with stated exceptions not applicable to judicial retirement benefits), are not subject to seizure upon execution or other process, North Dakota Stat., §28-22-19. Section 54-52-12, which exempted benefits from taxation and judicial process and prohibited assignment, was repealed by Chap. 286, §2 of the Laws of 1987.

SERVICE AFTER RETIREMENT

The chief judge may assign retired judges for temporary duty in any court or district under such rules and regulations as may be promulgated by the supreme court, North Dakota Constitution, Art. VI, §3.

The chief justice may appoint a retired judge, with his or her consent, to serve as a surrogate judge of the supreme court to aid and assist the court in the performance of judicial duties within the unified judicial system as the chief justice may assign, North Dakota Statutes, §27-17-03(1).

A retired judge of the supreme court or the district court is also eligible to serve as a master and to be compensated for services rendered in any civil case or other judicial proceeding. He or she is also eligible to serve as legal counsel and to be compensated for services rendered in the office of the attorney general, in any executive department, commission, or bureau of the state, and for any committee of the legislative assembly, North Dakota Statutes, §27-17-03(6).

The chief justice is authorized to assign retired judges for temporary duty in any court or district with consent of the retired judge to perform such specific duties as may be assigned for a term not to exceed one year, subject, however, to renewal, North Dakota Administrative Rule 15. The chief justice, with the approval of the supreme court and with the consent of a retired supreme court justice, retired district court judge, or surrogate judge, may assign such judge to serve on panels of the court of appeals in a particular case or cases when the case load of the supreme court so requires.

A retired judge may be assigned to serve on the temporary court of appeals established by §27-02.1-01.[3] He or she may not sit on any case he or she participated in while serving at the district court level or which originated in his or her judicial district, North Dakota Statutes, §27-02.1-02(2). A retired judge may not serve as a member of the Commission on Judicial Conduct, North Dakota Stat., §27-23-02.

Each judge of a court of record, including surrogate judges, must complete at least forty-five hours of continuing judicial education, at least three of which must be in judicial ethics, during each three-year period of service, commencing July 1, 1993, North Dakota Administrative Rules 36, Rule 4.

PAY AND EMOLUMENTS

A retired judge assigned to serve on the temporary court of appeals is entitled to receive compensation for each day of service in an amount equal to five percent of the gross monthly salary as provided for a regularly elected or appointed justice of the supreme court, or one-half the daily compensation for services of one-half day or less, North Dakota Statutes, §27-02.1-02(4).

---

[3] The section was enacted in 1987, effective until January 1, 1990, but has been extended periodically and is now effective until January 1, 2000.

A surrogate judge is entitled to receive compensation for each day of service in an amount equal to five percent of the gross monthly salary as provided for a regularly elected or appointed justice or judge of the court to which the services are rendered, or one-half that daily compensation for services of one-half day or less, North Dakota Statutes, §27-17-03(3). However, a surrogate judge shall not receive for his service during a calendar year a sum of money which, when added to his retirement pay, exceeds the annual salary of a judge of the court on which he qualified for retirement, *Id*, subd. 4. A surrogate judge is also entitled to reimbursement for travel expenses necessarily incurred in the performance of judicial duties, as regularly elected or appointed and qualified judges are entitled to receive, *Id*, subd. 5; see also §44-08-04.2. Mileage and travel expenses of state employees are governed by North Dakota Stat., § 54-06-09.

OHIO

MANDATORY RETIREMENT PROVISIONS APPLICABLE GENERALLY

No judge shall be elected or appointed to office if on or before the day he is to assume the office he shall have attained the age of seventy, Ohio Constitution, Article IV, §6(C).

Under the Ohio State Constitution, judges may be removed from office, by concurrent resolution of both houses of the general assembly, if two-thirds of the members, elected to each house, concur therein, Ohio Const., Art. IV, §17. Under Ohio's state law, judges may be, upon written and sworn complaint and after reasonable notice thereof and an opportunity to be heard, retired for disability, Ohio Const., Art. II, §38, Ohio Rev. Code, §2701.11. Grounds for retirement for disability exist when it is found on clear and convincing evidence[4] that the judge has a permanent mental disability which prohibits the discharging of the duties of his office, *Id*, or a physical disability which so impairs his or her faculties as to prevent the proper discharge of judicial duties for more than six months; and failure to be present in court or perform any judicial functions for six months raises a presumption of physical disability, Supreme Ct. Rules Gov. Jud. III(2) through (5), see also, Ohio Rev. Code, §§2701.11, 2701.12(B) and (C).

RETIREMENT PROVISIONS RE PARTICULAR COURTS

None.

OPTIONAL PROVISIONS FOR RETIREMENT

A judge may retire when he has reached age sixty-five or has completed thirty years of service. Ohio. Rev. Code, §3309.36. Retirement benefits are

---

[4] Compare §2701.11, which requires only that two-thirds of the members of the commission find that there is substantial credible evidence in support of the complaint.

available at a reduced level to judges who have not attained the above age or service requirements but have completed at least five years of service at age sixty. *Id.*

Ohio Rev. Code, §145.35 provides for disability retirement upon application of a member of the retirement system, a person acting on the member's behalf, or the member's employer, provided the member is not receiving age or service retirement benefits and has not been paid his or her accumulated contributions. The section requires that the application be made within two years from the date the member's services terminated, unless the retirement board finds that the medical records demonstrate conclusively that at the expiration of the two-year period the member was physically or mentally incapacitated and unable to make application. Examination by a board-selected physician is required, who determines whether the member is incapacitated by a disability condition either permanent or presumed to be permanent, that is, expected to last for a continuous period of not less than twelve months following filing of the application, and the board concurs in that determination. Ohio Rev. Code, §145.362 provides that the member is considered to be on leave of absence during the first five years following the effective date of the disability benefit. The board may require the employee to undergo medical examination, and if he or she is found capable of remaining in service similar to that from which he or she was found disabled, the disability benefit is terminated and the member, if the leave of absence has not expired, may be restored to his or her previous position. The board may also terminate the disability benefit at the request of the recipient.

Increase in retirement allowance, pensions, or other benefits which became effective prior to June 30, 1968, is provided for in Ohio Rev. Code, §145.322, the percentage of increase depending on the calendar year in which the benefit became effective. Section 145.323 requires that beginning April 1, 1971, the Retirement System Board increase each allowance, pension, or benefit by the average percentage change in the U.S. Department of Labor City Average for Urban Wage Earners and Clerical Workers: "all items 1982–1984 = 100" for the twelve calendar months prior to January 1 of the next preceding year, not, however to exceed three percent in any year, and the allowance, pension, or benefit not to exceed the limit established by 26 U.S.C.A. 415 as amended. Any such excess may, however, be accumulated and used to determine increases in subsequent years.

With stated exceptions (for example, a retirement pension under the auspices of an insider as defined in Ohio Rev. Code, §2329.66.2), a payment under any pension or annuity for disability, age, or length of service is exempt from execution, garnishment, attachment, or sale to satisfy a judgment or order, Ohio Rev. Code, §2329.66(A)(10). The exemption includes a federal pension or annuity, In Re Storer, 58 F.3d 1125, cert.-den.116 S.Ct. 520. See also §145.56, which exempts such pension or annuity from state, county, municipal, or local tax except school tax, and §145.75, which exempts employees' deferred compensation from legal process.

SERVICE AFTER RETIREMENT

Any voluntarily retired judge, or judge retired under Article IV, §6 of the Ohio Constitution, may be assigned with his or her consent by the chief justice of the supreme court to active duty as a judge, Ohio Constitution, Article IV, §6(C); Ohio Rev. Code, §141.16.

Any full-time municipal court judge who voluntarily retired, or judge retired under Article IV, §6(c) of the Ohio Constitution and who is not engaged in the practice of law, may be assigned with his or her consent by the chief justice of the supreme court to serve as a judge on any municipal or county court, M.C., Sup. R. Rule 13(A).

Any voluntarily retired judge, or judge retired under Article IV, §6 of the Ohio Constitution, may register with the clerk of any one or more of the courts of common pleas, municipal court, or county court for purposes of receiving referrals for adjudication of civil actions or for submission of particular issues in such an action, Ohio Rev. Code, §2701.10. The parties to any civil action may agree to have their case referred in full or in part to a registered judge. The parties must enter into a written agreement with the retired judge, in which they undertake to pay all costs and expenses of the proceeding and agree upon the amount of compensation to be paid such judge and the manner of payment, Ohio Rev. Code, §2701.10(B)(1). The retired judge so selected has all the powers of an active judge of the court, and his or her judgment or determination is subject to appeal as would be that of an active judge of the court, Ohio Rev. Code, §2701.10(C) and (D).

S.C.R. Gov. Jud. IV(3) requires retired judges serving pursuant to assignment to complete twenty-four hours of continuing legal education in every two years, but permits the Supreme Court Commission to grant temporary exemption from that requirement to a judge suffering severe, prolonged illness or disability, or as to whom the commission finds the special circumstances unique to the judge constitute good cause for so doing, or may approve a substitute program for a judge who has a permanent physical disability which makes attendance at such programs difficult.

PAY AND EMOLUMENTS

Any voluntarily retired judge or judge retired under Article IV, §6 of the Ohio Constitution called to active service shall receive the established compensation for such office computed on a per diem basis, in addition to any retirement benefits to which he may be entitled, Ohio Constitution, Article IV, §6(C); Ohio Rev. Code, §§141.16, 2743.04(B).

Any retired, full-time municipal court judge who is assigned to active duty shall receive actual and necessary expenses, plus the established compensation for a judge of the court to which he or she is assigned, computed on a per diem basis, in addition to any retirement benefits to which he or she may be entitled, M.C. Sup. R. Rule 13(B)(2), or, if he or she is a retired full-time municipal court judge who also is an active judge of the court of appeals or court of common pleas, fifty dollars, *id*(3).

OKLAHOMA

Oklahoma Constitution Article VII, Section 11(c) authorizes the legislature to provide by statute for the retirement of justices and judges automatically at a prescribed age or after a certain number of years of service, or both, but no such statute has been enacted.

Constitution Article VII-A, §1 authorizes compulsory retirement from office, with or without compensation for mental or physical disability preventing the proper performance of official duty, or incompetence to perform the duties of the office. The Rules of the Court on the Judiciary (Oklahoma Statutes, Article 5, Chapter 1, Appendix 7, Rule 8) prescribe the procedure for compulsory retirement for mental or physical disability or incompetence, on petition verified by the chief justice of the supreme court, the governor, the attorney general, the executive secretary of the Oklahoma State Bar Association or the Speaker of the House of Representatives (*id.*) When a justice or judge is ordered by the Court on the Judiciary to retire from office with compensation for reason of physical disability preventing performance of official duty, the compensation may not exceed seventy percent of the average monthly salary based on the last three years of active service and found applicable to such justice or judge at the time of retirement, Oklahoma Statutes, Title 20, §1102A(A). (Note, however, that while subdivision A of §1102A speaks of a justice or judge "ordered to retire from office" and, therefore, apparently deals with involuntary retirement for disability, subdivision C of that section, discussed under Optional Provisions for Retirement, below, is limited by its wording to a justice or judge who "make[s] application to the Court on the Judiciary for a determination of disability retirement benefits.")

RETIREMENT PROVISIONS RE PARTICULAR COURTS

None, the justices and judges of all present courts being covered by Oklahoma Statutes, Title 20, §1102(A), discussed under Optional Provisions for Retirement below. See, also, last paragraph of Service After Retirement.

OPTIONAL PROVISIONS FOR RETIREMENT

Oklahoma Statutes, Title 20, §1102, permits any justice or judge of the supreme court, court of criminal appeals, workers' compensation court, court of appeals or district court to elect to retire when he or she has served as justice or judge of any of said courts for eight years or longer and reached or passed the age of seventy, or has served for ten years or longer and reached or passed the age of sixty-five, or has served for twenty years or longer and reached or passed the age of sixty years, or whose sum of years of service and age equal or exceeds eighty, and may elect whether his or her retirement shall become effective immediately or at a specified time within his or her term or upon expiration of the term. Desire to retire is, under this section, evidenced by a written declaration filed with the governor, who endorses his approval thereon if the above specified conditions are met. In determining the periods of time above mentioned, a major fraction of a year is counted as a whole year (*id.*)

Voluntary retirement for disability is provided for in Oklahoma Statutes, §1102A(C), which provides that the justice or judge apply for such retirement to the Court on the Judiciary, which shall require that the justice or judge be examined by two recognized physicians selected by that court to determine the extent of the disability. Upon receipt of the report of the physicians, the court determines whether the justice or judge has a disability preventing proper performance of official duties. A disabled retiree is required to be examined once each year for three years following the start of his or her disability benefits by two physicians selected by the court, and if he or she is found no longer disabled by the physicians, the court shall terminate his or her disability benefits, but he or she shall then be entitled to receive such other benefits as he or she is entitled to by law.

Under Oklahoma Statutes, Title 20, §1103(C), a justice or judge who withdrew his or her retirement fund contributions upon prior termination of employment may, by repaying the amount withdrawn, plus interest at ten percent from the time of withdrawal, procure reinstatement of service credit for the prior years during which he or she previously served; and §1103F allows a member of the Uniform Retirement System for Justices and Judges, who is not receiving retirement benefits from the other Oklahoma retirement system(s), to transfer credited service accumulated while a member of such other system(s). Note, however, that under the last sentence of Oklahoma Statutes, Title 20, §1102A, as to any retired justice or judge elected or appointed to any political or judicial office, his or her retirement compensation is suspended during the period of time such office is held and reinstated when he or she leaves such office.

Under the conditions set forth in Oklahoma Statutes, §§1102B, 1103A and 1103B, a justice or judge may elect to bring his or her spouse under the survivor benefit of the State Judicial Retirement System, and the surviving spouse of a deceased justice or judge then becomes eligible under Oklahoma Statutes, §1102A(B), if the justice or judge had at least eight years of service and the spouse was married to him or her on the day of the termination of his or her employment and had been so married for at least three years immediately preceding his or her death, to receive survivor benefits, Oklahoma Statutes, §1102A(B)(1) and (2); but remarriage of the surviving spouse prior to reaching sixty years of age disqualifies the spouse from receiving such benefits, Oklahoma Statutes, §1102A(B)(4). Oklahoma Statutes, §1102A(C) permits a surviving spouse to apply to the Court on the Judiciary for disability retirement benefits, and if after physical examination the court finds the spouse disabled, the court shall order disability retirement benefits. To be noted, however, is that disability, as to a surviving spouse, is not defined.

Oklahoma Statutes, Title 20, §1104A increased benefits being paid a retired member on June 30, 1979 by ten percent; §1104D enacted a ten percent increase in benefits being paid beginning October 1, 1982; §1104E established the method for computation of the increase for members receiving benefits on July 1, 1994; and Title 62, §1001 made such an increase subject on and after July 1, 1995 to the effect of the increase on the retirement fund as computed pursuant to that section.

Oklahoma Statutes, Title 20, §1111, exempts any benefit or right accruing to any person under the Uniform Retirement System for Justices and Judges from execution, garnishment, attachment, or any other process or claim and not subject to assignment, except by a qualified domestic order which meets the requirements for such an order spelled out in that section.

SERVICE AFTER RETIREMENT

Const. Art. VII, §11, provides that any retired justice or judge may, in the discretion of the supreme court, be assigned to judicial service, and Oklahoma Statutes, Title 20, §1107, permitted justices or judges who held the status of supernumerary judge (abolished by Oklahoma Statutes, Title 20,

§1105), upon written application to the court administrator, to be assigned judicial duties by the supreme court.

Oklahoma Statutes, Title 20, §103.1 authorizes the chief justice of the supreme court to appoint temporary judges or judges pro tempore, and in Carter v. State of Oklahoma, 879 P.2d 1234, cert. den. 115 S.Ct. 1149, that section was held to authorize appointment of an active retired judge who had been defeated for reelection as a district court judge.

PAY AND EMOLUMENTS

Constitution Article VII, Section 11, provides that the compensation of retired justices or judges for service after retirement be fixed by statute, and Oklahoma Statutes, Title 20, §1104B(E) and (F) provide that a justice or judge so assigned shall receive a per diem of not more than $200, plus necessary expenses pursuant to the State Travel Reimbursement Act (Oklahoma Statutes, Title 74, §§500.1 and 500.2[C][1]) as determined by the supreme court, and shall be provided with office space, necessary equipment, and support staff as appropriate.

Oklahoma Statutes, Title 20, §1102E establishes a $4,000 death benefit to be paid upon death of a retired member to his or her beneficiary or estate, but §1108A requires that claims for such benefit be made within three years of the date of death of such member.

OREGON

Article VII, Section 1a of the Constitution mandates that a judge of any court retire at the end of the calendar year in which he attains the age of seventy-five years, but provides that the legislature may fix a lesser age for mandatory retirement not less than the end of the calendar year in which the judge becomes seventy years of age. Oregon Revised Statutes (ORS) §238.525 mirrors the constitutional provision, requiring retirement of a judge member of the Public Employees' Retirement System (PERS) at the end of the calendar year in which he or she reaches age seventy-five.

Involuntary retirement is likewise within legislative authority, Const. Art VII, §1a, empowering that body to authorize or require retirement of judges for physical or mental disability or any other cause rendering a judge incapable of performing judicial duties. See also Constitution Art. VII, §20, which provides that the governor may remove a judge of the supreme court upon the joint resolution of the General Assembly in which two-thirds in each house concurs for incompetency, corruption, malfeasance, delinquency in office, or other sufficient cause stated in the resolution.

Prior to August 1, 1991, there was a Judges Retirement Fund, but ORS §238.055 provided that as of that date the fund ceased to exist, after that date those receiving benefits from that fund became retired members of the Public Employees' Retirement System, and after that date any judge who would have become eligible to receive retirement pay from the Judges Retirement Fund upon retirement became a member of PERS, except that the eligibility to receive retirement pay or pension was determined by ORS §§1.314 to 1.380.

Involuntary retirement of judges for disability is dealt with in ORS §1.310 and §238.555. The provisions of §1.310 define judge to include any judge of the supreme court, the court of appeals, the tax court, or of any circuit or district court, and define disabled to mean so incapacitated physically or mentally as to be unable to discharge the duties of judicial office,[5] and authorizes the filing by named state and bar association officials of a request for investigation, of which the named judge receives a copy. If the judge does not resign, the Commission on Judicial Disability and Fitness makes an investigation, and if it finds the judge is in fact disabled, makes written findings of fact, from which the judge may appeal to the supreme court. That court conducts a proceeding de novo on the record, but may also remand to the commission for additional findings. Pursuant to ORS §1.425 the commission may direct the judge prior to hearing to submit to physical examination by a doctor, or up to three doctors, appointed by the commission or to a mental evaluation by one, two, or three physicians, psychologists, or other mental health professionals, or both, and if the judge fails to submit to examination, may consider that as evidence that the judge has a disability. The supreme court reviews the record on the law and the facts, and may retire the judge. ORS §238.555 provides that a judge retired under §1.310 receives such retirement allowance as he or she is entitled to under §238.555.

Both ORS §§238.320 and 238.555 deal with disability retirement. Section 238.320 states that a member who is found disabled "shall receive a disability retirement allowance," but in subd. (5) measures the time within which an "inactive member" must apply for such allowance from his or her "date of separation from service." It is unclear, therefore, whether retirement for disability under the section may be involuntarily imposed. Section 238.555, on the other hand, states that a member who meets its conditions "shall be retired," and, therefore, it is unclear whether it authorizes voluntary application by a member for disability retirement. (See also the second paragraph of Optional Provisions for Retirement, below.)

RETIREMENT PROVISIONS RE PARTICULAR COURTS

None.

OPTIONAL PROVISIONS FOR RETIREMENT

Service retirement is provided for in ORS §238.535, which requires that prior to age sixty a judge member elect to retire either at age sixty-five or

---

[5] Note, however, the apparent inconsistency of ORS §1.303, which in subd.(1)(c) defines

thereafter, having contributed to PERS during each of five calendar years, or at age sixty or thereafter, having contributed to PERS during each of five calendar years. A judge who fails to elect prior to age sixty may only retire at age sixty-five or thereafter, and an election made prior to age sixty becomes irrevocable when the judge attains age sixty. A judge who retires at age sixty or thereafter is retired on a reduced service allowance and must serve as a pro tem judge, without compensation, for thirty-five days per year for a period of five years from the member's date of retirement, but may be relieved of that requirement for good cause, including physical or mental incapacities that prevent the judge from discharging the duties of judicial office. Note that ORS §238-435(3) provides that as to a person establishing membership in PERS on or after January 1, 1996, normal retirement age is sixty. Prior thereto, ORS §238.005(18) defines normal retirement age as fifty-eight for employees other than police officers and firefighters.

Retirement for disability is allowed for both accidental injury or disease sustained while in actual performance of duty and not self-inflicted, ORS §238.555, and mental or physical incapacity for an extended duration from a cause other than accidental injury or disease so sustained, ORS §238.320(3), but in the latter case application by a judge who has separated from service must be made within five calendar years after separation from service, ORS §238.320(5).[6] A judge who has not attained age sixty-five, who has six or more years of service as a judge, and is found to be mentally or physically incapacitated for an extended duration, and thereby unable to perform any work for which qualified from cause other than accidental injury or disease, is retired on a pension equal to the service retirement allowance to which he or she would have been entitled had the judge served continuously until age sixty-five, but not less than forty-five percent of his or her final average salary, ORS §238.555. ORS §238.335 empowers the board to require medical examination by all applicants for disability retirement and to discontinue allowance for any person who refuses to submit to such examination; and §238.340 provides that if the

---

disability to mean a physical or mental condition of a judge including but not limited to impairment derived in whole or in part from habitual or excessive use of intoxicants, drugs, or controlled substances, that significantly interferes with his or her capacity to perform judicial duties, and provides for a procedure different from that of §1.310, and for removal rather than retirement, or, as provided in ORS §§1.425 and 1.435, for temporary suspension.

[6] See fifth paragraph of Mandatory Retirement Provisions Applicable Generally, above.

board determines that a disability retiree is not so incapacitated to the extent that he or she is disabled from performance of any work for which he or she is qualified, the disability retirement is canceled forthwith and the judge is eligible for reemployment. Both §§238.335 and 238.340 apply to disability retirement pursuant to §238.555. In making its determinations, the board may conduct hearings, and subpoena and examine witnesses and records; but ORS §238.655, which so provides, states that the procedures in such hearings shall be informal.

Cost of living adjustment of retirement allowances is dealt with in ORS §238.360, which provides for an increase or decrease in the allowance as of July 1 of each year based on the consumer price index (Portland area-all items) for July, and in §238.575, which requires that the monthly retirement allowance or pension payable to a judge member be readjusted to reflect the increase or decrease in cost of living required by §238.360, and that as to a judge member who retired in 1984 or thereafter, the retirement allowance be increased in varying percentage based on the year in which the judge retired.

Exemption of a pension, annuity, or retirement allowance from taxes, other than inheritance tax and state personal income tax, and from execution, garnishment, attachment, or other process, or the operation of any bankruptcy or insolvency laws, is provided for by ORS §238.445, which also makes such interests unassignable. However, ORS §238.445 excepts from such exemption a support obligation, and §238.465 also excepts a court decree of annulment or dissolution of marriage or separation or settlement agreement incident thereto. Note, however, that ORS §316.157 provides for a tax credit of an amount equal to the lesser of the tax liability of the taxpayer or nine percent of net pension income for taxable years after January 1, 1995, based on the age attained by the taxpayer during specified years after 1995. (See also Bresman v. Bresman, 42 Or. App. 739, 601 P.2d 851 construing §237.201, which is essentially identical to §238.445, holding pension funds exempt from legal process for the collection of delinquent support payments.)

SERVICE AFTER RETIREMENT

Section 1a(2) of the constitution authorizes the legislature to provide for recalling retired judges for temporary active service in the court from which retired, and Section 2(a) provides that the legislature may empower the supreme court to appoint retired judges of the supreme court as temporary members of the supreme court. ORS §1.300 provides that a judge who retires from the district court, circuit court, tax court, court of appeals or supreme court (other than one involuntarily retired, see ORS §1.310[7]), may be designated by the supreme court as a senior judge. A senior judge is eligible, with his or her consent, for temporary assignment to a state court when the supreme court determines that it is necessary for efficient administration of justice. A retiree from the supreme court may be assigned to any state court. A retiree from a court other than the supreme court may be assigned to any state court other than the supreme court, the duration of either such assignment being as stated in the assignment order, except as is necessary to complete a cause or to settle a transcript for appeal. A retiree appointed a senior judge has all the powers and duties of a regularly elected and qualified judge while serving under assignment. Note, however, that ORS §238.535(c) requires service by a retiree as a judge pro tem, without compensation, for thirty-five days a year for five years. See also ORS §1.635, which permits appointment of any "eligible person" to serve as a judge pro tem of the tax court, circuit court, or district court. No definition of "eligible person" has been found, but presumably it would include a retired judge of the respective courts.

PAY AND EMOLUMENTS

A senior judge assigned under ORS §1.300 shall receive as compensation for each day the senior judge is actually engaged in the performance of duties under the assignment an amount equal to five percent of the gross monthly salary of a regularly elected and qualified judge of the court to which the senior judge is assigned, or one-half of that daily compensation for services of half a day or less. However, the judge shall not receive an amount during a calendar year which, when added to his retirement benefits, exceeds the annual salary of a judge of the court from which the senior judge retired. The senior judge will also be reimbursed for expenses necessarily incurred in the performance of duties under an assignment in a court outside the county in which the senior judge regularly resides, ORS §1.300(5) and (6).

A judge who retires at age sixty as provided in ORS §238.535 is, as noted above, required to serve as a judge pro tem for thirty-five days during each year for five years after retiring, without compensation, but is reimbursed for expenses incurred in providing such services, *id*, subd (c).

PENNSYLVANIA

Pennsylvania Constitution Article V, §16(b) mandates retirement of justices, judges, and justices of the peace upon attaining seventy years of age; see also, 42 Pennsylvania Consolidated Statutes Annotated, §3351.

Any judge may be compulsorily retired by the supreme court if, after investigation by the Judicial Conduct Board (formerly the Judicial Inquiry and Review Board, see Const. Art. V, §24) and an opportunity of the judge to be heard, it finds probable cause that the judge suffers from a disability seriously interfering with the performance of his or her duties and files formal charges with the Court of Judicial Discipline. The charges then become a matter of public record. They must be proven by clear and convincing evidence. The decision of the court is then subject to review by the supreme court, or, if a justice of the supreme court is the subject of the charges, by a special court. Unless the supreme court or the special court holds the finding of mental or physical disability clearly erroneous, or the recommended sanction unlawful, it may order removal from office, retirement, suspension, or other limitation of the activities of the justice, judge, or justice of the peace. A judge who is compulsorily retired has the same rights and privileges as if he or she were retired for age, Const. Art. 5, §§18(a)(9), (b)(5), (c)(1) and (2), (d)(1); 42 Pa. C.S.A. §§3331-3332, 3334. Note, too, Rule 33 of the Rules of Procedure of the Judicial Conduct Board, which provides that the board may require a physical, psychiatric, or psychological examination of the judicial officer, and that the unjustified failure to submit to such examination may be considered as evidence of physical or mental disability, and Rule 601 of the Rules of Procedure of the Court of Judicial Discipline, which contains a similar provision. Note also that 71 Pa. C.S.A., §5908(b) requires an annuitant receiving a disability annuity to submit a written statement within thirty days of the close of each calendar quarter of all income earned during that quarter, that the failure to do so may result in the board refusing to make further payments, and if the member's refusal to do so continues for six months, the member's rights to disability annuity payments in excess of any annuity to which he or she is otherwise entitled are forfeited; and that §5908(c) requires that a disability annuitant submit to a medical examination by a physician or physicians nominated by the board, with like penalties for the member's refusal or failure to do so. Moreover, §5908(d) places on the member the burden of establishing continued disability.

RETIREMENT PROVISIONS RE PARTICULAR COURTS

None.

OPTIONAL PROVISIONS FOR RETIREMENT

Title 42, Chap. 33, Subchap. D, deals with retirement of Judicial Officers. However, it contains only two sections: §3351 (referred to in Mandatory Retirement section above), which provides that judges and district judges shall be retired at age seventy, and §3352, which provides that former and retired judges and district judges shall receive such compensation as shall be provided by or pursuant to statute. Title 71, Part XXV, deals with Retirement for State Employees and Officers and, in §5102, defines "member of the judiciary" to mean "any justice of the supreme court, any judge of the Superior Court, the Commonwealth Court, any court of common pleas, the Municipal Court and the Traffic Court of Philadelphia or any community court."

The only provisions dealing with the age and/or years of service that entitles a judge to retire with benefits are contained in the statutes relating to the "Retirement of State Employees and Officers," contained in Title 71. Superannuation annuitant is defined by 71 Pa. C.S.A. §5102 as one whose annuity first becomes payable on or after attainment of superannuation age, and "superannuation age" as "any age upon accrual of 35 eligibility points or age 60"; and in 71 Pa. C.S.A., §5307 defines "eligibility points" as one point for each year of credited service as a member of the State Employees' Retirement System or the Public School Employees' Retirement System, including fractional points for fractional parts of a year of such service. The annuity does not become effective, however, until the member files an application for it, 71 Pa. C.S.A., §5907(h). Note, however, that a member who terminates service and is not a disability annuitant may opt to receive an immediate annuity or to withdraw his or her total deductions to the retirement system, or, if he or she has ten or more eligibility points, to vest his or her retirement rights until attainment of superannuation age for subsequent exercise, 71 Pa. C.S.A., §§5907(f) and 5309.

A disability annuity may be voluntarily applied for by the member or a person legally authorized to act on his or her behalf, with or without a supplement, if the disability is service connected, 71 Pa. C.S.A., §5907(k), if he or she has credit for at least five years of service, provided the board finds him or her mentally or physically incapable of continuing to perform his or her duties as a judge, and qualified in accordance with the provisions of §5905(c)(i); 71 Pa. C.S.A. §5308(c). Section 5905(c)(i) requires the board to have the application reviewed by the medical examiner, and after consideration of his report respecting permanency and the need for subsequent reviews, the board then makes a finding of disability and whether it is service connected or not, the effective date of disability, and the terms and conditions regarding subsequent reviews.

The right of a retiree to any benefits is exempt from state or municipal tax, levy and sale, garnishment, attachment, spouse election, or any other process, except for setoff by the commonwealth for repayment of money owed on account of employment or on account of a loan from a credit union which has been satisfied by the board from the fund, and is unassignable, except to the commonwealth as above noted, to a credit union as security for a loan, to forfeiture under the Pension Forfeiture Act, or to attachment as set forth in a qualified domestic relations order, 71 Pa. C.S.A., §§5953 and 5953.1-5953.4.

Service After Retirement

A former judge (i.e. one who vacates office upon expiration of his term or resigns prior thereto, 45 Pa. C.S.A., §3352[b]) or a retired judge, who has not since his or her last judicial duty engaged in the practice of law and does not intend to engage in the practice of law in the future, who has not been defeated for re-election and his served as a judge (whether or not continuously or on the same court) for an aggregate of at least ten years, except that any justice or judge having an aggregate of six years, who is required to retire at age seventy, may, with his or her consent, be assigned on temporary judicial duty by the chief justice of the supreme court, Const. Art. V, §16(c); 42 Pa.C.S.A. §4121(b), Pa. R.J.A. No. 701(a). A senior district justice who was not defeated for reelection or suspended or removed from office may, with his or her consent, be assigned on temporary magisterial service, 42 Pa.C.S.A. §4122(b).

A senior judge of the Philadelphia Municipal Court who has not been defeated for reelection or suspended or removed from office and who has served an aggregate of four years as an elected judge and who is required to retire at age seventy may, with his or her consent, be assigned temporary judicial service to that court, 42 Pa.C.S.A. §4124.

42 Pa. C.S.A., §3118 requires that district court judges must attend continuing legal education courses for 32 hours per year, but makes no mention of retired judges.

PAY AND EMOLUMENTS

Compensation for senior judges was fixed by 42 Pa. C.S.A., §3581(h) at $275 per day, but subdivision (i) of that section (which expires January 1, 2001) provides for an annual cost of living adjustment equal to the percentage increase in the Consumer Price Index for Urban Workers for the preceding twelve-month period. Note, however, that 71 Pa. C.S.A., §§5708 through 5708.4 deal with additional monthly supplemental annuities and special supplemental postretirement annuities computed for various years as provided in those sections, and that effective January 1, 1997 and each January 1, thereafter, 65 P.S., §366.2a(i) requires that the annual salary of various judges and justices, including senior judges, is increased by the percentage change in the Consumer Price Index for All Urban Consumers for the Pennsylvania, New Jersey, Delaware, and Maryland area for the most recent twelve-month period for which figures have been officially reported by the U.S. Bureau of Labor Statistics. In any calendar year the amount a senior judge earns when added to his retirement benefits may not exceed the compensation payable by the commonwealth to a judge in active service on the court from which said senior judge retired, 65 P.S. §366.2a(h). Retired judges are also reimbursed for travel, lodging, and subsistence expenses as provided by Rules of the supreme court, 42 Pa. C.S.A., §§4122(b) and 4123, Pa. R.J.A. No. 701(i).

A senior district justice shall be paid a per diem salary at the same annual rate as is applicable in the district where he or she is temporarily assigned and shall receive expenses at the same per diem rate as other justices temporarily assigned, 42 Pa.C.S.A. §4122(b).

RHODE ISLAND

The Rhode Island Constitution and statutes are silent regarding a mandatory retirement age for justices of the supreme court and lower courts.

Article XI, §3, of the Constitution does, however, permit removal of a judicial officer found to be incapacitated, and R.I. Stat., §§8-16-4 through 8-16-14 establish the Commission on Judicial Tenure and Discipline and authorize it, upon receiving a verified statement indicating that a judge has a physical or mental disability that seriously interferes, and will continue to interfere, with the performance of his or her duties, or, on its own, to make a preliminary investigation, if it finds substantial evidence thereof to hold a public hearing on notice to the judge, and if it recommends retirement, requires that it file its certified recommendations and a transcript of the hearing with the supreme court. If the judge has not reached retirement age, its recommendations may include that his or her pension rights become effective as of the date of retirement.

After such hearings as the supreme court deems necessary, it takes such action as it deems necessary to give effect to such of the commission's recommendations for retirement for disability or incapacity as it affirms or modifies, but if it endorses the recommendation for advancement of the judge's retirement date must forward that recommendation to the general assembly for legislative action. Note, however, that R.I. Stat., §§8-16-7(b) and 8-16-9(a) provide that a justice of the supreme court may not be retired for disability without his or her consent, but if consent is withheld, a further recommendation is then made to the speaker of the house of representatives to initiate proceedings for removal of the judge pursuant to Const. Art X, Sec. 4; and Art. XI. R.I. Stat., §8-16-9(b) provides that a judge retired for disability or incapacity shall be deemed to have retired voluntarily.

R.I. Stat., §8-16-9(c) requires that if the supreme court rejects the recommendation of the commission its decision be published, and §8-16-14 provides that if the judge complained against retained counsel and the complaint is dismissed by the commission, the judge is entitled to have his or her reasonable counsel fee paid by the state.

RETIREMENT PROVISIONS RE PARTICULAR COURTS

Retirement of workmen's compensation court judges is dealt with in R.I. Stat., §§28-30-15(a) and 28-30-16(a), which provide, respectively, for retirement on reduced pay or on full pay based upon the same age and service requirement provided for in §§8-3-7(a) and 8-3-8(a) discussed in the Optional Provisions section below. Note, however, that the provision for cost of living adjustment of the retirement compensation for workmen's compensation judges is computed similarly to that for the judges discussed in the last paragraph of the Optional Provisions section below, except that R.I. Stat., §28-30-18 provides that the worker's compensation judges adjustment *is* compounded.

OPTIONAL PROVISIONS FOR RETIREMENT

Rhode Island has a system known as the Employees' Retirement System of the State of Rhode Island, R.I. Stat., Title 36, Chaps. 8, 9 & 10 (hereafter "ERS"), but also provides for retirement of judges of various courts in statutes relating to the courts dealt with in Title 8, Chaps. 3 and 16 and Title 28, Chap. 30 (hereafter "Judicial System"). R.I. Stat., §36-9-5 provides that a justice or judge of the supreme court, superior court, family court, district court, administrative adjudication court, or workmen's compensation court who prior to becoming a justice or judge was a member of the ERS may remain a member of that system by filing a waiver of all benefits under §§8-3-7 to 8-3-11 or 28-30-15 to 28-30-18, both inclusive, and making contributions based on his or her salary as such justice or judge, and is then eligible for benefits under the ERS. There are material differences between the two systems, however. The judicial system provides for mandatory disability retirement, but no provision for disability retirement on application of the judge or justice has been found, whereas the ERS makes provision for both ordinary and accidental disability on application of the member, the department head, or a person active on the member's behalf, R.I. Stat., §§36-10-12 and 36-10-14, subject to annual medical examination while the disabled member is under the minimum age for service retirement, R.I. Stat., §39-10-17.

Any justice of the supreme court, the superior court, the family court, or the district court, or any combination thereof, who has served for twenty years and reached age sixty-five, or has served for fifteen years and reached age seventy, may retire at the same annual salary he or she was receiving at the time of retirement, R.I. Stat., §8-3-8(a). Note, however, that §8-8-10 provides that a district court judge retiring under the same age and service requirements receives a pension of only three-quarters of the salary he or she was receiving at the time of retirement.

A justice who has served on those courts, or any combination thereof, for twenty years, or has served for ten years and reached age sixty-five, may retire and thereafter receive a pension of three-quarters of the annual salary he or she was receiving at the time of retirement, R.I. Stat., §8-3-7(a).

A justice of such courts whose combined service as a member of the general assembly, a justice, and a general officer, is twenty years or more and who has retired, resigned, or completed such service, upon reaching age sixty-two receives a pension of three-quarters of the highest annual salary he or she was receiving during such service, R.I. Stat., §8-3-12.

A judge or justice who elected to remain a member of the ERS and waived benefits under the Judicial System may retire upon written application, provided that on his or her retirement date the member has attained age sixty and completed at least ten years of total service or who, regardless of age, has completed twenty-eight years of total service, R.I. Stat., §36-10-9(a), and except as to a member retiring for ordinary or accidental disability, or a member of the municipal retirement system who retired pursuant to R.I. Stat., §§45-21-19 through 22 under that system for ordinary or accidental disability, the member shall have been a contributing member of ERS for at least ten years, R.I. Stat., §36-10-9(c).

All justices of the supreme court, superior court, family court, or district court who retired after January 1, 1970, who receive a retirement allowance, or their surviving spouses, shall, as of the third anniversary date of such retirement, receive a cost of living retirement adjustment equal to three percent of the original retirement allowance and in each succeeding year an additional three percent of the original allowance, not compounded, R.I. Stat., §8-3-15(a). However, a retired judge assigned to duty does not receive credit for such service in the computation of the amount receivable by him or her or his or her surviving spouse, Bulman v. Kane, n.o.r., 519 A.2d 1123.

ERS benefits are exempt from municipal or state tax, except for personal income tax, R.I. Stat., §36-10-32, and under §36-10-34 are exempt from lien, attachment, or garnishment, and are not transferable or assignable, except that a governmental agency by which the member was employed which has a claim against the member has the right to payment at the time any refund of contributions is made to the member. No similar provisions of the Judicial System for exemption from tax or execution has been found.

SERVICE AFTER RETIREMENT

Any justice of the supreme court who retired pursuant to §8-3-8(a), shall at the direction of the chief justice of the supreme court, subject to the retiree's physical and mental competence, be assigned to perform such services as an associate justice of the supreme court as the chief justice of the supreme court shall prescribe, R.I. Stat., §8-3-8(c).

Any justice of the supreme court, the superior court, the family court, or the district court, or any combination thereof, who became such on or *before* July 2, 1997 and who has served for twenty years, or has served for ten years and reached age sixty-five, may retire and receive for life three-fourths the salary he or she was receiving at the time of retirement pursuant to §8-3-7(a), or who has served for twenty years, or for ten years and reached age sixty-five, may retire and receive for life three-fourths of his or her average highest three consecutive years of compensation, §8-3-7.1(a). Such a judge who became such *after* July 2, 1977 and has served for twenty years and reached age sixty-five, or for fifteen years and reached age seventy, may retire and receive for life the full amount of the annual salary he or she was receiving at the time of retirement, §8-3-8(a), or who has served for twenty years and reached age sixty-five, or for fifteen years and reached age seventy, may retire and receive annually for life a sum equal to his or her average highest three consecutive years of compensation, §8-3-8.1(a). Under each of those sections and under §36-9-5 (re judges who opted to remain in the public employees retirement system) the judge *may*, at his or her request and at the direction of the chief justice of the supreme court, subject to the retiree's physical and mental competence, be assigned to perform such services as an associate justice of the Superior Court, the family court, or the district court, as the presiding justice of the Superior Court or the chief judge of family court or the district court shall prescribe, R.I. Stat., §8-3-7(b). Likewise, a retired judge of the workman's compensation court *may*, at his or her request and at the direction of the chief judge of said court, subject to physical and mental competence, be assigned to serve as a judge of said court, R.I. Stat., §28-30-15(b). Note, however, that R.I. Stat., §8-3-8(b) provides that any justice of the supreme court, the superior court, the family court or the district court who retired pursuant to §8-3-8(a), *shall* at the direction of the chief justice of the supreme court, subject to the retiree's physical and mental competence, be assigned to perform such services as an associate justice of the superior court, the family court, or the district court, as the presiding justice of the superior court or the chief judge of the family court or the district court shall prescribe, and that §8-3-8(c) also provides that a retired justice of the supreme court *shall*, at the direction of the chief justice of the supreme court, subject to the same conditions, be assigned to perform such services as an associate justice of the supreme court as the chief justice of that court shall prescribe.

R.I. Stat., §8-17-1, establishes a program of litigating civil trials, including domestic relations matters, whereby the litigants, by agreement, may retain the services of any retired justice of the supreme court or superior court, or retired judge of the family court or district court, to hear the merits of the issues before the court, all without a jury. Such a trial shall be conducted in private, the cost of the proceedings shall be borne by the parties, and any judgements issued thereunder shall have the same effect as judgements of a court of competent jurisdiction and may be appealed to the supreme court.

While Rhode Island has a system of mandatory continuing legal education, it does not apply to state and federal court judges, magistrates and masters whose duties are full time, and presumably therefore applies to a retired judge sitting by assignment, unless the assignment requires full-time duty, Supreme Court Rules, Rules 3.2(b)(3) and 5.05.

PAY AND EMOLUMENTS

Any justice or judge of the supreme court, superior court, family court, district court who retired pursuant to §8-3-7, §8-3-8 or §8-3-12, and who shall subsequently be assigned to perform such services in accordance with §§8-3-7 or 8-3-8, shall receive while performing such service, in addition to his or her retirement pension, the difference in pay and fringe benefits between what he or she was entitled to receive prior to exercising his or her options available under §8-3-11 (to receive only three-fourths of retirement pay in consideration of his or her surviving spouse's receiving one-half of the judge's retirement pay during the surviving spouse's lifetime or until he or she remarries) and what a judge or justice with comparable state service time is receiving as a justice or judge of the court to which he/she is assigned, or a justice or judge of the court from which he/she retired, whichever is greater, R.I. Stat., §8-3-10.

SOUTH CAROLINA

The Retirement System for Judges contained in South Carolina Code Annotated, Title 9, Chap. 8, defines the judges covered by the system to mean "a justice of the supreme court or a judge of the court of appeals, circuit or family court," S.C.C.A. §9-8-10(17), and in §9-8-60 provides that any member of the system may retire upon written application "not later than his [or her] attaining age seventy-two."

South Carolina Constitution, Article V, §17, gives its supreme court the power to remove or retire any judge from office after hearing upon a finding of disability seriously interfering with the performance of his or her duties, which is, or is likely to become, of a permanent character.

Retirement Provisions re Particular Courts

Probate judges may elect to participate in the Police Officer Retirement System or to remain under the regular state retiring system, S.C.C.A., §9-11-25.

Optional Provisions for Retirement

S.C.C.A., §9-8-60, permits any member of the system to retire prior to age seventy-two, provided he or she makes written application for retirement and meets the provisions of that section concerning age and years of credited service, or who has completed twenty-five years of credited service regardless of age.

S.C.C.A., §9-8-60(3) provides that a member who has a minimum of five years of credited service, upon application, "shall be permitted to retire" when it is proven to the satisfaction of the supreme court, or a majority thereof, that the member is totally and permanently disabled, physically or mentally, or both, from rendering useful and efficient service. The five-year minimum is not required, however, if the member is disabled as a result of an injury arising out of and in the course of his or her duties on or after July 1, 1985, if the medical board certifies that the member is mentally or physically incapacitated from further performance of duty, that the incapacity is likely to be permanent, and that the member should be retired.

S.C.C.A. §9-8-190 exempts retirement benefits from state or municipal tax, except income and estate taxes, and from legal process, and makes them unassignable except to beneficiaries.

SERVICE AFTER RETIREMENT

A justice or judge drawing retirement pay who engages in the practice of law may not serve as a justice or judge in any court in the state. Within thirty days of retirement, a retired judge or justice must make an irrevocable election as to whether he or she wishes to engage in the practice of law or be eligible for appointment by the chief justice as a judge or justice in the courts of the state, S.C.C.A., §9-8-120(4).

To be eligible for appointment, a retired justice or judge must have been screened within two years of his or her appointment and found qualified to serve, but if he or she retired before the expiration of his or her then current term, screening is not required until that term would have expired, S.C.C.A., §14-1-215. Provided he or she is willing to accept assignment and has been screened and found qualified to serve, a retired judge or justice from the supreme court, court of appeals, or circuit court may be assigned to preside in any circuit court; a retired judge or justice from the supreme court or court of appeals may be assigned to act as an associate justice or judge in any proceeding before the supreme court or court of appeals; and a retired judge from the family court may be assigned to preside over any official proceeding in any family court. Such assignments are made by the chief justice of the supreme court, S.C.C.A., §§9-8-120(3), 14-1-215.

The parties to an appeal in a civil case may agree to arbitration of the appeal before three arbitrators selected by the parties, who may be retired justices, retired judges, active or retired attorneys, or a combination thereof, who consent in writing to serve, S.C. Rules of Appellate Practice, Rule 223.

To be noted also is S.C.C.A., §14-5-170, which provides that when "no other disengaged circuit judge is available to hold such courts," the governor shall immediately commission as a special judge a person learned in the law recommended by the supreme court, or by the chief justice if that court is not in session, to hold the courts of the circuit or any special session thereof which the chief justice may order, and that a special judge so appointed has all the powers and duties that a regular judge would have. The section does not preclude appointment of a retired justice or judge, but since the chief justice is involved in both the assignment of retired justices or judges and the appointment of special judges, it seems doubtful that a retired justice or judge would be appointed a special judge.

PAY AND EMOLUMENTS

A retired justice or judge serving as an acting associate justice or judge serves without pay, except for his or her actual expenses while serving; but if his or her judicial duties extend beyond three consecutive months, he or she receives, in addition to retirement pay for each full month of service, the difference between retirement pay and active pay, S.C.C.A., §9-8-120(3). A retired justice or judge serving as an arbitrator under S.C. App. Ct. Rule 223 receives actual expenses and compensation of $150 per case acted on. A special judge appointed pursuant to S.C.C.A., §14-5-170 receives a per diem of $150 for each day of trial, and for not more than five additional days expended in preparation of his or her decree, plus necessary expenses, S.C.C.A., §14-5-200.

SOUTH DAKOTA

South Dakota Codified Laws, §16-1-41 as to supreme court justices, and §16-6-31 as to circuit court judges provide, that the justice or judge is automatically retired on the first Tuesday after the first Monday of January next after the general election at which members of the legislature are elected immediately following the attainment of age seventy of such justice or judge, but also permit the justice or judge to conclude all matters pending before him or her unless the supreme court makes other provisions for the disposition of such matters. There is, however, no similar provision with respect to magistrate judges who, under S.D.C.L., §16-12A-41, are subject to removal only upon recommendation of the Judicial Qualifications Commission and action of the supreme court thereon, as to which see next paragraph.

Disability that seriously interferes with the performance of his or her judicial duties (see also, S.D.C.L., §3-12-47[26] defining "disability") is a ground for involuntary retirement of a justice or judge after investigation and hearing, pursuant to Constitution Article V, Section 9. Under that section a justice or judge may be retired or removed for habitual intemperance or disability that seriously interferes with the performance of duties. Investigation and hearing are conducted by the Judicial Qualification Commission pursuant to Rules of Procedure adopted by the supreme court. Under those rules (which appear in S.D.C.L as an Appendix to Chapter 16-1A) the commission prepares a report stating its findings of fact and recommendation concerning retirement, which is then reviewed by the supreme court. A member eligible to receive a disability allowance must report in writing no later than May 31 following the end of each calendar year in which a disability allowance is paid, other than the year in which the member dies or converts to a normal or early retirement benefit, any earned income of the member, and failure to file such a report suspends the disability allowance until such filing is made, S.D.C.L., §3-12-143.

Retirement Provisions re Particular Courts

None.

Optional Provisions for Retirement

All justices, judges, and law-trained magistrates are members of the South Dakota Retirement System, S.D.C.L., §3-12-62. Normal retirement is defined by S.D.C.L., §3-12-47(48) as "the termination of employment of a member with five or more years of credited service on or after his normal retirement age for any cause other than death," and normal retirement age for justices, judges and magistrate judges is age sixty-five, *id.* (49).

A retired justice or judge who leaves employment as such after five years of credited service but does not withdraw his or her accumulated contributions is said to be "vested", *id.* (73), and is entitled to an annuity payable at normal retirement age or can retire during the ten years preceding his or her normal retirement age on a reduced allowance, S.D.C.L., §3-12-106, but is not entitled to disability benefits (S.D.C.L., §3-12-47[73]). A nonvested member who has terminated employment and left his or her contributions in the system who does not return to employment with a governmental unit having employees who are members of the retirement system within five years of such termination must withdraw his or her accumulated contributions with interest, and membership in the system terminates, S.D.C.L., §3-12-79. But if a person whose contributions have been refunded since July 1, 1974 reenters the system, his or her credited service forfeited when the contributions were refunded is reinstated if he or she redeposits the refunded contributions with compound interest within two years after reentry to the system, S.D.C.L., §3-12-80. And if a person who retired on a reduced allowance pursuant to §3-12-106 becomes employed prior to normal retirement age as a full-time employee by a governmental unit having employees who are members of the retirement system, his or her annuity is suspended during such employment, S.D.C.L., §3-12-111.

Voluntary retirement for disability is provided for in S.D.C.L., §3-12-98, which requires that if application therefor is not filed with the administrator within three years of the date on which the member's service ended, the right to disability benefits is forfeited. Section 3-12-100 provides that the board of trustees shall set the criteria for determining the disability of members and that the methods of doing so be applied uniformly and consistently; and §3-12-141 requires that no such application be determined until the employer has certified to the retirement system that it is unable to provide comparable level employment. When a person receiving disability allowance reaches age sixty-five, or if over age sixty at the time of commencement of disability after a period of five years, the disability allowance is terminated, and he or she receives the allowance payable for service retirement at that age, S.D.C.L., §3-12-103; and if a person who received a disability allowance returns to employment prior to normal retirement age, his or her credited service shall include the time of disability (*id*). A member who withdraws from the retirement system and within twelve months thereafter becomes a permanent full-time justice, judge, or magistrate, must have at least three years of contributory service since the date of last withdrawal, unless the member was disabled by accidental means while performing his or her usual duties. As to a member eligible to receive a disability allowance, see the concluding sentence under Mandatory Retirement, above.

As to increase in benefits for a retiree, see S.D.C.L. §§3-12-47, 3-12-124 and 13-12-125.

The rights of any member of the South Dakota Retirement system are exempt from any state, county, municipal, or other local tax and from execution, garnishment, attachment, operation of bankruptcy or insolvency laws, or any other process of law, and are unassignable except as required by applicable law, including a qualified domestic relations order as defined in the Internal Revenue Code, S.D.C.L, §3-12-115.

SERVICE AFTER RETIREMENT

Constitution Article V, Section 11, provides that the chief justice of the supreme court is the administrative head of the unified judicial system and empowers him or her to authorize retired justices and judges to perform any judicial duties to the extent provided by law and as directed by the supreme court. S.D.C.L., §16-1-5 provides that retired justices and judges, with their consent, may be authorized by the chief justice to act in place of disqualified justices, vacancies, or other necessities as determined by the chief justice. S.D.C.L., §16-6-32 permits the chief justice to authorize a retired justice or judge to preside in any action or proceeding, or over any term of court, in the circuit court, with the same effect as though he or she were a regularly elected or appointed judge; and §16-12A-101 provides that the chief justice may authorize a retired justice or judge, with his or her consent, to preside in any action or proceeding, or any term of court, in the magistrate court with the same effect as though he or she was a regularly appointed magistrate.

Pay and Emoluments

No provision for compensation of a retired justice or judge sitting by assignment, other than his or her retirement benefits, has been found, but S.D.C.L., §§16-1-5,16-6-32 and 16-12A-10.1 each directs the supreme court to provide for reimbursement of the expenses of a retired justice or judge appointed under the provisions of the respective section.

TENNESSEE

Tennessee Code Annotated (TCA) provides in §8-34-715 that a state judge shall receive full retirement credit for service rendered after such judge's seventieth birthday, but neither the Tennessee Constitution nor any statute establishes a mandatory retirement age for a judge of any court.

Involuntary retirement for disability is provided for in TCA Article 17, Chapter 5,[7] which in its various sections sets forth a multi-stage procedure. Article 17 provides in §17-2-116(a)(2) that if a judge or chancellor does not himself or herself certify the disability to the governor, and the chief justice of the supreme court determines that he or she is disabled as to prevent carrying out the duties of office for a period of ninety days or more, the chief judge has authority to certify the disability to the governor. Section 17-5-101[1][A]) creates the Court of the Judiciary and authorizes it to inquire into the physical, mental, and/or moral fitness of any judge, and on its own or pursuant to the complaint of anyone having reason to believe a judge is disabled, to investigate and take appropriate action, including recommendation of removal from office when it finds that an active judge is suffering from any disability, physical or mental, which is, or is likely to become, permanent and which would substantially interfere with the prompt, orderly, and efficient performance of judicial duty (TCA, §17-5-303). Under TCA §§17-5-303 through 17-5-311, if the court's disciplinary counsel finds the information would not constitute disability, he shall dismiss the complaint subject to review by the court's investigative panel; or, if he finds it would constitute disability, he conducts a preliminary

---

[7] To be noted is that TCA, §8-34-701 repealed Title 17, Chapter 2 (Judges' Retirement System) and Title 17, Chapter 5 (Retirement System for County-paid Judges) as of July 1, 1972, the date as of which the Consolidated Retirement System was created by TCA, §§8-34-201 and 202. However, §§8-34-703 and 709 preserved the rights of prior class members, and §8-34-707 preserved the rights of a member of a superseded system to ordinary or accidental disability retirement under the superseded system. To be noted also is that TCA, §17-2-109 ff. regarding special and substitute judges, and §17-5-101 ff. regarding the Court of the Judiciary, have been amended as recently as 1995 and 1996.

investigation and recommends investigation by the court's investigative panel, which then either dismisses the complaint or authorizes a full investigation. Notice is then given the judge, and after his response the panel may dismiss or direct disciplinary counsel to file formal charges, which the judge has thirty days to answer. Unless the judge consents to retirement or removal, the matter is then tried before a hearing panel of the Court of the Judiciary, which issues formal findings of fact and an opinion. If the court report recommends removal from office, the judge may appeal to the supreme court, the judgment of which is final unless it affirms the recommendation for removal, in which event the question of removal is referred to the General Assembly for final determination, and a joint House and Senate committee hears the appeal de novo, based on the record and argument of counsel, but without hearing any additional evidence. Complaints to the Court on the Judiciary and its proceedings prior to the filing of formal charges are confidential.

RETIREMENT PROVISIONS RE PARTICULAR COURTS

Tennessee has a consolidated retirement system, the provisions of which relating to judges are referred to above and are also discussed under Optional Provisions for Retirement. County judges taking office after July 1, 1977 may become members of the consolidated system if the county in which they are employed is participating in the system, and county judges elected or appointed to full time positions taking office after June 30, 1981 may participate in the consolidated system under the conditions set forth in TCA, §8-35-116. "County judge" is defined in TCA, §8-34-101(7) as a person who is or was a judge of a general session court, trial justice court, county judge, probate judge, or judge of a juvenile and/or domestic relations court, and whose compensation is paid wholly by a county of the state. City judges may also become members of the consolidated system if the municipality adopts a resolution so providing, TCA, §8-35-234.

OPTIONAL PROVISIONS FOR RETIREMENT

Prior to July 1, 1972 there were separate retirement systems, one of which was the Judicial Retirement System, which as of that date were superseded by the Consolidated Retirement System. A person who became a judge on or after July 1, 1972 became a member of the consolidated system as a condition of employment, a person who on June 30, 1972 was a member of a superseded system became a member of the consolidated system as of July 1, 1972, and any person who on June 30, 1972 was not a member of a superseded system who was a state judge or a county judge could elect to become a member of the consolidated system by filing with the board of trustees within ninety days after July 1, 1972 an election to become a member, TCA, §8-35-101. TCA, §8-35-105 classified employees by group, of which only Groups 3 and 4 covered judges[8], Group 3 covering all state judges and county judge and Group 4 covering state judges entering service after September 1, 1990 and transferring membership from the superseded system as provided in TCA, §8-34-711.

Service retirement requires for a Group 3 judge attainment of sixty-five years of age or attainment of fifty-five years of age and completion of twenty-four years of creditable service, and for a Group 4 judge attainment of sixty-five years of age with eight years of creditable service or attainment of fifty-five years of age with twenty-four years of creditable service, TCA, §8-36-201; see also §8-36-204(a). For early service retirement with a reduced allowance, a Group 3 judge must have attained fifty-five years of age with eight years of service, and a Group 4 judge must have attained sixty years of age with eight years of service, TCA, §8-36-301; see also §8-36-204(b)(1).

Voluntary retirement for disability is available upon application by any Group 3 or 4 judge who has completed eight years of creditable service, payable at nine-tenths of service retirement allowance until the member reaches service retirement age, at which time the judge becomes entitled to a full service retirement allowance, TCA, §8-34-501. Accidental disability retirement allowance is available to a Group 1 or 2 member, but no provision for such an allowance for judges is made.

Disability is defined by TCA, §8-34-101 Subds. 13, 27 and 43 to mean the inability to engage in any substantial gainful activity by reason of a medically determinable physical or mental impairment, which is both totally and permanently disabling and which can be expected to last for a continuous period of not less than twelve months. Disability is determined

---

[8] TCA, §8-34-601(c) speaks of "[a]ny Group 1, Group 3 or Group 4 state judge," but since TCA, §8-35-105 defines Group 1 as teachers and general employees, and §8-34-101(18), which defines general employee, expressly states that the term "does not include any . . . state judge, county judge," it is not clear to whom the "Group 1 judge" classification applies.

by the board of trustees after examination of medical records by the medical board, TCA, §8-36-504. Primary in the determination is the severity of impairment, but when medical factors alone are not determinative, consideration of vocational factors, including the individual's age, education, training, and work experience must be considered, and if they indicate that the individual is capable of retraining for other employment within a twelve-month period, the individual shall not be considered disabled, *id.* A disability retiree who has not attained retirement age may be required to submit annually to examination by a physician or physicians designated by the board of trustees, and should any disability beneficiary who has not attained the age of sixty refuse for ninety days to submit to such annual examination, his or her monthly retirement benefits may be suspended by the board of trustees, TCA, §8-36-505. Should the medical board certify that the disability beneficiary is able to engage in substantial gainful activities, and should the board of trustees concur, the board may suspend or reduce his or her monthly benefit, and if the board determines that he or she is in fact engaged in such activity, the monthly benefit shall be suspended; but if the beneficiary's earning capacity is later changed, the monthly benefit may be restored if the evidence substantiates that he or she is no longer able to engage in gainful activity, TCA, §8-36-506. A disability retiree who has not yet attained service retirement age may be required to report on an annual basis income other than retirement benefits, and should the board determine from such reports that the disability retiree is able to engage in gainful employment, the amount of his or her disability benefit may be reduced at the discretion of the board, *id.*

Cost of living adjustment in retirement allowance is provided for in TCA, §8-36-701, which directs an increase or decrease in allowance as of the end of each calendar year based upon the difference between the Consumer Price Index (all items—United States city average) and 100 percent, provided the percentage thus determined is at least equal to one percent but not to exceed three percent, or, if the beneficiary at retirement elects an actuarially reduced benefit, not to exceed six percent, and provided further that the retiree has been retired for a minimum of twelve months on July 1 next following the December 31 as of which the percentage is determined.

Retirement allowances and other benefits and the accumulated contributions of members, as well as the cash and assets of the retirement fund, are exempt from any state, county, or municipal tax and are not subject to execution, attachment, garnishment, or other process whatsoever. Nor is any assignment thereof enforceable in any court, TCA, §8-36-111, except with respect to claims of the state against a member who is terminated and who elects to withdraw his or her accumulated contributions, or against a member who elects to retire, whose debt to the state may be satisfied from the member's monthly benefits, TCA, §§8-36-113, 8-36-114. To be noted, however, is TCA, §26-2-104, which provides that moneys received by a resident of Tennessee as a pension from the state or any subdivision or municipality, before receipt, or while in his or her hands or upon deposit in the bank, are exempt from execution, attachment, or garnishment by a creditor, other than the state, except for an order for assignment of support or the claim of an alternate payee with a qualified domestic relations order.

SERVICE AFTER RETIREMENT

Const. Art. VI, Section 11, authorizes the legislature to provide that special judges may be appointed to hold any court the judge of which is unable or fails to attend or sit; or to hear any cause in which the judge may be incompetent. The wording of that section and the definition of incompetency in TCA, §17-2-101 make clear that incompetency does not include disability, but the reference to a judge who is unable to attend or sit makes clear that the legislature is authorized to provide for special judges in case of disability. It has done so in a number of statutes, some of which refer specifically to retired judges, others of which do not mention, and thus, apparently, do not exclude retired judges who meet the qualifications called for by the statute.

Statutes that authorize appointment of special judges for reasons other than incompetency of an active judge, and permit appointment of retired judges, are: TCA, §17-2-109, which authorizes the chief justice of the supreme court, when litigation in any chancery, circuit, criminal, or appellate court becomes congested or delay in disposition of litigation becomes imminent, to assign a retired chancellor or judge to assist in removal of the congestion or delay; TCA, §17-2-121, which authorizes the parties to a complex civil case or one desired to be disposed of expeditiously to agree to employ a retired or former judge to hear the case without a jury and provides that judgment may be entered on the findings of the retired or former judge and that the judgment may be appealed as in any other civil case; and TCA, §8-36-806, which empowers the chief justice of the supreme court to assign any retired state judge to hold any court to relieve congested dockets or sit for a judge who may be incapacitated or who may be absent because of illness or otherwise. To be noted with respect to §8-36-806 is that §17-2-109(c) states that nothing in that section shall be construed to interfere with the appointment of special chancellors or judges as provided elsewhere by statute.

TCA, §17-2-116 makes no mention of retired judges but appears to be broad enough to include them. It provides that when a judge of the circuit court, criminal court, other special courts, a court of general sessions, or a chancellor is unable from sickness or other physical disability to hold court, the governor shall appoint and commission a special judge having the same qualifications as the regular judge to hold court during the absence or disability of the regular judge; and if a judge or chancellor does not certify such disability to the governor, and the chief justice of the supreme court determines that he or she is so disabled as to prevent carrying out the duties of his or her office for ninety days or more, the chief justice has authority to certify such disability to the governor, and the governor shall appoint a special judge having the same qualifications as the regular judge or chancellor to hold court during such disability and until the chief justice certifies to the governor that the judge or chancellor is no longer disabled. TCA, §17-2-118 likewise makes no mention of retired judges and refers to appointees pursuant to its provisions as "substitute judges" rather than "special judges." It permits a judge of a state trial court of record who by reason of illness, physical incapacitation, or absence related to the judge's office himself to appoint as a substitute judge a person possessed of all of the qualifications of a judge of the court to which the substitute is appointed and as to whom all litigants present at the beginning of the proceeding consent, to hold court, but not for more than three days unless a trial commenced during that period requires more time to complete.

TCA, §17-2-301 ff. provides for designation of a retired supreme court justice, judge of an intermediate appellate court, or judge of a state court of record as a senior justice or judge, provided the justice or judge makes written request for such designation, accompanied by evidence that as of the date of retirement he or she does not suffer from a permanent physical or mental disability that would substantially interfere with performance of duties, and a written agreement that he or she will not engage in the practice of law while so serving and will be available to perform judicial duties for at least an aggregate period of thirty weeks out of each successive twelve-month period, §17-2-302. Designation is for a term of four years unless the justice or judge has reached seventy years of age, in which latter event the term is for two years or such shorter period deemed proper by the supreme court. Senior justices and judges are eligible for reappointment, and the supreme court's decision on designation or renewal is final and not subject to review, §17-2-303. Status as a senior justice or judge terminates upon (1) expiration of the term, (2) when the judge or justice so requires, (3) the Court on the Judiciary so orders, or (4) the justice or judge declines more than three assignments without good cause within any calendar year, §17-2-306. As stated in §17-2-308, the provisions of this part of the statute are in addition to Chapter 17 and §§8-36-806 and 16-3-502(2).

Continuing legal education of at least fifteen hours per year is required for all attorneys by Supreme Court Rule 21, which permits attorneys over age sixty-five to petition for exemption. The rule makes no mention of judges or retired judges.

PAY AND EMOLUMENTS

TCA, §17-2-111 provides that a retired justice or judge appointed pursuant to §§17-2-109, 17-2-110 or 16-3-502(2)[9] receive his or her regular salary plus expenses as certified by the judge or justice pursuant to supreme court rule. Under §17-2-117 a special judge or chancellor appointed pursuant to §17-2-116 draws the same salary and receives the same emoluments as the regular judge or chancellor has. Pursuant to §17-2-305 a senior justice or judge receives, in addition to his or her retirement allowance, an annual salary equal to the lesser of fifty percent of the current annual compensation of the office from which he or she retired or the difference between the annual retirement allowance and such current annual compensation, as well as office space and equipment, secretarial and research assistance, and a law library; and if assigned to a court outside his or her county of residence, reimbursement for travel expenses the same as provided to an active justice or judge.

A retired state judge assigned to duty pursuant to TCA, §8-36-806 is paid, in addition to the retirement allowance for the period during which he or she sits as a judge, the difference between his or her retirement allowance for the period and the amount he or she would receive for that

---

[9] Section should refer to subd. 3, which authorizes the Supreme Court to direct the administrative director of the court to assign retired judges to appropriate judicial duties.

period if he or she were an active judge of the same court. The section makes no mention of expenses. To be noted, however, is that TCA, §8-26-101, which makes no mention of retired judges assigned to duty pursuant to §8-36-806, provides that justices of the supreme court, judges of the intermediate appellate court, criminal court judges, circuit court judges, and chancellors shall be reimbursed for necessary office rent, supply and equipment expense, and travel expenses pursuant to policies and guidelines promulgated by the supreme court.

TEXAS

Texas Constitution, Art. 5, §1-a(1) provides that the office of justices and judges of the Appellate Courts and District and Criminal District Courts "shall become vacant when the incumbent reaches the age of seventy-five (75) years or such earlier age, not less than seventy (70) years as the Legislature may prescribe, but, in the case of an incumbent whose term of office includes the effective date of this Amendment, this provision shall not prevent him from serving the remainder of said term nor be applicable to him before his period or periods of judicial service shall have reached a total of ten (10) years." No statute providing for earlier mandatory retirement of such judges has been enacted. The effective date of the Amendment was November 2, 1948.

Constitution Art. 5, §1-a(6)(B) provides for involuntary retirement or removal from office of a justice or judge for disability seriously interfering with the performance of his or her duties, which is likely to become permanent in nature.

Retirement Provisions re Particular Courts

None.

Optional Provisions for Retirement

Retirement based on age and years of service is provided for in V.A.T.S. Government Code, §834.101, under which a member of the retirement system may apply for service retirement if (1) he or she is at least sixty-five years old, currently holds a judicial office, and has at least ten years of service credited in the system, or (2) is at least sixty-five years old and has at least twelve years of service, continuous or otherwise, regardless of whether he or she currently holds a judicial office, or (3) has at least twenty years of service, the most recently performed of which was for a continuous period of at least ten years, regardless of whether the member currently holds a judicial office, or (4) may retire on a reduced pension under (1) or (2) above, if the member is at least sixty years old, *id.*, §834.101; see also §§832.003, 834.002. Application must be filed with the board of trustees of the retirement system, *id.*, §834.002, and the chief justice of the supreme court must certify that the applicant is entitled to the pension (*id.*, §834.003). Statutory probate judges are county officials but; since there are 254 counties in the state, review of their voluntary retirement provisions has not been undertaken.

A member of the retirement system may apply for disability retirement, V.A.T.S. Government Code, §834.002, regardless of age, provided the member has at least seven years of service credit in the retirement system, (*id.*, §834.201[a]) and he or she files with the supreme court written reports of two physicians licensed to practice in Texas, "fully reporting" (sic) the claimed physical incapacity, (*id.*, §834.202[a]). The chief justice may appoint a physician licensed in Texas to make such additional medical investigation as the court finds necessary (*id.*, §834.202[b]). If the chief justice does not find a claimed physical incapacity to have been caused by or resulting from intemperate use of alcohol or narcotic drugs, and certifies that the member is mentally or physically incapacitated for further performance of regular judicial duties (*id.*,§834.201[b], [c]), the member is entitled to a disability retirement annuity payable for the duration of the disability (*id.*, §834.203).

Service After Retirement

Texas has had two different retirement systems for judges: the Judicial Retirement System of Texas Plan One and the Judicial Retirement System of Texas Plan Two, V.A.T.S. Government Code, §§832.001, 837.001. Both relate to judges or justices of the supreme court, the court of criminal appeals, a court of appeals, or a district court (*id*).

Assignment to judicial duties of retirees who are members of Plan One is governed by Government Code, Chapter 74; assignment of retirees who are members of Plan Two is governed by Government Code, Chapter 75; and assignment of statutory probate judges is governed by Government Code, Chapter 25. Those provisions speak of assignment not only of retirees, but also "former judges," the distinction being, apparently, between retirement on the one hand and failure to run for reelection, failure of reelection, or resignation (other than resignation after notice that the Judicial Conduct Commission has instituted formal proceedings against the former judge, Government Code, §74.055[c][4]) on the other, see Lanford v. Fourteenth Court of Appeals, 847 S.W.2d 581; Jackson v. State, 567 S.W.2d 222; Whittington v. Whittington, 638 S.W.2d 92; Op. Atty. Gen. 1986, No. JM 586.

To be eligible for assignment, a retired or former judge must have served for at least forty-eight months in a district, statutory county, or appellate court, unless he or she is a former district judge who has served on more than one district court, must have developed substantial experience in one or more of criminal, civil, or domestic relations cases, not have been removed from office or resigned after initiation of proceedings against him or her, certify to the presiding judge of the administrative region willingness not to appear and plead as an attorney in any Texas court for a period of two years, and demonstrate annually that he or she has during the past calendar year completed the educational requirements for active district and statutory court judges, *id.*, §§74.055, 75.115. The certificate of willingness not to appear or plead as an attorney may be revoked at the end of any two-year period, but if not revoked, recertification for subsequent two-year periods takes effect by operation of law, *id.*, §74.0551.

Note, however, that the qualifications of senior district court judges of the First Administrative Judicial Region omits the requirements for certification of willingness not to appear and plead as an attorney, and of completion of education courses, but adds provisions that the judge have served as judge of a district court for twelve years, not necessarily consecutively, and that he or she be sixty-five years of age or younger, *id.*, §75.104. The election by a retiree to serve as a senior judge may be made to the chief justice not later than the ninetieth day after the date of the person's retirement, or, after the ninetieth day, by petition addressed to the supreme court. If made within the ninety-day period, the election is effective upon approval by the chief justice, but if made after the ninety-day period is effective only upon approval by the court of the election petition, *id.*, §75.001. A retiree assigned pursuant to Chapter 74 or 75 has all of the powers of a judge of the court to which he or she has been assigned, *id.*, §§74.059(a), 75.001(c). The assignment continues only during the period for which the retiree or former judge has certified a willingness to serve, *id.*, §§74.056(d), 75.003(b).

Assignments of retired and former judges are made by the chief justice or the presiding judge of an administrative district, *id.*, §§74.056, 74.057, 75.002, but V.A.T.S Government Code, §26.023, permits a county judge who is going to be absent from the county or absent because of incapacity to appoint a retired judge as a special judge to sit during his or her absence. Retired statutory probate judges may be assigned to judicial duty by the presiding judge of the statutory probate court, V.A.T.S., §25.0022(j). The multiple and complex provisions for assignment of retired or former judges of various courts need not be spelled out, except to note that a retired district judge, a former judge with at least twelve years service as a district judge, or a retired appellate judge with judicial experience on a district court, may be assigned as a presiding judge of the district court, *id.*, §74.045 (see also §75.109), and that a retired judge seventy-five years of age or older may serve as such a presiding judge or in other active duty assignments, Wexlin v. Calvert, 460 S.W.2d 398. Thus retired judges are eligible for service after retirement without limitation as to age. Also to be noted is that §74.053, which permits a party to a civil case to disqualify the assigned judge by simply filing an objection before the first hearing or trial, including pretrial hearings over which the assigned judge is to preside, limits each party to a case to one objection for that case as to a retired judge, though not as to a former judge, State ex rel Holmes v. Lanford, 837 S.W.2d 705; see, Garcia v. Employers Insurance of Wausau, 856 S.W.2d 507, 509, writ denied. That §74.053 applies to assignments of a judge or justice under Government Code, Chapter 74 or 75 was specifically stated in Section 9 of the 1991 amendment of it, Chapter 785, 72nd Legislature.

However, the assignment provisions are strictly construed. Only after his or her election to serve becomes effective does a retired judge or justice who elects as provided in §75.001 to become a judicial officer or senior judge have jurisdiction to act; any action prior thereto is absolutely void, Lone Star Industries v. Ater, 845 S.W.2d 334, 335-336, rehearing overruled; Houston General Insurance Co. v. Ater, 843 S.W.2d 225, 226, rehearing overruled; see also State ex rel Holmes v. Lanford, *supra.*

Finally, under V.A.T.S., Civil Practice and Remedies, Title 7, Chapter 151, which is entitled Alternate Methods of Dispute Resolution, a retired or former district, statutory county court, or appellate court judge who has served at least four years in a district, statutory county court or appellate court, has developed substantial experience in his or her area of specialty, has not been removed from office or resigned while under investigation for discipline or removal, and annually demonstrates that in the past calendar year he or she has completed at least five days of continuing legal education may, in civil or family law matters, on agreement of the parties and the filing by each party of a motion so requesting, be designated by the judge in whose court the case is pending, as a special judge, with all the powers of a district court judge, except as to holding in contempt a person other than a witness before him or her, to hear the case. The special judge's verdict stands as a verdict of the district court and may be appealed as an order of that court.

With respect to the various statutory provisions referred to in this section on Service After Retirement, Constitution, Art. V, §1-a(6)(c) must be kept in mind. It provides that "[u]nder the law relating to the removal of an active Justice or Judge, the Commission and the review tribunal may prohibit a retired or former Judge from holding judicial office in the future or from sitting on a court of this State by assignment." Under that provision, the services of a retired or former judge or justice may be terminated for disability.

V.A.T.S Government Code §834.004 exempts all Plan One (which prior to September 1, 1995 was referred to as the Judicial Retirement System of Texas) payments to retirees from garnishment and state and local taxation.

PAY AND EMOLUMENTS

A retired judge of the supreme court, of the court of criminal appeals, or of a court of appeals who is assigned out of the county of his or her residence, receives the same salary and expenses and per diem that the regular judge receives for such services, V.A.T.S. Government Code, §§74.003(c), the salary being determined pro rata for the period of time that the judge or justice actually sits as the assigned judge, id., §74.061(c); and a former judge or justice receives the same salary and expenses that the regular judge is entitled to receive for the services actually performed, id., §74.061(d). A retired or former district judge or retired appellate judge who is assigned as a presiding judge receives a salary depending on the number of districts courts and statutory county courts in the administrative district over which he or she presides, id., §74.051(c). He or she is also entitled to receive travel and other expenses incurred in attending meetings of the judges or continuing judicial education courses, id., §74.062.

A senior district judge for the First Administrative Judicial District who is a retiree is entitled to compensation, salary, and expenses equal to the highest amounts paid to any regular district court judge in the state, less any annuity that the judge receives from the retirement system, *id.*, §75.109(b), and during a period of assignment to all per diem allowances paid to judges sitting outside the county of their residence, *id.*, §75.110(d), as well as actual expenses incurred in going to and returning from the assignment and living expenses incurred during assignment, *id.*, §75.114. He or she is, however, entitled to receive retirement benefits during the period of assignment, but not to retirement credit for the time served during the assignment, *id.*, §75.112(a).

A former or retired judge of a statutory probate court assigned to sit as a judge of said court is entitled to daily compensation equal to that of a judge of a statutory probate court in the county to which he or she is assigned, *id.*, Chap 25, §25.0022(p), plus reasonable and necessary expenses for travel, lodging, and food, *id.*, §25.0022(q), and if assigned to a county outside that of his or her residence, twenty-five dollars for each day or fraction of a day served, *id.*, §25.0022(t) and actual and necessary expenses for travel to and from meetings and those incurred while attending the meeting, *id.*, §25.0022(u).

The compensation of a special judge appointed to sit in a county in which there is no statutory county court at law or statutory probate court and all duties devolve upon the county judge is, for each day he or she sits as a special judge, 1/365th of the county judge's annual salary, *id.*, §§26.021, 26.026.

The compensation of a special judge sitting in alternative dispute resolution proceedings must be agreed upon by the special judge and the parties, is set forth in the motion for referral, and is paid by the parties in equal shares, V.A.T.S., Civil Practice and Procedure, Title 7, §§151.002, 151.009.

UTAH

Constitution Article VIII, Section 15, states that the legislature may provide standards for the mandatory retirement of justices and judges from office, and Utah Code Annotated (UCA) §49-6-801, see also §49-6-203, requires that a judge or justice of a court of record retire upon attaining the age of seventy-five years, but permits a judge or justice who is sixty-five or older on July 1, 1996 to serve until December 31 of the year in which he or she would have been subject to a retention election. UCA §78-5-137(5) requires a county or municipal justice court judge to retire upon attaining the age of seventy-five years, but bars such a judge who is serving on July 1, 1996 and who reached seventy-five before that date, or on or before the first Monday in February 1999 (county justice court judge), or on or before the first Monday in February 2000 (municipal justice court judge), from reelection or reappointment.

Involuntary retirement of any justice or judge for disability is provided for in Const. Art. VIII, §13 and in the Judicial Code (UCA §§78-7-28 through 78-7-30). Section 13 of the Constitution authorizes the Judicial Conduct Commission to retire involuntarily any justice or judge for disability that seriously interferes with the performance of judicial duties; and UCA §78-7-28(1)(d) repeats that language, as does §78-7-29, adding, however, the words "and which is, or is likely to become, of a permanent character" and making its provisions applicable to a "justice, judge or justice court judge of any court of this state." It also apparently makes its procedural provisions applicable not only to involuntary retirement, but also to an application by such a judicial officer desiring to retire on grounds of disability who certifies to the Judicial Conduct Commission his or her request for retirement.[10]

---

[10] Initially, the Judges Retirement Act provided for disability retirement of justices and judges in §§49-6-501 and 49-6-502. These sections were repealed effective July 1, 1987, but the rights of justices and judges who had retired under those provisions were protected when the Public Employees Disability Act was enacted in 1987 (see UCA §§49-9-403[1][a][ii] and 49-9-408[3]). As to the applicability of the latter act to disability retirement of justices and judges, see Optional Provisions for Retirement, below.

The procedure for determination of the right to disability retirement is prescribed in UCA §§78-7-29 and 78-7-30. Those sections require an investigation by the Judicial Conduct Commission, after which the matter may be set for formal hearing, notice thereof being given the justice or judge, which may include the identity of the complainant, any findings or order being upon majority vote of the quorum of the commission; or, alternatively, the commission may appoint as special masters three justices or judges of courts of record to hear and report. Action by the commission must be based upon the recommendations of one or more medical examiners or physicians as well as examination of statements submitted by the bar or judicial associations, certifying that the judge is disabled as above defined, and should be retired. The supreme court then reviews the record on the law and the facts and may take additional evidence. If the court orders retirement, the justice, judge, or justice court judge shall retire with the same right and privileges as if he or she retired pursuant to statute. The proceedings are confidential until the supreme court enters its final order, unless it orders otherwise, or the judge or justice complained against so requests; but in the event of dismissal, the complainant must be so informed without the consent of the judge or justice complained against.

RETIREMENT PROVISIONS RE PARTICULAR COURTS

As to mandatory retirement of county justice court and municipal justice court judges, see discussion above.

OPTIONAL PROVISIONS FOR RETIREMENT

Retirement of justices and judges of courts of record is provided for in two acts: the Judges Retirement Act, UCA §§49-6-101 ff. and the Judges Noncontributory Retirement Act, UCA §§49-6a-101 ff., the differences being that in the noncontributory system contributions are made entirely by the employer, §49-6a-301(1), and that justices and judges of courts of record appointed after July 1, 1997, automatically become members of the noncontributory system, UCA §49-6a-203; a justice or judge of a court of record appointed prior to that date becomes a member of the contributory system, UCA §49-6-203, but may elect to participate in the noncontributory system, provided he or she does so prior to January 1, 1998. Both cover justices and judges of courts of record, §§49-6-201 and 49-6a-201, and provide for a retirement benefit calculated in the same way, the language of §§49-6-402 and 49-6a-402 dealing with benefit calculation being identical.

Normal retirement age is defined as sixty-five years of age, §§49-6-103(3) and 49-6a-103(3), but a member of either may retire if, on or before the effective date of proposed retirement, he or she has at least six years of service and is seventy years of age or older, or has at least ten years of service and is sixty-two years of age or older, or has at least twenty years of service and is fifty-five years of age or older, or, regardless of age, has twenty-five years of service, UCA §§49-6-401, 49-6a-401.

Voluntary retirement for disability is authorized by UCA §78-7-29(1), which states that any justice, judge, or justice court judge desiring to retire on grounds of disability shall certify to the Judicial Conduct Commission his or her request for retirement and the nature of the disability. Subdivision 2 of that section requires that the approval or disapproval of such an application be based upon the evaluation of one or more medical examiners, and examinations of statements submitted by committees of the bar or judicial associations, certifying that the justice, judge, or justice court judge is mentally or physically disabled and totally incapacitated from further performance of his duties and that the incapacity is likely to continue and to be permanent. UCA §78-7-30, which details the Judicial Conduct Commission procedures, discussed under Mandatory Retirement above, is, however, limited by its express wording to *involuntary* retirement. Furthermore, while the Public Employees Disability Act's definition of "employee" in UCA §49-9-103 appears to include judicial full-time employees (see §§49-9-403[1][a][ii] and 49-9-408[3] discussed under Mandatory Provisions above), UCA §49-9-401(1) turns upon "receipt of proof by the board *from an employer* that an employee has become totally disabled as a result of (a) accidental bodily injury which is the sole cause of disability and is sustained while [the Act] is in force, (b) disease or illness causing total disability commencing while [the Act] is in force, or (c) physical injury resulting from external force or violence as a result of the performance of duty" (emphasis supplied). In view of the italicized words, it is unclear whether subd. (1)(b)'s reference to disease or illness covers an application for voluntary retirement. In any event, if it does apply, the benefit payable is reduced by amounts received from listed third-party sources; and the employee is required to apply at the earliest eligible age for all retirement benefits to which he or she may be entitled, UCA §49-9-402.

Cost of living increase or decrease based on the Consumer Price Index is provided for in both Judicial Retirement Acts (UCA §49-6-601, see also 49-6-103[1][b][ii] and UCA §49-6a-501, see also 49-6a-103[1][b][ii]) after one year of retirement, in each case not to exceed four percent of the monthly allowance, except that any excess over four percent may be accumulated over two or more years and used to make subsequent annual adjustments when the cost of living adjustment is less than four percent. The Public Employees Disability Act also provides in §49-9-404 for an annual adjustment to reflect changes in the Consumer Price Index not exceeding adjustments made to retirees under the system which covered the employee at the time of disability.

In statutory provisions applicable to all retirement plans, UCA §49-1-608 exempts benefits accrued or paid to any beneficiary from any state, county, or municipal tax, except for benefits subject to federal income tax which have not been taxed; and §49-1-609 exempts such benefits from attachment, execution, garnishment, or other legal or equitable process, and provides that they are not subject to alienation or assignment, except pursuant to an order of court with respect to a domestic relations matter, and as to offset of an amount owed by a member to the system.

SERVICE AFTER RETIREMENT

Const. Art VIII, §4 and UCA §78-2-4 empowers the supreme court by rule to authorize retired justices and judges to perform any judicial duties, and UCA §§78-5-137(6) and 138 makes similar provision with respect to retired justice court judges if physically and mentally able to perform the duties of the office. Rule 11-201 (see also Rule 3-113) governs the appointment of justices and judges who have served on any court of record who elect to take senior status after voluntary retirement, are physically and mentally able to perform the duties of judicial office, are neither actively practicing law nor been so engaged since retirement, and are willing to accept, or adjudicate, at least two cases during each calendar year of his or her term. Such judges are appointed for a term not exceeding three years unless otherwise determined by the supreme court, at the conclusion of which he or she may apply for an additional term. The chief justice may assign such judges to any appropriate case or matter, or for a specified period of time, with the consent of the judge. Rule 11-203 deals with appointment of senior justice court judges, who must have served in office in either a municipality or a county for not less than five years and voluntarily left office by retirement, resignation, or election not to seek retention, who elect to take senior status by application to the Board of Justice Court judges, and are physically and mentally competent to perform the duties of office. Such an applicant is appointed by the mayor, town president, or county commission chairperson to act as a temporary justice court judge in the county of his or her residence or an adjacent county, to preside over individual cases or for specified periods of time.

Continuing judicial education of justices and judges and justice court judges is provided for in UCA §§78-3-21(4)(c)(1), 78-3-24(12), 78-5-127, and Rules 3-403 and 9-103. Indeed, §78-5-127 authorizes removal of a justice court judge who does not attend such courses for two consecutive years, and §78-7-28(2) permits involuntary retirement from office of a justice, judge, or justice court judge who fails to obtain and maintain certification for attendance at required training courses. Although none of those provisions expressly refers to senior judges, it may well be that such judges, while serving on active duty as senior judges, are within their provisions. (See discussion under Pay and Emoluments, below).

PAY AND EMOLUMENTS

Rule 3-113 requires that active senior judges be compensated for the performance of judicial duties at an hourly rate equal to that of a district judge and be paid in half-day increments, and for attendance at educational functions, travel, and expenses. Note, however, that UCA §78-5-137(6)(b) provides only that a retired justice court judge receive reasonable compensation for services performed after retirement as set by local ordinance of the municipality or county.

VERMONT

Constitution Chap. II, §35 provides that all justices of the supreme court and judges of all subordinate courts shall be retired at the end of the calendar year in which they attain seventy years of age or at the end of the term of election [sic] during which they attain seventy years of age, as the case may be. Constitution, Chap. II, §34 establishes a six-year term of office, which may be continued for another six years unless a majority of the members of the General Assembly vote against continuation. It thus appears that a justice or judge elected or continued in office at age sixty-nine can retain his or her seat until age seventy-six, although no court decision so holding has been found.

Mandatory retirement has been held not to violate the constitutional right to equal protection, since it furthered a legitimate state interest, Aronstam v. Horican, 132 Vt. 538, 325 A.2d 361. In Equal Employment Opportunity Commission v. Vermont, 904 F.2d 794, the Second Circuit ruled that the mandatory retirement age as applied to appointed judges was preempted by the Age Discrimination in Employment Act. Query, however, whether in view of Gregory v. Ashcroft, 501 U.S. 452, and the Second Circuit's decision in Tranello v. Frey, 962 F.2d 244, holding that Act not preempted with respect to an appointed deputy county attorney of New York, its Equal Employment Opportunity Commission decision has not been impliedly overruled.

V.S.A., Title 3, Chap. 16, §455(11)(D) defines member of the Vermont Employees' Retirement System to include justices of the supreme court, superior court judges, district judges, and probate judges elected prior to July 1, 1987, and §455(11)(E) includes probate judges elected or appointed for the first time on or after January 1, 1991. Section 460 authorizes the retirement board to retire any member judge who has had five or more years of creditable service on application of his or her department head on ordinary disability retirement, provided the medical board, after medical examination, certifies that the judge should be retired because he or she is mentally or physically incapacitated for the further performance of duty, that such incapacity has existed since the judge's separation from service, and is likely to be permanent. Section 462 provides that once each year during the first five years following retirement on ordinary disability, and once in every three-year period thereafter, the board may, and upon the judge's application shall, require a judge retired for ordinary disability who has not reached normal retirement age to undergo a medical examination by the medical board or a physician designated by it. Should the judge refuse to undergo such examination, his or her retirement allowance may be discontinued until he does, and if the refusal continues for one year, his or her right to a pension may be revoked by the board.

Section 461 authorizes the board to retire any member judge on application of his or her department head on accidental and occupationally related disability if it finds on the evidence before it, including a report of the medical board after examination, that the judge should be retired because he or she is mentally or physically incapacitated for further performance of duty as a natural and proximate result of an accident occurring at a definite time and place during the course of performance of duty as a judge, and was not the result of his or her negligence or willful misconduct.

RETIREMENT PROVISIONS RE PARTICULAR COURTS

None.

OPTIONAL PROVISIONS FOR RETIREMENT

V.S.A., Title 3, Chap. 16, §455(13) defines "normal retirement date" for judges as the first day of the calendar month next following attainment of age sixty-two and completion of ten years of creditable service. Section 459 provides that a judge who has reached normal retirement age may retire by applying to the board, and subdivision (b)(3) of that section directs that a judge shall receive an allowance in addition to the normal retirement allowance, after twelve years of service as a supreme court justice, a superior judge, or a district judge, or any combination thereof that will make the total allowance equal to two-fifths of their salary at retirement and, for each year of service in excess of twelve, an amount equal to three and one-third percent of such salary shall be added, not, however, to exceed the salary at retirement.

Subdivision (c)(1) of Section 459 permits a judge who has not reached normal retirement date but who has completed thirty years of creditable service, or who has attained age fifty-five and completed five years of such service, to retire on an early retirement allowance which, under subdivision (c)(3) is equal to the normal retirement allowance reduced by one quarter of one percent for each month the judge is under age sixty-two at the time of early retirement.

The provisions of §§460, 461 and 462 outlined in the Mandatory Retirement section above apply as well to a judge who applies for ordinary disability retirement or accidental and occupationally related disability retirement, provided he or she does so not later than ninety days, or longer for cause shown, after the judge may have separated from service.

Section 470 provides that as of June 30 in each year, commencing June 30, 1972, the post retirement allowance payable to a judge shall be increased or decreased to the nearest one-tenth of a percent, in the ratio of the average of the Consumer Price Index for the month ending on that date to the average of that Index for the month ending on June 30, 1971, or the month ending on June 30 of the most recent year subsequent thereto as of which an increase or decrease in retirement allowance was made.

V.S.A., Title 3, Chap 16, §476 exempts a member's annuity, pension, or retirement allowance from any law relating to bankruptcy or insolvency and from attachment, execution, or other process of court, but not from taxation, including income tax. It also provides that, except as expressly provided in Chapter 16 (essentially relating to assignment to a beneficiary), no assignment of any interest in the member's funds in the retirement system shall be valid.

SERVICE AFTER RETIREMENT

Regardless of the court in which he or she served, a retired justice or judge, with his or her consent, may be specially assigned by the chief justice to any court, including the supreme court, but preference must be given to superior judges to sit in superior court and to district judges to sit in district courts, V.S.A., Title 4, Ch. 1, §22.

PAY AND EMOLUMENTS

A specially assigned retired justice or judge is entitled to a per diem equal
to the daily compensation authorized for the judicial position to which he
or she is assigned, plus necessary expenses, in addition to his or her retirement compensation, not, however, in total to exceed the annual salary of
a superior court judge. V.S.A., Title 4, Ch. 1, §23. A retiree who has
completed at least twenty years of state service and is insured for group
life insurance on his or her retirement date is covered by $5,000 of such
insurance, the premium for which is prorated on the same basis as for an
active judge, his or her share of which may, if the retiree so directs, be
deducted from his or her retirement allowance, V.S.A., Title 3, Ch. 16,
§479; Title 3, Ch. 21, §631(a)(9), §633. Retirees also retain group medical
benefits in the plan provided by the state for active state employees,
V.S.A., Title 3, Ch. 16, §479 (a)(1).

VIRGINIA

Virginia Constitution, Art. 6, §9 provides that the General Assembly may provide for a mandatory retirement age for judges, beyond which age they shall not serve, regardless of the term to which elected or appointed. Accordingly, all judges who attain seventy years of age are required to retire twenty days after the convening of the next regular session of the General Assembly, Va. Code Ann., §51.1-305(B1). This provision applies only to those judges who are elected or appointed to an original or subsequent term commencing after July 1, 1993. *Id.*

The Virginia Constitution mandates that the General Assembly shall create a Judicial Inquiry and Review Commission to investigate charges which would be the basis for retirement of a judge. Upon the filing of a complaint by the commission, the supreme court shall conduct a hearing, and upon a finding of disability that is, or is likely to be, permanent and that seriously interferes with the performance by the judge of his duties, shall retire such judge from office, Virginia Constitution, Art. 6, §10. A judge retired under this provision shall be considered for the purpose of retirement benefits to have retired voluntarily. *Id.*

Retirement Provisions re Particular Courts

None.

Optional Provisions for Retirement

A judge may opt to retire before he reaches age seventy, Va. Code. Ann., §51.1-305(B). According to this provision, a judge who has either (1) attained fifty-five years of age with five or more years of creditable service or (2) has met the retirement requirements of the previous system of July 1, 1970, may retire with benefits. *Id.*

Voluntary retirement for disability is dealt with by Va. Code Ann., §51.1-156. Under its provisions, a member while in service, or within ninety days after termination of service, may retire for disability compensable under the Virginia Workers' Compensation Act by giving the board written notice of the date the retirement is to become effective. If the cause is not compensable under the Workers' Compensation Act, disability retirement is available only to a member who has not withdrawn his or her contributions to the retirement system, upon the giving of such notice. In either case, the ninety-day notification period may be waived by the board. Note, however, that a member who has been on leave of absence without pay for more than twenty-four months is not entitled to retire under the section. The Medical Board determines, after a medical examination or review of pertinent medical records, whether the member is mentally or physically incapacitated for further performance of duty, the incapacity is likely to be permanent, and whether the member should be retired. If the condition existed at the time the member became a member, the medical evidence must convince the board that the preexisting condition has worsened substantially. If no Workers' Compensation is awarded because the person causing the disability settles with the member, the Workers' Compensation Commission determines whether the member's disability is from a cause compensable under the Workers' Compensation Act.

Retirement benefits are increased annually based on the increase in the United States Consumer Price Index over the preceding year, up to three percent, plus one-half of such additional increase up to seven percent, Va. Code Ann., §51.1-166, subd. 8.

Judges who are members of the Judicial Retirement System are expressly excluded from the Virginia Retirement System by the definition of "state employee" in Va. Code Ann., §51.1-124.3. But while §51.1-124.4 exempts benefits payable under the latter system from state, county, or municipal tax and from execution, garnishment, or other process, except for a debt to the employer or child or spousal support and, with a limited exception, makes them not assignable, except as to division of marital property, the sections governing the Judicial Retirement System (§51.1-300 ff) contain no similar prohibitions.

Service After Retirement

The chief justice of the supreme court may call upon any judge of a district court who is retired to perform, for a period not to exceed ninety days at any one time, such judicial duties in any district court as the chief justice shall deem in the public interest for the expeditious disposition of the business of such court, Va. Code Ann., §16.1-69.22:1(A). Any retired judge who has not yet reached age seventy must accept such recall and perform the duties assigned. It is in the discretion of any judge who has attained age seventy whether to accept such recall, Va. Code Ann., §16.1-69.22:1(B). As of June 1, 1998, if funds are provided there will be an amendment to this section which provides that only retired district court judges who have completed the training program required by the Judicial Council of Virginia shall be eligible to perform judicial duties in a family court.

The chief justice of the supreme court may call upon any judge or justice of a court of record who is retired to (1) hear any case for the duration of the case or (2) to perform, for a period not to exceed ninety days at any one time, such judicial duties in any court of record as the chief justice shall deem in the public interest for the expeditious disposition of the business of such court, Va. Code Ann., §17-7.01(A). Any retired judge who has not yet reached age seventy must accept such recall and perform the duties assigned. It is in the discretion of any judge who has attained age seventy whether to accept such recall, Va. Code Ann., §17-7.01(B).

The State Corporation Commission may call upon any member who is retired under the Judicial Retirement System to perform, for a period not to exceed ninety days at any one time, such duties for the commission as it deems in the public interest for the expeditious deposition of its business, Va. Code Ann., §12.1-11.1(A). Any retired judge who has not yet reached age seventy must accept such recall and perform the duties assigned, but it is within the discretion of a retired judge who has attained age seventy whether to accept such recall, Va. Code Ann., §12.1-11.1(B).

Any chief judge or judge of the court of appeals who is eligible to retire for other than disability may, with consent of a majority of the members of the court, retire and be known as a senior judge. The appointment is for a year, and there is no limit to the number of terms a senior judge may serve. He may terminate his senior status, or it may be terminated by a majority of the members of the court. Only three retired judges shall serve as senior judges at any one time, Va. Code Ann., §17-116.01:1.

No former justice or judge of a court of record, and no former full-time judge of a court not of record, who is retired and receiving retirement benefits under the Judicial Retirement System shall appear as counsel in any case in any court of the commonwealth, Va. Code Ann., §51.1-309;

and that provision applies to all retired judges eligible to recall for judicial service, Rules of Supreme Court, Part 6, Sec. III, Canon 8, subd. B.

Continuing education is mandated by Rules of Sup. Ct., Part 6, Sec. IV, §§13.2, 17, but retired judges do not appear to be within its provisions, which speak only of "active lawyers."

Pay and Emoluments

Any retired judge recalled to service shall be reimbursed for actual expenses incurred during such service and shall be paid a per diem of $150 for each day he actually sits, exclusive of travel time, Va. Code Ann., §14.1-39.1.

A senior judge, in addition to retirement benefits, shall receive as compensation a sum equal to onefourth the total compensation of an active judge of the court of appeals for a similar period of service. He shall also be furnished with an office, secretary, telephone, and supplies, Va. Code Ann., §17-116.01:1(c).

WASHINGTON

Mandatory Retirement Provisions Applicable Generally

Constitution Article IV, Section 3(a) requires a judge of the supreme court or the superior court to retire at the end of the calendar year in which he or she attains age seventy-five, but authorizes the legislature to fix a lesser age for mandatory retirement not earlier than the end of the year in which such judge attains the age of seventy. To be noted also are: Constitution, Article IV, Section 30, which provides that retirement of judges of the court of appeals shall be provided by statute; Revised Code of Washington, §2.10.100(3), which provides that any member of the Judicial Retirement System who attains the age of seventy-five years shall be retired at the end of the calendar year in which the member attains that age; and R.C.W., §3.74.030, which mandates that district judges retire at age seventy-five.

Involuntary retirement for disability is also authorized by Section 2(a) of Article IV of the Constitution, which provides that the legislature by general law may authorize or require retirement of judges for physical or mental disability or any cause rendering judges incapable of performing their judicial duties. To be noted also is Section 9 of Constitution Article IV, which authorizes the legislature by joint resolution, in which three-quarters of the members of each house concur, to remove judges for incompetence or other sufficient cause stated in such resolution.

Involuntary retirement for disability is, under Constitution Article IV, Section 31, first considered by the Commission on Judicial Conduct (as to which see R.C.W., §2.64.010), based on a complaint to the commission or other reason for it to believe that a justice or judge should be retired, notice to the justice or judge, a confidential investigation to determine whether there is probable cause for a public hearing; and if the commission recommends to the supreme court after hearing that the judge or justice be retired for a disability that is permanent or likely to become permanent and that severely interferes with the performance of judicial duties, the supreme court may retire the judge or justice, after a hearing upon notice to review the findings of the commission. Such a retirement is, however, treated as a voluntary retirement, R.C.W., §41.40.200(2). As to periodic medical examination and restoration to active service of a member previously retired for disability, see Optional Provisions section below.

RETIREMENT PROVISIONS RE PARTICULAR COURTS

None except, as noted in the Mandatory Retirement section above, judges of the district court must retire when they attain seventy-five, whereas other judges who are member of the Judicial Retirement System are permitted to serve until the end of the year in which age seventy-five is attained.

OPTIONAL PROVISIONS FOR RETIREMENT

There are two systems for retirement of judges. R.C.W., §2.10.040 provides that judges first appointed or elected on or after July 1, 1988, shall not be members of the Judicial Retirement System provided for in R.C.W. Chapters 2.04 (re: Supreme Court), 2.06 (re: Courts of Appeals), and 2.08 (re: Superior Court) judges, but may become members of the Public Employees' Retirement System under R.C.W. Chap. 41.40. Judges appointed prior to that date holding credit toward retirement benefits under Chapter 41.40 are allowed to make an irrevocable choice, filed in writing, to continue coverage under "that chapter" (sic) and to be permanently excluded from coverage under the Judicial Retirement System, R.C.W., §2.10.040; and a former member of the retirement system who was not serving as a judge on July 1, 1988, has one year after reentering service as a judge to file his or her written election, (id). However, a judge who was not serving as a judge on July 1, 1988, had not retired under the judicial retirement system, and subsequently reacquires membership in the Public Employees' Retirement System, may transfer to that system all periods of time served as a judge. R.C.W., §41.40.098.

Retirement for service or age of judges of the supreme court, court of appeals, or superior court is dealt with by R.C.W., §2.12.010, which authorizes a judge of those courts who has served for eighteen years in the aggregate, or served ten years in the aggregate and attained age seventy or more, to file notice of his or her retirement and of the date it will commence; and §2.12.012, which permits a judge of those courts who has served as a judge of any of such courts for an aggregate of twelve years to retire and receive a partial pension at age seventy or eighteen years after commencement of service, whichever shall first occur. As to court of appeal judges, see also R.C.W., §2.06.100. Note, however, that R.C.W., §2.10.100(2) permits any member of the Judicial Retirement System who has completed fifteen years of service to retire but provides that he or she is not eligible to receive a retirement allowance until he or she attains age sixty.

A person receiving retirement benefits from the Judicial Retirement System, who after retiring is appointed or elected to the supreme court, court of appeals, or superior court, again becomes a member of the system, and his or her retirement benefits cease; but pro tempore service as a judge of a court of record is not appointment within the meaning of the section (R.C.W., §2.10.230), and when the judge leaves the office to which he or she was thus appointed or elected, his or her benefits are recomputed or restored (*id*).

For members of the Pubic Employees' Retirement System, R.C.W., §41.40.630 defines normal retirement as at least five service credit years and attainment of at least age sixty-five, and early retirement as at least twenty service credit years and attainment of age fifty-five, but a member taking early retirement receives a retirement allowance actuarially reduced to reflect the difference between the number of years at retirement and age sixty-five. To be noted, however, are: R.C.W., §41.40.150, which provides that a member who separates from service before age sixty ceases to be a member of the system, unless the member has completed five years of service, in which event he or she may either remain a member for the exclusive purpose of receiving a retirement allowance to begin upon attainment of age sixty-five, or elect to receive a reduced allowance on or after age sixty; and R.C.W., §41.40.180, which permits retirement with five years of service at age sixty, or after twenty-five years of service and attained age of fifty-five, or after thirty years of service without limitation as to age. A member who has left service and withdrawn his or her accumulated contribution receives service credit for the prior service upon reentry to the system by restoring all withdrawn accumulated contributions together with interest since the time of withdrawal, such restoration to be completed within five years of resumption of service or prior to retirement, whichever first occurs, R.C.W., §41.40.740.

Voluntary retirement for physical or mental disability may be authorized by the legislature, Constitution, Article IV, §3(a), and has been authorized under both systems. As to members of the Judicial Retirement System, R.C.W., §2.12.020 permits a judge of the supreme court, court of appeals or superior court who has served as a judge of any of those courts and believes he or she "has become physically or otherwise permanently incapacitated for the full and efficient performance of the duties of his [or her] office," to apply to the director of retirement systems for retirement. The verified application is then sent to the governor, who appoints three physicians to examine the judge and report their findings to the governor. If the majority of the physicians report to the governor their opinion that the judge has become permanently incapacitated and the governor approves their report, he files the report, with his or her approval endorsed thereon, with the director and with the administrator for the courts, and the applicant is deemed to have retired from the date of the filing and is entitled to benefits as if he had retired under the provisions of R.C.W., §2.12.010. As to members of the Public Employees' System, the statutes differentiate between disability in line of duty, and nonduty disability. R.C.W., §41.40.200 permits a judge who is a member of the system and has become totally incapacitated for duty as the natural and proximate result of an accident occurring in the actual performance of duty to apply for disability retirement. A member so retired who has attained age sixty receives a service retirement allowance regardless of creditable service, R.C.W., §41.40.210, but before age sixty receives a pension of two-thirds his or her average final salary, but not to exceed $4,200 per annum, R.C.W., §41.40.220(1), and credit for service for the period prior to age sixty he or she was out of service due to disability (*id* [2]), and, upon attainment of age sixty, receives a service retirement allowance (*id*). As to a judge who becomes totally and permanently incapacitated for duty as a result of causes occurring not in the performance of his or her duty, the judge may, pursuant to R.C.W., §41.40.230, apply for disability retirement; and if it is found after medical examination that the member is mentally or physically incapacitated for further performance of duty, that the incapacity is likely to be permanent, and that the member should be retired, the member will, pursuant to R.C.W., §41.40.235, receive a nonduty disability retirement allowance equal to two percent of average final compensation for each service credit year, reduced, however, by two percent of itself for each year or fraction thereof that his or her age is less than fifty-five years, the allowance not, however, to exceed sixty percent of average final compensation.

A judge who became a member of the system prior to September 30,

1977, who is retired for disability and who has not attained age sixty, may be required by the department to, and upon the member's application shall, undergo a medical examination once each year during the first five years following retirement and at least once in every three years thereafter. If the medical advisor reports, and the department concurs, that the member is no longer totally incapacitated for duty as a result of the injury or illness for which disability was granted, or that he or she is engaged in a gainful occupation, the disability pension or retirement allowance shall cease, except that if the compensation of the gainful employment is less than the member's compensation earnable at the date of disability, the disability benefits continue in an amount which, added to such compensation, does not exceed his or her compensation at the date of separation, adjusted July 1 of each year by the ratio of the average U.S. Consumer Price Index for the calendar year prior to the adjustment to the average Consumer Price Index for the calendar year in which separation occurred, but in no event shall the adjustment result in an amount less than the amount earnable at the date of separation, R.C.W., §41.40.310; and the reinstated member again becomes a member required to contribute to the system in the same manner as prior to disability retirement, his or her prior service and membership service is restored to full force and effect, and, except as to a nonduty disability retiree, is given service credit for the time out of service due to disability, R.C.W., §41.40.320.

Note, however, that a judge who receives a disability allowance and who became a member of the system on or after October 1, 1997 (see R.C.W., §41.40.610), is subject to comprehensive medical examinations as required by the department, and if such an examination reveals that the member has recovered from the incapacitating disability and the member is offered reemployment at comparable compensation, the member ceases to be eligible for such allowance (R.C.W., §41.40.670).

Under both systems the pension, annuity, or retirement allowance is exempt from state and local taxation, is not subject to execution, garnishment, attachment, or other judicial process, and is unassignable except for spousal maintenance, child support, and other specified orders, R.C.W., §2.12.090 and R.C.W., §§41.40.052, 41.50.530; see also §§2.10.180 and 2.14.100. Both systems also provide for annual increase of the retirement allowance based upon the Consumer Price Index of the U.S. Department of Labor for urban wage earners and clerical workers, R.C.W., §§ 2.10.170, 2.12.057, 41.40.197, 41.40.640, 41.50.760.

A person receiving benefits under the Judicial Retirement System, who is appointed (other than for pro tempore service) or elected to the supreme court, court of appeals, or superior court, again becomes a member of the system and his or her other retirement benefits cease, R.C.W., §2.10.230, but upon again leaving office receives recomputed benefits not less than was being paid at the time his or her benefits ceased (*id*). For similar but not identical provisions applicable to judicial and other members of the Public Employees' Retirement System, see R.C.W., §41.40.150 and §41.40.740.

Both systems also provide that a retiree may elect to have his or her benefits remaining unpaid when he or she dies paid to his or her estate, or to such other person, persons, trust, or organization as he or she designates in writing, or, if no such person or persons be living at the retiree's death, to his or her estate, but requires consent of the member's spouse unless a dissolution order was filed at least thirty days prior to the member's retirement, R.C.W., §§2.10.146, 41.40.660. R.C.W., §2.12.030 provides that a surviving spouse who has been married for *three* years to a supreme court, court of appeals or superior court judge who has retired or is eligible for retirement at the time of death, and had served on any of such courts for an aggregate of ten or more years, or an aggregate of twelve years if pension rights are based upon R.C.W., §2.12.012 (which permits retirement after twelve years on a partial pension but does not authorize payment until attainment of age seventy or eighteen years after commencement of judicial service, whichever shall first occur), shall be paid an amount equal to one-half the retirement pay of the judge as long as the surviving spouse remains unmarried. Compare, however, R.C.W., §2.10.140, which provides that a surviving spouse of a judge who dies after retiring shall receive a monthly allowance equal to forty percent of the retirement allowance the judge was receiving, but conditions the right to such allowance on the spouse having been married to the judge for a minimum of *two* years at the time of death.

As to the rights of a surviving spouse or of a beneficiary designated by a judge when the judge dies before the date of retirement, see R.C.W., §§2.10.144 and 41.40.270.

SERVICE AFTER RETIREMENT

Constitution Article IV, Section 2(a), empowers a majority of the supreme court to authorize a retired judge of courts of record to perform temporarily judicial duties in the supreme court, and Article IV, Section 7, and R.C.W., §2.08.160, provide that a case in the superior court may be tried by a judge pro tempore, agreed upon in writing by the parties litigant or their attorneys, such agreement being unnecessary, however, when a previously elected judge of the superior court retires leaving a pending case in which he or she has made discretionary rulings, in which case the judge may continue to act as a judge pro tempore. In Zachman v. Whirlpool Financial Corp., 123 Wash.2d 667, 869 P.2d 1078, the supreme court held the latter provision applicable to a judge "retired" by reelection defeat.

R.C.W., §2.04.240 authorizes a majority of the supreme court to appoint any retired judge of a court of record to serve as a judge pro tempore of the supreme court, and R.C.W., §2.06.150 authorizes the chief justice of the supreme court to appoint any retired judge of a court of record to serve as judge pro tempore of the court of appeals, but provides that no judge so appointed may serve on the court of appeals more than ninety days in any one year. Note, further, that no retired judge is eligible to receive a service or disability retirement allowance if he or she is employed as a pro tempore judge for more than 810 hours in a calendar year, and that when the employment which caused the suspension of such benefits terminates, the benefits are actuarially recomputed upon reinstatement, R.C.W., §2.10.155(3). If a retired judge accepts appointment or election to a judicial office, his retirement pay is suspended, but he then receives the full salary pertaining to such office, subject, however, to contribution to the Judges Retirement Fund, R.C.W., §2.12.040.

Under the Public Employees' Retirement System, a Plan II retiree (which includes judges, R.C.W., §41.40.010[34]) may work in any position that normally requires five or more months of service a year (R.C.W., §41.40.010[23]) on a temporary basis for up to five months in a calendar year (R.C.W., §41.40.690[1][b]), but if his or her retiree benefits are suspended under that provision, the benefits are reinstated when the employment which caused the suspension terminates, but upon reinstatement, the benefits are actuarially recomputed, id (2).

PAY AND EMOLUMENTS

A retired judge of a court of record serving as a judge pro tempore of the supreme court receives during the period of his or her service as such an amount equal to the salary of a regularly elected judge of the court in which he or she last served, less the retirement pay accrued to him or her during such period, plus reimbursement for subsistence, lodging, and travel expenses, R.C.W., §2.04.250. Under R.C.W., §2.06.160 a retired judge of a court of record serving as a judge pro tempore of the court of appeals receives compensation for each day of such service in the amount of sixty percent of 1/250th the annual salary of a court of appeals judge; and, under R.C.W., §2.08.180, a judge who has retired from the supreme court, court of appeals, or superior court, serving as judge pro tempore to try a case in the superior court, receives compensation for such services in like portion of the annual salary of a superior court judge. Payments for subsistence, lodging, and compensation pursuant to 2.04.250 and 2.06.160 are made only for time away from the judge's usual residence and only for time actually devoted to sitting on cases heard by the judge pro tempore and in research and preparation of a written opinion, R.C.W., §2.28.160.

WEST VIRGINIA

MANDATORY RETIREMENT PROVISIONS APPLICABLE GENERALLY

Nothing in the West Virginia Constitution or statutes mandates that a judge of its court retire at a given age.

Involuntary retirement for disability is provided for, however. Constitution Article VIII provides that justices of the supreme court of appeals (§2), of the circuit courts (§5), and magistrate courts (§10) may be retired as authorized in Article VIII, and in Section 8 authorizes the supreme court of appeals to retire any such justice, judge, or magistrate who is eligible for retirement under the Judges Retirement System or substituted retirement system for justices, judges, or magistrates who, because of advancing years and attendant physical or mental incapacity, should not, in the opinion of the supreme court of appeals, continue to serve as such, but that no justice of the supreme court of appeals may be so retired unless all of the other justices concur in such retirement. West Virginia Code, §6-6-2, states that any justice, judge, or magistrate may be retired for such incapacity in the manner provided in Article VIII, Section 8, of the Constitution and by rules prescribed, adopted, promulgated, and amended pursuant thereto, and Rule 4.12 of the Rules of Judicial Disciplinary Procedure authorizes the Judicial Hearing Board to recommend, or the supreme court of appeals to impose, "involuntary retirement for a judge because of advancing years and attendant physical or mental incapacity and who is eligible to receive retirement benefits under the judges' retirement system or the public employees' retirement system." As to involuntary retirement for disability under the public employees' retirement system, see Optional Provisions for Retirement below.

RETIREMENT PROVISIONS RE PARTICULAR COURTS

None.

OPTIONAL PROVISIONS FOR RETIREMENT

There are two systems for retirement of judges. W.V.C., §51-9-5(a) permits a judge to elect in writing within thirty days after he or she takes office not to become a member or make payments or contributions to the Judges Retirement System. A judge who so elects is permitted thereafter to become such member by paying into the judges' retirement fund all contributions the judge would have been required to pay, together with interest at a rate determined by the state auditor to be reasonable for the prior period, as if the judge had not elected not to be a member of the system. Service credit may be transferred between the Judges Retirement System and the Public Employees' Retirement System in order to allow full flexibility of choice of option by a judge or judicial member (*id* [b]). A judge whose services have terminated, otherwise than by retirement, may obtain a refund of his or her contributions to the fund without interest; doing so terminates his or her rights to benefits of the system, but he or she may reenter the system after subsequent appointment or election to a qualified judgeship, W.V.C., §51-9-12.

The Public Employees' Retirement System is provided for in Chapter 5, Article 10, of the West Virginia Code. Section 5-10-2(6) expressly includes judges of the state court of claims. Section 5-10-17(b) provides that membership in the system shall not include any person who is a member of, or has been retired by, the judges retirement system, but, as above noted, transfer between the Judges Retirement System and the Public Employees' Retirement System is permissible.

Under the Judges Retirement System any judge of a court of record who shall have served as such for not less than sixteen full years and shall have reached age sixty-five, or who shall have served as a judge of that court and other courts of record for a period of sixteen full years or more (whether continuously or not, and whether the judge shall be in office when he or she becomes eligible for benefits) and shall have reached age sixty-five, or who has served as a judge of a court of record for a period of not less than twenty-four full years regardless of age, upon tender of his or her resignation to the governor and the governor's determination that the judge is entitled to retirement benefits and his acceptance of such resignation, is entitled to annual retirement benefits as long as he or she shall live, based upon the salary of the office as it may be changed during the period of retirement, equal to seventy-five percent of the highest annual salary of such office for any one calendar year during the period of his or her retirement, (W.V.C., §§51-9-6, 51-9-9). Further, a judge of a court of record who has served not less than eight full years after attaining age sixty-five and who has made payment into the judges retirement fund is, subject to the same terms concerning resignation and acceptance thereof, entitled to a like retirement benefit; and if such judge becomes incapacitated to perform his or her duties before expiration of his or her term and after serving for six years thereof, he or she receives the annual retirement benefit so long as he or she may live, (W.V.C., §51-9-6a).

The Judges Retirement System also provides in W.V.C., §51-9-6b(a) for payment to the surviving spouse of a judge who is eligible at the time of his or her death for retirement benefits, or who has, at death, actually served five years or more as a sitting judge of any court of record, exclusive of other service credit to which the judge may otherwise be entitled, and who dies while in office or after resignation or retirement from office, of an annuity of forty percent of the annual salary of the office which the judge held at his or her death or from which he or she resigned or retired, or if the said salary is increased or decreased while the annuitant is receiving such annuity, in the amount of forty percent of the new salary, such annuity to terminate on the death or remarriage of the spouse. Under W.V.C., §51-9-6b(b) if there be no surviving spouse, or if a surviving spouse dies while receiving benefits as provided in subsection (a), leaving him or her surviving a dependent child or children of the deceased judge, such child or children shall receive an amount equal to twenty percent of the salary of the office the judge held at the time of his or her death, which shall continue as to each child until he or she attains eighteen years of age, or so long as the child remains a full-time student, twenty-three years of age; and in the event there are three or more dependent children who survive the judge, each child's annuity is proratably reduced so that the aggregate received by all dependent children does not exceed forty percent of such salary, continuing for such time as each such child is eligible to receive such annuity subject to increase or decrease proportionately, if the salary of judges is increased or decreased while the annuitant is receiving benefits, to like increases or decreases.

A member of the Public Employees' Retirement System who has attained age sixty and has five or more years of credited service, during at least one year of which he or she was a contributing member of the system, or, if he or she became a member after June 1, 1986, all five years were as a contributory member, may retire by filing application with the board of trustees, W.J.C., §5-10-20. Any member with five or more years of credited service of which at least three are contributory who leaves employment prior to age sixty for any reason except disability or death is entitled to an annuity, provided he or she does not withdraw the contributions, the annuity to begin on the first day of the month next following the filing of his or her application, on or after his or her attainment of sixty-two years, W.V.C., §5-10-21(a). A member who qualifies under subdivision (a) and has ten or more years of credited service and has attained age fifty-five at the date of separation may, prior to the effective date of retirement, elect to receive a reduced annuity commencing on the first day of any calendar month between his or her date of separation and attainment of age sixty-two, *id*(b), or, if he or she has twenty or more years of credited service, commencing on the first day of the calendar month between his or her fifty-fifth birthday and attainment of age sixty-two, *id*(c). A member may elect to receive his or her annuity as a straight life annuity payable for life, or as a reduced annuity payable for life, and upon his or her death paid to such person having an insurable interest in the judge's life as the judge nominates, or upon the judge's death payable as to one-half the reduced annuity to a person having an insurable interest in the judge's life as the judge nominates, through the life of such person, W.V.C., §5-10-24.

Voluntary retirement for disability is provided for by both systems. A member of the Judges Retirement System who has served for ten full years, or, if over the age of sixty-five, for at least six years, as a judge of a court of record, who becomes physically or mentally incapacitated to perform the duties of his or her office during the remainder of his or her term, may make written application to the governor for retirement, which tenders his or her resignation as such judge on condition of being retired with pay. If the governor after such investigation as he deems advisable determines that the disability exists and that the public service is suffering and will continue to suffer by reason of such disability, he accepts the resignation and directs retirement of the judge for the unexpired portion of the judge's term. The judge is then paid annual retirement pay for the remainder of his or her unexpired term equal to the annual salary the judge was receiving at the time of retirement, in lieu of retirement benefits which the judge may otherwise have received; and after the end of the term, even though not then sixty-five years of age, the judge shall be paid the retirement benefits for which provision is made in W.V.C., §51-9-6, discussed above, W.V.C., §51-9-8. As to procedure for the governor's determination, see also §51-9-9. To be noted, however, are W.V.C., §51-8-8(b), which states that no judge is eligible for disability retirement unless disabled to such an extent as to preclude the judge from engaging in the practice of law during all of the period of disability, and W.V.C., §51-9-13, which provides that no judge "who has become physically incapacitated" to perform his or her duties, and remained so for one year without making application for retirement, is entitled to retirement pay or retirement benefits under any section of Chapter 51, Article 9.

Disability retirement of members of the Public Employees' Retirement System is provided for in W.V.C., §§5-10-25 and 5-10-26. Section 25(a) provides for such retirement "[u]pon the application of a member or former member . . . or his present or past employing authority," of a member or former member who is or was in the employ of a participating public employer who has ten or more years of credited service, of which at least three is contributory service, and "becomes totally and permanently incapacitated for employment by reason of a personal injury or disease." Such a member may be retired by the board of trustees if after medical examination the medical committee reports that he or she is physically or mentally totally incapacitated for employment, that the incapacity will probably be permanent, and that the member or former member should be retired. The above service requirements are waived, however, if the disability is the natural and proximate result of an injury or disease arising out of and in the course of his or her actual performance of duty and he or she receives workmen's compensation on account of such physical or mental disability, *id*.(b). A retiree for disability pursuant to Section 25 who has not attained age sixty may be required, pursuant to W.V.C., §5-10-26, to undergo a medical examination by a board-selected physician at least once each year for the first five years after retirement and at least once in each three-year period thereafter, or may be so examined upon his or her own application. Should the retiree refuse to submit to such examination, the board may discontinue his or her disability annuity until withdrawal of such refusal, and should the refusal continue for one year, the annuity may be revoked. If the physician reports that the retiree is physically able and capable of resuming employment, and the board concurs, he or she is returned to employment and again becomes a member of the system, *id*(a) and (b). If the disability retiree who has not attained age sixty becomes engaged in gainful occupation, business, or employment, his or her disability annuity is reduced so that it, together with the earnings from such occupation, business, or employment, equals his or her annual rate of compensation at the time of retirement, *id*(c).

To be noted with respect to disability retirement is W.V.C., Chapter 5, Article 10D, which established a consolidated public retirement board to administer, beginning July 1, 1991, all public retirement systems, including the Public Employees' Retirement System and the Judges Retirement System, W.V.C., §5-10D-1(a) and (b), and which in §5-10D-5 provides that the board may not award disability retirement to a member of any plan that it administers if the member is seeking to retire based on a disability that existed at the time the member joined the public retirement plan. However, West Virginia's Attorney General has opined (Gen. Op. 7/11/94 #2) that this provision contravenes the federal Americans With Disabilities Act, and it may be argued that it is inconsistent with W.V.C., §5-10-17(b), which states that the membership of the Public Employees' Retirement System shall not include any person who is a member of, or who has been retired by, the Judges Retirement System.

A judge retired for disability under the judges retirement system may not practice law, and if he or she does so, retirement pay or benefits are suspended for such time only as he or she is engaged in the practice of law, W.V.C., §51-9-7. With respect to the Public Employees' Retirement System, W.V.C., §5-10-26(c), discussed above, would appear to have similar though not identical effect as to a judge who is a member of that system.

Under both systems the right of a retiree or other person to benefits is not subject to execution, attachment, garnishment, or the operation of bankruptcy or insolvency laws and is not assignable, W.V.C.,§§5-10-46, 51-9-14, except that under §5-10-46 a participating public employer has the right of setoff for a claim arising from embezzlement by, or fraud of, a member, retiree or beneficiary. The Public Employees' Retirement System also exempts the annuities and other benefits payable by it, and its assets, from state, county, and municipal taxes, W.V.C., §5-10-47, but no similar provision as to the Judges Retirement System has been found.

SERVICE AFTER RETIREMENT

Constitution Article VIII, Section 8, provides that a retired judge may be recalled, with his or her permission and the approval of the supreme court of appeals, by the chief justice of the supreme court of appeals for temporary assignment as a justice of the supreme court of appeals, judge of an intermediate appellate court, a circuit court, or a magistrate court.

W.V.C., §§51-9-10 and 50-1-6a deal with service after retirement of judges and magistrates. Section 51-9-10 authorizes the supreme court of appeals to create a panel of senior judges to utilize the talent and expertise of former circuit court judges and supreme court justices, with the objective of reducing caseloads and providing speedier trials, and §50-1-6a contains like provisions with respect to a panel of senior magistrates. To be noted also is W.V.C., §51-2-4, which provides that if the circuit court judge thinks the public interest requires it, he may appoint a special term, and that any such special term may be held by a special judge elected by the attorneys practicing in the court. The section does not specifically mention retired judges, but neither does it exclude them from serving as a special judge if elected by such attorneys.

Rule 7 of the Judicial Disciplinary Procedure Rules defines "judges" to include justices of the supreme court of appeals and circuit court judges, both active and in senior status, but makes no mention of magistrates, and Rule 7.14 requires "judges" to complete a minimum of thirty hours of continuing legal education during every two years.

Pay and Emoluments

With respect to senior judges, W.V.C., §51-9-10, states that reasonable payment shall be made to justices and judges serving as senior judges, but that the per diem and retirement compensation of a senior judge shall not exceed the salary of a sitting judge, and allowances shall also be made for necessary expenses as provided for special judges.

W.V.C., §50-10-6a, likewise provides for reasonable payment to a senior magistrate on a per diem basis, the per diem and retirement compensation not to exceed the salary of a sitting magistrate, and for allowance for necessary expenses pursuant to travel regulations of the supreme court of appeals.

WISCONSIN

Wisconsin Constitution Article VII, Section 24(2), provides that unless assigned temporary service, no person may serve as a supreme court justice or judge of a court of record beyond the July 31 following the date on which such person attains the age of not less than seventy years, which the legislature shall prescribe by law. The legislature has not prescribed a higher age beyond which regular justices or judges cannot serve. However, as to a reserve judge (defined in Service After Retirement section below) it was held in State ex rel Godfrey v. Gollmar, 76 Wis.2d 417, 251 N.W.2d 438, that reserve judges, as distinguished from regular justices and judges, could serve after the age of seventy.

Involuntary removal for cause or for disability of a justice or judge by the supreme court pursuant to procedures established by the legislature is authorized by Const. Art. VII, Sec. 11.[11] Those procedures are spelled out in W.S.A., §§757.81 to 757.99, which established a judicial commission empowered to remove judges for misconduct or disability, permanent or temporary. Permanent disability is defined in §757.81(6) as a physical or mental incapacity which impairs the ability of a judge to substantially perform the duties of his or her judicial office and which is likely to be of a permanent or continuing nature, as is temporary disability (§757.81[7]) in the case of a municipal court judge or a judge of a court of record other than the supreme court, except that it need only be found likely to exist for a period of one year or less, and in relation to a supreme court justice the impairment need only be likely to exist for a period of six months or less.

---

[11] Const. Art. VII, Sec. 13 provides that any justice or judge may be removed from office by address of both houses of the legislature if two-thirds of all members elected to each house concur, and the justice or judge is served with a copy of the charges and had an opportunity of being heard. The section does not define "charges," but since section 11 speaks of "removal for cause or disability," presumably section 13 will be construed not to include removal by the legislature for disability.

If the commission finds probable cause that a judge has a disability, W.S.A., §757-87 permits it, before it files a formal petition, by a majority of its total membership not disqualified from voting, to request a jury hearing before a jury of six persons, of whom five-sixths must agree on all questions that must be answered to arrive at a verdict. If a jury is not requested, the issue of permanent disability is heard by a panel of three court of appeals judges, or two court of appeals judges and one reserve judge selected by the chief judge of the court of appeals on the basis of length of service as a court of appeals judge. W.S.A., §757.89, requires that the allegations of the petition be proven to a reasonable certainty by clear, satisfactory, and convincing evidence and if the hearing is before a jury, the presiding judge must instruct the jury regarding applicable law, and file the jury verdict and his or her recommendation of appropriate action concerning the disability with the supreme court. If the hearing is before a panel, its findings of fact, conclusions of law, and recommendations regarding appropriate action are filed with the supreme court. In either case the supreme court makes the final determination of appropriate action in cases of permanent disability, W.S.A., §757.91. If the judge is found not to have a permanent disability, the judge is reimbursed for reasonable attorneys' fees.

To be noted is that effective May 1, 1992 the provisions of §§757.85 through 757.99 discussed above were made applicable to court commissioners as well as judges. As to reserve judges and court commissioners, see the section on Service After Retirement below.

RETIREMENT PROVISIONS RE PARTICULAR COURTS

Municipal court judges are dealt with in statutes separate from justices and judges of other courts of record, but since such statutory provisions are identical with those concerning justices and judges of other courts, the sections relating to municipal court judges are cited in the following sections of this report below, together with those relating to judges of other courts.

OPTIONAL PROVISIONS FOR RETIREMENT

W.S.A., Chapter 40, deals with the Public Employee Trust Fund and includes as Subchapter II (§§40.20-40.30) the Wisconsin Retirement System. Section 40.02 (24) defines "elected office" to mean a participating employee who is a supreme court justice, court of appeals judge, circuit judge, or "state, county or municipal official elected by vote of the people," which presumably includes municipal judges so elected. "Participating employee" is defined by *id* (46) as one who is currently serving or is on a leave of absence, and "normal retirement" date means for an elected official the date on which he or she attains age sixty-two, *id* (42)(b). A participant first covered under the Wisconsin Retirement System after January 1, 1990 who is not on authorized leave of absence, who has attained the age of fifty-five and has creditable service of at least five years, may retire at a reduced annuity pursuant to his or her application in accordance with actuarial tables in effect on the effective date of his or her retirement, W.S.A., §40.23(1)(a) and (am). Note, however, that while Constitution, Article IV, Sec. 26, proscribes legislative increase of compensation to a public officer, it specifically excepts in subdivision (3) increase of retirement system benefits when provided by a legislative act passed by a three-fourths vote of all members of both houses of the legislature.

Voluntary retirement for disability is provided for in W.S.A., §40.63, which makes the requirement of five years creditable service inapplicable to an application for disability retirement prior to the normal retirement date, but imposes lesser creditable service requirements, requires that the employee be unable to engage in any substantial gainful activity by reason of medically determinable physical or mental impairment which can be expected to result in death or to be of long-continued and indefinite duration as certified by at least two licensed and practicing physicians approved or appointed by the Department of Employee Trust Funds, that the employer have certified that the employee is not entitled to any earnings from it, the termination of active service was due to disability, and no other employment which is substantial gainful activity has intervened since the termination. The department's report may be appealed to the retirement system board by either the applicant or the employer. If the application by a participant aged fifty-five or over is disapproved, the applicant may request that the date that would have been the effective date of the disability annuity shall be the retirement annuity effective date. If the disability annuity is approved, the board may require that the annuitant be examined by a physician designated or approved by the board during any calendar year the annuity is being paid, and may terminate the annuity if the physician's report indicates that the annuitant is no longer disabled, as that term is above defined, or if the annuitant refuses to submit to such an examination or to submit information concerning earnings or compensation when requested by the department. Substantial gainful activity is defined by subdivision 11 of the section as employment for which the annual compensation exceeds, for determinations made in the calendar year commencing January 1, 1982, $3,600, or, for determinations made in subsequent years, the amount applied in the previous calendar year increased by the salary index.

W.S.A., §40.08 exempts all benefits under any plan administered by the department from any tax, other than a tax on income, levied by the state or any subdivision of the state, and provides that such benefits shall not be assignable, in law or in equity, or subject to execution, levy, attachment, garnishment, or other legal process, except that a participant's rights and benefits under the retirement system may be divided pursuant to a qualified domestic relations order which meets the requirements spelled out in W.S.A., §40.08(1m); see also W.S.A., §815.18(3)(j), (6)(b) and (13)(f) and (h); and as to retirement benefits from retirement systems of cities of the first class, see also W.S.A., §66.81, which is not as broad in scope as W.S.A., §40.08 referred to above.

SERVICE AFTER RETIREMENT

Constitution, Art. VII, Sec. 24(3) provides that a person who has served as a supreme court justice or a judge of a court of record may, as provided by law, serve as a judge of any court of record except the supreme court on a temporary basis if assigned by the chief justice of the supreme court.

W.S.A., §753.075 deals with appointment of reserve judges, either as a permanent reserve judge, defined as a judge appointed by the chief justice to serve for a period of six months, or a temporary reserve judge appointed by the chief justice to carry out specified duties on a day-to-day basis as the chief justice directs. Permanent reserve judges perform the same duties as other judges and may be appointed for subsequent periods, *id*, subd.(1). The chief justice of the supreme court may appoint as a reserve judge of the court of appeals or the circuit court for any county any person who, as of August 1, 1978 had served a total of eight or more years as a supreme court justice or circuit judge, or who has served four or more years as a judge or justice of any court or courts of record, and who was not defeated at the most recent time he or she sought reelection to judicial office, *id*, subd (2). The director of state courts is also authorized to assign retired judges to service as reserve judges, S.C.R. 70.10 and 70.23. To be eligible for appointment by the chief justice, a chief judge or the director of state courts, however, a retired judge must have on file a consent to serve as a reserve judge, S.C.R. 70.35. W.S.A., §860.065, which deals with municipal court procedure, provides in subd. 1 that a judge of a municipal court for any municipality within a judicial administrative district may be appointed by the chief judge of that district as a temporary reserve judge to perform specified duties on a day-to-day basis as the chief judge directs, and, in subd. 2, that any person who has served eight or more years as a municipal judge or served four or more years as a municipal judge and was not defeated at the most recent time he or she sought election to judicial office, may be so appointed.

Supreme Court Rule 11.07 bars a reserve judge who has served as a circuit judge or as a court of appeals judge from appearing for a period of one year after service in the court of which he or she is a former member, and S.C.R. 32.08 provides that to be eligible for appointment or reappointment as a reserve judge, a person otherwise entitled to appointment must have earned five credits by attending judicial education programs, unless that requirement is waived by the director of state courts for good cause. With respect to a former municipal judge or former circuit court judge note, however, that W.S.A., §755.18 provides that the continuing judicial education requirement does not apply during the six-month period following the date on which the judge receives his or her appointment; and with respect to municipal judges, compare W.S.A., §800.065, which makes a municipal judge appointed as a temporary reserve judge subject to §755.18.

Any former judge of an inferior court of record may be appointed as a full-time or part-time court commissioner, W.S.A., §757.68(4), and any retired or former circuit or county court judge may be appointed to act in conciliation matters with full authority to hear, determine, and report findings to the court, W.S.A., §807.09. A retired circuit court judge appointed a conciliator pursuant to that section may be appointed court commissioner and continues in that position until a successor is appointed and qualifies, W.S.A., §757.68(3).

PAY AND EMOLUMENTS

Permanent reserve judges receive compensation equal to that paid for the six-month period to a judge of the court to which assigned, but the combined amount of such compensation, together with retirement annuities received by him or her during any one calendar month, may not exceed one-twelfth of the yearly compensation of a circuit court judge, W.S.A., §753.075(3)(b). As enacted, the subdivision also included social security in the combined amount, but in Raskin v. Moran, 684 F.2d 472, that provision was held in violation of the supremacy clause of the federal constitution.

Temporary reserve judges receive a per diem of $225, and commencing August 2, 1994, and every August 2 thereafter, that per diem is increased by the same percentage increase as the total percentage increase in circuit court judges' salaries authorized during the preceding twelve-month period ending on August 1. While serving outside the county of his or her residence, a temporary reserve judge also receives actual and necessary expenses incurred in discharge of judicial duties, W.S.A., §753.075. Note, however, that as to municipal court judges serving as temporary reserve judges, W.S.A., §800.065 provides that they shall receive compensation in an amount agreed to by contract between the municipality and the temporary reserve judge.

Reserve judges are also entitled to payment of a per diem and reimbursement of expenses incurred in attending judicial education programs, S.C.R. 32.08.

The compensation of a court commissioner serving as a facilitator is such reasonable amount as may be fixed by the court, not exceeding the hourly equivalent of the salary of a judge of the court, W.S.A., §814.68(1).

The compensation of a conciliator appointed under W.S.A., §807.09 is fixed and provided for by the county board, *id*, subd.2.

WYOMING

MANDATORY RETIREMENT PROVISIONS APPLICABLE GENERALLY

Constitution Article V, Section 5, requires the legislature to provide for voluntary retirement of justices and judges of the supreme court and district courts and provides that it may do so for any other court. It then provides that "the office of every such justice and judge shall become vacant when the incumbent reaches the age of 70 years, as the legislature may prescribe." Wyoming Statutes Annotated (WSA) §5-1-106(a) mandates that a judge of the supreme court or district courts retire when he or she attains the age of seventy (see also §5-1-106[e]), but the statutes that relate to county judges, municipal judges, and justices of the peace (§§5-4-104, 5-5-110, 5-6-104) only fix the term of the judgeships and contain no mandatory retirement provision. No case construing the words "every such justice and judge" in the constitution to apply to judges of county or municipal courts or justices of the peace has been found, but, as discussed in Retirement Provisions re Particular Courts below, it appears that they are not subject to the seventy-year age limit.

Constitution Article V, Section 6(g), requires that the code of judicial conduct provide for the mandatory retirement of a judicial officer (defined in subd.[j] as all members of the judicial branch performing judicial functions) for any disability that seriously interferes with the performance of the duties of the office and is, or is likely to become, permanent, but that a judicial officer so retired shall be considered to have retired voluntarily without loss of retirement benefits. In view of the broad definition of judicial officer, it appears that judges of the county and municipal courts are subject to mandatory retirement for disability.

The procedure by which a determination is made that a judge should, or should not, be retired for disability is contained in the "Rules for the Commission on Judicial Conduct and Ethics." Rule 2(b) defines judge to include a judicial officer serving full or part time, including a retired judge who has been given a general or special appointment to hear cases by the supreme court. The commission functions through an investigatory panel which reviews complaints concerning a judge (Rule 10[b]), may order the judge to have physical or mental examinations by independent examiners, (*id*), failure to submit to which may be considered by the panel unless due to circumstances beyond the judge's control (Rule 13[d]), an adjudicatory panel which conducts formal hearings and makes adjudicatory findings (Rule 3), and a hearing before the full commission, which if it finds a disability within the above definition by the greater weight of the evidence, recommends to the supreme court that the judge be retired for disability (Rules 9, 19[d], 21). The judge may then file with the supreme court a petition to modify or reject the commission's recommendation for retirement. All proceedings and papers are confidential until the commission files the record of its proceedings with the supreme court (Rule 7).

RETIREMENT PROVISIONS RE PARTICULAR COURTS

WSA §9-3-402(a) defines employer to include the "state judicial branch," but "member" to exclude employees covered by other retirement plans, including the supreme court and district court justices pension plan. The latter plan is discussed under Optional Provisions for Retirement below. Therefore, the following paragraphs under this heading relate to judges of the county courts, municipal courts, and justices of the peace.

As already noted in the discussion of Mandatory Retirement Provisions, judges of the county courts, municipal courts, and justices of the peace appear to be subject to mandatory retirement at age seventy, although they are otherwise covered by the Wyoming Retirement Act as to normal and disability retirement, and although the Retirement Act contains no provision for mandatory retirement at age seventy of members covered by it.

Normal retirement of such judges and justices is permitted after at least four years of service and at least sixty-five years of age, or where combined total of years of service credit and years of age equals at least eighty-five, and early retirement at a reduced benefit is permitted after the member has at least four years of service and has reached at least fifty, but not yet sixty, years of age, or at least twenty-five years of service and is not yet fifty years of age, WSA §9-3-415.

Voluntary retirement for disability is dealt with in the retirement act in WSA §9-3-422, which permits a member who has ten or more years of service credit, during which contributions have been paid, to retire because of illness or injury outside of or in the scope of employment on account of total or partial disability, in accordance with rules and regulations adopted by the board. Total disability is defined in WSA §9-3-402(v) as a disability condition that renders the member unable to engage in any occupation for which he or she is reasonably suited by training or experience and which is reasonably expected to last at least twelve months; and partial disability is defined as a disability condition that renders a member unable to perform the occupation for which he or she is reasonably suited by training or experience but still allows him or her to function in other employment and which is reasonably expected to last at least twelve months. As to procedure, WSA §9-3-411 provides that any person aggrieved by any ruling of the retirement board is entitled to a hearing before the board after giving reasonable notice, and that the decision of the board after hearing is subject to review in accordance with the Wyoming Administrative Procedure Act. WSA §9-3-422(a) authorizes the board to adopt rules and regulations and to require physician reports, medical examinations, functional capacity evaluations, vocational examinations, and other necessary reports and examinations, at the cost of the retirement system; and §9-3-423 permits the board to require a disability retiree to submit to such examinations once each year for the first five years, and once in every three-year period thereafter, the benefit to be discontinued if he or she refuses to do so, and requires any member receiving a partial or total disability benefit who has not reached age sixty to report to the board annually his or her total earnings for the preceding calendar year from gainful employment and workers compensation benefits.

OPTIONAL PROVISIONS FOR RETIREMENT

A judge of the supreme court or of a district court is eligible to retire when he or she has served as a judge of either or both courts for (1) not less than eighteen years; (2) not less than fifteen years and is sixty-five years or older; (3) not less than twelve years and is seventy or older; (4) not less than six consecutive years and is sixty-five or older; (5) less than six years but continuously from the date of appointment to the age of seventy years; (6) not less than twelve years and is fifty-five or older; (7) not less than six years and dies in office or is retired by the supreme court for disability, WSA §5-1-106(a).

With respect to disability retirement, while WSA §5-1-106(a)(vii) recognizes, as discussed under Mandatory Provisions above, that a judge of the supreme court or of a district court may be *involuntarily* retired for disability, no provision for *voluntary* retirement of such judges for disability has been found. As noted above in Retirement Provisions for Particular Courts, WSA §9-3-422 provides for such retirement for members of the Wyoming Retirement System, and §9-3-402(a)(vi)(R) defines "employer or participating employer" to include "the state judicial branch." However, because subd. (vii) which defines "member" expressly states in subsection (F)(I) that member does *not* mean employees covered by the supreme court and district court justices' pension plan, but subdivision (x) defines "employee" to mean an employee of a participating employer, it appears that judges of the county court, municipal courts, and justices of the peace may voluntarily retire for disability pursuant to §9-3-422.

Cost of living adjustment is dealt with in WSA §§9-3-419 and 9-3-425. Section 9-3-419, in subd. (a) provides for increases for member service prior to July 1, 1975, and in subd. (b) requires increase effective July 1, 1997 and each July 1 thereafter, based on the increase in the Wyoming cost of living for the preceding calendar year as determined by the state's division of economic analysis, not, however, to exceed 1.5 percent except that any increase which exceeds 1.5 percent is accumulated and added to future years' increase in the cost of living. The only provision for an increase in the pension of judges of the supreme court and district courts is contained in WSA §5-1-106(b), which provides for a retiree's pension of fifty percent of the salary currently authorized by law for judges of the court from which they retired but "shall increase or diminish proportionately as salaries of judges of the respective courts change."

Exemption of benefits from state, county, or municipal tax, and from execution or attachment or any other process whatsoever, is dealt with in WSA §9-3-426, which also states that benefits are not assignable, except pursuant to a qualified domestic relations order approving a property settlement agreement made pursuant to the law of any state relating to child or spousal support or to marital property rights of a spouse, former spouse, or other dependent of a member. In view of the §9-3-402(vii) definition of member, discussed above, it would appear that judges of the supreme court and the district court are not covered by §9-3-426. They may, however, be exempt from execution pursuant to WSA §1-20-110(ii) as to the retirement fund, though apparently not as to benefits.

SERVICE AFTER RETIREMENT

Const. Art. V, §5, empowers the legislature to provide for reassignment to active duty of retired justices and judges of the supreme court, district courts, and any other courts, where and when needed. WSA §5-1-106(f) states that any justice of the supreme court or district court judge, who has retired and is not practicing law, may, with his or her consent, at the request of a district court judge with the consent of the chief justice, or by the chief justice, be assigned to service on any court; and §5-3-107 provides that if a judge of the district court dies or is unable to perform the duties of the office, the chief justice of the supreme court may assign any retired judge of the state to perform judicial functions in his or her place until a successor for such district has been appointed or elected.

A retired judge is required to comply with the Code of Judicial Conduct while serving as a judge, with certain exceptions, Application of the Code of Judicial Conduct, Wyoming Court Rules, page 847. Rules 3 and 7 of the Rules for Continuing Judicial Education require all judges of the supreme court, district judges, and county judges to complete fifteen hours of continuing judicial education, but make no mention of retired judges.

PAY AND EMOLUMENTS

A retired justice of the supreme court or judge of the district court receives as salary during any period of assignment the difference between his or her retirement allowance and the current compensation of a judge of the court to which he or she is assigned, and receives the same per diem and travel allowance allowed active judges or justices, WSA §5-1-106(f); and as to per diem and travel allowances for active judges, see WSA §§9-3-102 and 9-3-103. No provision similar to §5-1-106(f) applicable to judges of the county court, district court, or justices of the peace has been found.

www.ingramcontent.com/pod-product-compliance
Lightning Source LLC
Chambersburg PA
CBHW072056020426
42334CB00017B/1533